The Congressional Black Caucus, Minority Voting Rights, and the U.S. Supreme Court

The Congressional Black Caucus, Minority Voting Rights, and the U.S. Supreme Court

Christina R. Rivers

THE UNIVERSITY OF MICHIGAN PRESS

Ann Arbor

First paperback edition 2014
Copyright © by the University of Michigan 2012
All rights reserved

Published in the United States of America by
The University of Michigan Press
Printed and bound by CPI Group (UK) Ltd, Croydon, CR0 4YY

2017   2016   2015   2014   5   4   3   2

A CIP catalog record for this book is available from the British Library.

Library of Congress Cataloging-in-Publication Data

Rivers, Christina R.
    The Congressional Black Caucus, minority voting rights, and the U.S.
    Supreme Court / Christina R. Rivers.
        p.   cm.
    Includes bibliographical references and index.
        ISBN 978-0-472-11810-6 (cloth : alk. paper) — ISBN 978-0-472-02821-4 (e-book)
        1. Minorities—Suffrage—United States.   2. Congressional Black Caucus.
    3. African Americans—Suffrage.   I. Title.

    KF4893.R58   2012
    324.6'208996073—dc23

                                                    2012005028

ISBN 978-0-472-03582-3 (pbk. : alk. paper)

To Katie and J. B.
You're always with me.

Contents

Preface and Acknowledgments

"In the year 2007 Congress will once again convene to decide
whether or not Blacks should retain the right to vote. Does anyone
realize that . . . African-Americans are the only group of people who
still require permission under the U.S. Constitution to vote?! . . . Our
right to vote should no longer be up for discussion, review and/or
evaluation!"
>> —Message circulated via e-mail and the Internet, ca. 1998

"When President Bush met with . . . the Congressional Black Caucus,
Rep. Jesse Jackson Jr. . . . asked him if he would support extension
and strengthening of the Voting Rights Act when it comes up for
renewal in 2007. Bush responded that he did not support voting
rights for the District of Columbia. Jackson said that was not what he
asked; he asked about extending the [act]. Bush replied that he was
not aware of the act and would look at it when it got to his desk."
>> —*Chicago Sun-Times*, March 1, 2005

The Voting Rights Act of 1965 (VRA) is one of the crowning achievements
of the American civil rights movement. One of the most powerful cata-
lysts of democracy in this country, it has amplified thousands of political
voices that had long been muted by racial, ethnic, and language discrimination at the polls and elsewhere. Thanks to the VRA, the corpus of
elected officials is more diverse and thus more representative of the U.S.
population than at any other time in the country's history. Yet the act is
shrouded in ignorance. For example, the first epigraph comes from a message that circulated e-mail inboxes and the Internet for several years despite clarifications by civil rights organizations and the Justice Department. Even though most Americans believe that voting is a fundamental
right, the legislation that protects this right for so many is often misunderstood to the point of hysteria or barely registers on the national radar.

Moreover, since the 1990s the VRA—and minority voting rights—has been caught in an increasingly intense cross fire between the Congressional Black Caucus and the Supreme Court over the meaning and scope of the act.

My own ignorance about the VRA eventually compelled me to learn more about it. As a literal child of the 1960s, I do not recall the events that led to the act's passage. I grew up in San Diego and lived for the first ten years of my adulthood in Orange County, California—hardly hotbeds of political dissent or activism. Given my distance from the front lines of the civil rights movement, my memories of it derive largely from what was on television news and from eavesdropping on grown-ups, whose commentaries were generally not intended for juvenile ears. Like so many who benefited from the civil rights movement without contributing to it, I understood little about my voting rights and took them for granted. It probably did not help that I cut my political teeth on a tortured series of events including the ragged culmination of the Vietnam War, the revelation of the Pentagon Papers, the ensuing Watergate scandal and impeachment proceedings against President Nixon, the oil crisis, and the Iranian hostage crisis. Along with many of my jaded peers, I relied more on *Saturday Night Live, Mad Magazine,* Richard Pryor, George Carlin, and the Fabulous Furry Freak Brothers for my political socialization than on family, teachers, or the mainstream news media. When I reached voting age, I exercised my right to the franchise, although I did so more out of curiosity and a sense of racial commitment than faith in or knowledge about the democratic process.

College did little to educate me on the topic of the VRA or minority voting rights more broadly. This is in part my fault. As a political science major, I was so completely taken with international relations, foreign languages, and study abroad that American politics were of no interest to me whatsoever. I petitioned out of the required introductory course in American government (with unexpectedly far-reaching ramifications, given that I now routinely teach such courses). In addition, course offerings on race and politics were rare at my undergraduate institution in the early 1980s. A decade later, while I was pursuing a master's degree in public policy, the topic of minority voting rights never came up. Not until the second year of my doctoral studies did I "discover" the VRA in a seminar on voting and democracy taught by Professor Kathryn Abrams. The year was 1993, the same year that the Supreme Court handed down its benchmark decision in *Shaw v. Reno.* So enlightening was Professor Abrams's instruction and so compelling was her concern about this new direction of the

Court's minority voting rights jurisprudence that I looked forward to the dismal morning slogs up Ithaca's icy, treacherous hills to get to her class. Her seminar triggered my interest in the Supreme Court's interpretation of the VRA, which lies at the core of this book.

Fortunately for me, Professor Abrams agreed to serve on my dissertation committee and to supervise my legal analysis of the districting cases. Another committee member, Walter Mebane, suggested that I look at the role of the Congressional Black Caucus (CBC) in various amendments of the VRA. This included the CBC's role as amicus curiae, or friend of the court, in voting rights cases. My committee chair, Theodore Lowi, has long extolled the relevance of the Court's early interpretations of the Fourteenth Amendment in the *Slaughter-House Cases* and *Strauder v. West Virginia* to contemporary litigation involving race and civil rights. His emphasis on these cases, along with subsequent readings in critical race theory, fueled my interest in the race-conscious roots not just of the Court's interpretation of that amendment but also of the Reconstruction framers' intent for it. My investigation of the evolution of the Court's Fourteenth Amendment jurisprudence, particularly regarding the Equal Protection Clause, shed light on the VRA's effect on the system of checks and balances, particularly the way the act has been buffeted between the Supreme Court's interpretation of it and the administration of it by the Department of Justice (DOJ). Finally, because a key provision of the VRA mandates federal oversight of certain states and regions, I became interested in how the act affects the system of federalism.

While tracing these constitutional roots in the broader context of American political development, I was consistently vexed by the lack of attention to blacks' participation in that development. So much of the scholarship on African Americans in the political system is anchored by the civil rights movement. The movement itself is often presented as an "awakening" of black politics. Given the extraordinary nature of the movement, such emphases are not surprising. However, they both minimize and mischaracterize black politics. To focus so much on the civil rights movement suggests that it is either the only significant instance of black political activism in American history or the only one worthy of study by political scientists. Such a focus also obscures the centrality of black political leadership, including that of black women, to American political development.

My vexation spurred me to delve more deeply into the foundations of black political thought and leadership. For this I am most grateful to Professor James Turner, who directed my independent study on this topic. He introduced me to black leaders in and the debates regarding abolition, emigration, self-separation, suffrage, electoral politics, and desegregation. Through these readings, I learned that the groundwork for the civil rights movement and for contemporary African American politics was laid by black activists well over a century ago.

The more familiar I have become with these voices, the more I am convinced that they are not simply voices of the past. Nor do they speak solely about the black experience in America. Although disagreement among leaders was common, virtually all were united in their commitment to the core American principles of liberty, equality, and democracy. Therefore, one of the goals of this book is to demonstrate how the observations of early black leaders provide a relevant and potentially unifying context for the study of contemporary American politics. In this respect, they offered sophisticated, nuanced alternatives to binary and often simplistic approaches that tend to characterize discussions of race in law, politics, and representation. It has been immensely fulfilling to listen to black political voices going as far back as 1830. It is an honor to introduce them to my students and now to readers of this book who may not have encountered them.

If there is one aspect of this book about which I am confident, it is that some of its readers will think that my perspectives on race, constitutional law, and representation are completely misguided. Knowing that I will take a few arrows, I am motivated by John Stuart Mill's belief that even those opinions seen as objectionable or wrong may ultimately point to the truth. So, along with providing readers with facts and insights that tend to be overlooked, this book takes as its overall goal the promotion of thinking beyond reactionary rhetoric, oversimplified analyses, and apologetic platitudes about race, representation, and democracy in America. If any of the contents herein promote meaningful debate over the scope and meaning of the VRA in a classroom, conference, legislative hearing, judicial proceeding, blog, Facebook discussion, or friendly bar, the risk of my being caught in the cross fire is well worth it.

I am a transplant to Chicago. Among its several nicknames, it is known as "the city of neighborhoods." Along those lines, I thank my "neighbors," both here and elsewhere, for their support of this project.

I am very grateful to Congressmen Bobby Scott (D-VA), Jim Sensenbrenner (R-WI), and Mel Watt (D-NC) for their comments on the role of the Congressional Black Caucus in amending the VRA. I initially sought to speak with Scott and Watt, given their membership in the caucus and their centrality on the committee that oversaw the 2006 reauthorization of the act. On Watt's enthusiastic recommendation, I also sought Sensenbrenner's input. All three men readily agreed to be interviewed, and all of them shared invaluable insights on the caucus's role specifically and on the various amendments of the act more generally. I am also indebted to Congressman Scott for his subsequent comments and clarifications. It was an honor and a delight to converse with these gentlemen, and this book is greatly enriched by their contributions.

I have benefited from the superb guidance of Melody Herr, acquisitions editor at the University of Michigan Press. She was instrumental in helping mold a dissertation of ideas into a more coherent and fully developed book manuscript. I also appreciate her assistance during my first foray into the often bewildering realm of academic book publishing. I cannot imagine having a better editor for this process. I also thank Susan Cronin, Ellen Goldlust-Gingrich, and Mary Hashman for their expert assistance, especially for their patience with my occasional bouts of hysteria about the whole process.

I am deeply indebted to the anonymous reviewers of my manuscript for their encouraging and extremely thorough comments. Their suggestions enabled me to make better connections across the disciplines of politics, history, and law. They also helped me condense what had become a bloated manuscript in some parts into a leaner and hopefully more efficient final product.

Some of the central arguments in this book have appeared in articles published in *Publius: The Journal of Federalism* and in *Southern Studies*. I appreciate the opportunity to revisit and further develop those arguments in this book.

I thank Dick Engstrom, Lorn Foster, Ted Lowi, Toni-Michelle Travis, and Jerome Ziegler for their mentorship over the years. I also thank them for providing me with valuable insights on my project and with exciting opportunities to contribute further scholarship on minority voting rights. In addition, I am grateful to Thomas Brunell and Julie Novkov for helping me improve various components of the manuscript. I am particularly grateful to David L. J. Reed and Brian Sales for sharing their passion for African American history and political thought and for engaging me in so many fruitful discussions of it both during and after my time in graduate school.

I thank my students, many of whom helped me develop my arguments, particularly my presentation of them, during my courses on African American politics, African American political thought, and voting rights law. Their energetic engagement with Court decisions and black political thinkers helped me refine many of my points and often confirmed that this project was worth completing.

I am particularly indebted to Teresa Galicia, my former student and now my ace research assistant, for her indispensable—and completely voluntary—efforts to help me complete this book. Not only did she gracefully endure my frequent disorganization and flakiness, but she motivated me with her intellectual curiosity, her determination, her good humor, and her insistence that I take up salsa dancing. Teresa is a woman of immense academic promise. It has been a privilege to work with her and a pleasure to become her friend. I am grateful as well for the excellent and speedy research assistance of Alexis Burson of DePaul University's library, which in turn helped me fortify one of the book's most important points. I also thank Joshua Covell and Angela Weir for their invaluable assistance in tending to copiers, printers, and scanners and for helping me compile the manuscript.

As I have pressed (or more often plodded) on with this project, I could not have asked for more supportive colleagues both in my department and elsewhere at DePaul. I am grateful for their consistent and loyal encouragement of my development as a scholar and a teacher. I am also grateful to DePaul University for funding a two-quarter research leave that allowed me to complete the initial manuscript.

It is difficult to find sufficient words with which to thank Andrea Anderson-Hamilton, Corina Espinoza, Adishi Gardner, Tonya Hopkins, Valerie Johnson, Azza Layton, Shiera Malik, Cathy May, and Chernoh Sesay Jr. for keeping my spirits up and my feet to the fire and for keeping me fed and watered. The same goes for the members of my family (two- and four-legged) and especially for their patience during my in absentia periods. I am especially grateful to Gilbert Rivers and Valerie Rivers-Bethel for their unwavering support and for demonstrating that one can indeed go home again. I would not have been able to complete this book without the encouragement, patience, laughter, and love of so many wonderful folk around me, and I am both honored and humbled by their presence in my life.

As grateful as I am to my neighbors for helping me strengthen this book, I alone am accountable for its weaknesses.

Introduction

"The glass through which black life is viewed by white Americans is inescapably befogged by the hot breath of history. True objectivity, where race is concerned, is as rare as a necklace of Hope diamonds."
—Hoyt Fuller

In 1993, the Supreme Court held in the redistricting case of *Shaw v. Reno* that the Equal Protection Clause of the Fourteenth Amendment entitles all voters to a color-blind redistricting process. On its face, this decision is emblematic of the Court's landmark decision in *Brown v. Board of Education.* Indeed, the *Shaw* decision was heralded as a pinnacle of objective, color-blind constitutionalism in the area of voting rights jurisprudence and as proof of the Court's commitment to leveling the electoral playing field for all voters. Other observers lamented the decision as well-intended but profoundly misguided. In particular, the Congressional Black Caucus (CBC) feared that invalidating remedial uses of race—such as the creation of the majority-minority[1] districts challenged in *Shaw*—would endanger the political power that blacks and other minorities had gained from the Voting Rights Act (VRA). Ironically, the *Shaw* decision put the caucus and the broader civil rights community (which is instrumental in promoting the concept of color blindness) in the position of objecting to color-blind voting jurisprudence, or at least to the *Shaw* majority's concept of it.

While this turn of events is relatively recent, conflicts over the role of race in the Constitution are not. Debates over color blindness, race consciousness, and equality are deeply entrenched in American law, politics, and society. The context of contemporary minority voting rights issues reaches at least to the Reconstruction era and the framing of the Fourteenth Amendment. From one perspective, that amendment sharply limits the use of racial classifications in public policies, regardless of the intent behind such classifications. Speaking very generally, those who endorse this position tend to be characterized as conservative. They also tend to be associated with an originalist interpretation of the Constitution—that is, close adherence to the text or to one's understanding of the framers' original intent of the law when it was written, rather than the current context. Again speaking very generally, this type of constitutional interpretation tends in turn to be associated with judicial restraint, or deference to precedent. The Court majority in *Shaw v. Reno* is often seen as an example of this position.

From an opposing perspective, the Fourteenth Amendment was intended not to exclude all uses of race but to prevent the use of racial classifications that have the intent or effect of disadvantaging a particular group, especially those with a history of being disadvantaged. Continuing to speak generally, adherents of this position tend to be classified as liberal and as proponents of interpretivism—that is, a more flexible reading of the Constitution that takes current contexts into account. Also generally speaking, interpretivists are typically seen as less beholden to precedent and thus as judicial activists. The dissenters in *Shaw* tend to be affiliated with this position.

Debates about voting and civil rights have long pitted color blindness and race consciousness as mutually exclusive concepts. The same goes for originalism versus interpretivism. At least with respect to minority voting rights, however, the CBC advocates a third approach to the Fourteenth Amendment. It has frequently contended that the amendment's framers primarily intended it to protect blacks. Consequently, the Equal Protection Clause *would* allow for remedial or preventive uses of race when designing districts or other electoral plans. In an effort to give a "new interpretation to the civil rights struggle that will enable [blacks] to . . . take part in" and articulate it, the caucus has advocated for a broader interpretation of the Fourteenth Amendment that takes the race-conscious aspects of its framing into account.[2] As a result, it becomes rather difficult to place the caucus neatly into a single ideological category. While its advocacy of original intent takes it toward the conservative pole of the binary, its race-conscious interpretation of that intent shifts it back toward the liberal end. Moreover, race consciousness is itself at odds with the color-blind rhetoric that defines the civil rights movement. With respect to the minority voting rights cases at issue in this book, the CBC may best be characterized as fusionist—that is, taking a race-conscious, originalist approach to racial equality, including constitutional and statutory provisions enacted to foster such equality.

Of course, ideological preferences and modes of constitutional interpretation are far too complicated to allow for such generalized comparisons. With respect to ideology, for example, even Martin Luther King Jr. promoted the concept of racial pride as well as black racial bloc voting.[3] With respect to modes of interpretation, the CBC, civil rights organizations, and a sizable host of other interests endorsed judicial restraint in *Grutter v. Bollinger,* the most recent case involving affirmative action in higher education, by defending the precedent of *Brown v. Board of Education.* Conservatives opposing such policies took a more activist approach that effectively called for a retreat from *Brown* and adherence to the newer precedent, *Shaw v. Reno.*[4] And, as subsequent chapters will illustrate in the context of voting rights, an individual justice's tendency toward activism or restraint may depend less on precedent or ideology than on his or her individual perceptions of race and racism.

The mutually exclusive binary approach to promoting and measuring racial equality fails further in light of the Court's first adjudications of the Fourteenth Amendment—decisions that put the justices in the same category as the CBC. In two of the Court's earliest interpretations of the amendment, the *Slaughter-House Cases* and *Strauder v. West Virginia,* the justices interpreted the framers' intent for the Fourteenth Amendment as protecting blacks, both as individuals and as a class, from discrimination by whites. Soon after those decisions, the Court shifted from an affirmatively race-conscious interpretation of the Equal Protection Clause to a jurisprudence that sustained laws that were facially neutral but racially discriminatory in intent and effect. Its decision in *Plessy v. Ferguson* is emblematic of that jurisprudence. The Court eventually reversed that trajectory in *Brown v. Board of Education* by embracing the concept of color blindness as enunciated by Justice John Marshall Harlan's dissent in *Plessy* and advanced by black civil rights activists.

There is no doubt that *Brown* and the jurisprudence that has emerged from it have helped equalize political processes. In the realm of minority voting rights, however, since 1993 the Court has treated racial classifications intended to remedy racial inequality as suspiciously as classifications intended to maintain such inequality. This approach, in turn, constrains the intent and scope of the Fourteenth Amendment as well as the VRA.[5] From this angle, the *Shaw* decision is neither originalist nor restrained. The majority in that case not only elided earlier holdings that the Fourteenth Amendment allows for remedial uses of race, it departed from a relatively recent precedent, *Thornburg v. Gingles,* that acknowledged that possibility with respect to redistricting.

This book focuses on the CBC's attempts to demonstrate the shortcomings of racially and ideologically binary approaches to law, race, and representation. It explores the caucus's contentions that (1) an originalist approach to the Fourteenth Amendment allows for remedially race-conscious districting and (2) the Reconstruction framers' intent should be central to current interpretations of that amendment. I first examine the caucus in the legislative realm, through its role in amending the VRA. I then examine the CBC in an external role, as it submits amicus curiae (friend of the court) briefs in cases involving minority voting rights. Drawing from the CBC's legislative and amicus positions, I argue that the Court majority's current voting rights jurisprudence tends to constrain rather than foster meaningful discussion of the role of race in constitutional law.

As chapter 1 shows, the majority overlooks the fact that color blindness meant very different things to the Fourteenth Amendment's framers and even to Justice Harlan's legendary *Plessy* dissent than contemporary articulations of it tend to mean. For example, today's advocates of color blindness tend to oversimplify the troubling but crucial reality that although the Reconstruction-era Congress and Court sanctioned ameliorative race-based measures, they also sanctioned racial segregation and subordination. In other words, their motives were not purely egalitarian or objective—legislators and justices recognized that legislating equality was difficult to achieve, much less enforce, in a polity that was unambiguously premised on white superiority. Even Harlan's dissent affirmed white supremacy. Yet because the binary approach frames color-blind and race-conscious measures as mutually exclusive, it minimizes the extent to which such measures are complementary approaches toward racial equality.

The debates over constitutional interpretation are echoed by similar discussions regarding the role of race in the VRA. Passed in 1965, on the heels of the Civil Rights Act of 1964, the VRA is lauded as the crown jewel of the civil rights movement. It was intended to fortify the Fifteenth Amendment after the latter had languished, ignored by the South and minimally enforced by Congress, for nearly a century. Accordingly, the VRA contains both remedial and preventive measures. This book concentrates on two key provisions designed to abate racial discrimination at the polls. Section 2, which is more substantive, protects minority political strength from being subordinated by white racial bloc voting and covers the entire country. Section 5, which is more procedural, requires certain states and jurisdictions (mostly but not exclusively in the former Confederate South) to get Justice Department approval for changes in their electoral plans before such plans can be enacted.[6] Although Section 5 has drawn steady criticism for imposing excess federal influence onto the states, it has been renewed each time the act has come up for reauthorization. Among the various reauthorizations, those of 1982 stand out for two reasons. Given abundant evidence of continued evasion of Section 5, Congress extended it beyond the typical five- or seven-year period for an unprecedented twenty-five years. In addition, Congress made Section 2 permanent. More important, it revised that provision in a way that made it easier for states to employ race-based measures to offset existing or prevent future racial discrimination at the polls.

In the 1990s and under the auspices of a color-blind interpretation of the Equal Protection Clause, the Court rendered a series of decisions that chipped away at Sections 2 and 5. Congress again renewed, most recently in 2006. After presenting copious evidence that racial discrimination in elections remains a serious problem, it left Sections 2 and 5 intact and again extended the latter for twenty-five years. Three years later, Section 5 was challenged in *Northwest Austin Municipal Utility District Number 1 v. Holder.* In that case, the Court decided (in an uncharacteristically overwhelming majority for such cases) not to strike down that provision. At the same time, it strongly signaled that Congress should reconsider how Section 5 can continue to be justified in light of the overall advancements made as a result of that provision. The use of race in districting was not explicitly at issue in *Northwest Austin,* nor was the Equal Protection Clause. Implicit in the Court's opinion, however, was the idea that Congress must envision the act more along the lines of the former's color-blind jurisprudence.

Before moving on to what this book intends to do, it is important to note what it does not do. This book does not evaluate the CBC's overall legislative performance.[7] It does not look solely at redistricting or present a quantitative analysis of the topic.[8] It does not evaluate the VRA, either in its entirety or key elements of it.[9] Finally, this is not a purely legal analysis of the debates over race, law, and representation.[10]

This book does present contemporary debates over race, law, and representation from overlooked vantage points. Toward that end, it illustrates the centrality of race to American legal and political development. This approach includes a revisitation of nineteenth-century black political leaders and their debates over the best paths to liberty, equality, and democracy. The goal here is to demonstrate that the CBC's efforts are best understood not solely in the context of contemporary voting rights issues but as contemporary expressions of the race-conscious tradition of black political thought dating back to at least 1830. (This book also pushes past the finding that studies of race have tended to garner less status in political science than in most other social science disciplines.)[11]

This book also revisits the early interpretation of the Equal Protection Clause to demonstrate its shifting interpretation over time. On this point, I do not purport to be neutral. Concepts of race, representation, power, and politics are simply too heavily freighted with normative implications, as are assessments of their intersections. By focusing on the CBC, early black political thinkers, and the evolution of the concept of equal protection, I break new ground and fortify the explanatory foundations on which normative conclusions about these intersections can be reached.

Drawing primarily from congressional hearings, Supreme Court opinions, and amicus curiae briefs submitted by the CBC in key redistricting cases, this book demonstrates how, since the early 1990s, various battles over the use of race in districting and other electoral arrangements constrain the enforcement of statutory and constitutional laws protecting minority voting rights. For example, Congress and the CBC have battled the Court over the scope of the VRA—specifically, the validity of majority-minority districting. Moreover, the Justice Department has conflicted with the Court over officials' interpretation of the role of race in the administration of the VRA. These conflicts came to a head after the 1990 redistricting and continue into the present, exposing a "bifurcated framework of [statutory] review" that does not simply divide authority over the VRA among the three branches of the federal government but that also stymies productive dialogue about the act's scope and purpose.[12]

Concurrent with these institutional battles are battles over federalism that pit the national government against state purview over electoral processes. To weed out discriminatory electoral plans, Section 5 requires states to get prior Department of Justice approval of any changes in their plans. Section 5 works in tandem with Section 2's purpose of preventing the weakening or "dilution" of minority voting strength in states and regions covered by Section 5. On the one hand, Section 5 clearly compromises state power to enact electoral plans that invidiously discriminate against minority voters. On the other, the Court's interpretations of both provisions also limit state power to enact electoral plans intended to protect or preserve minority political power. Thus, not only are states constrained by the VRA, they are squeezed between conflicting institutional interpretations of the act at the federal level.

With respect to checks and balances, this book illustrates how the CBC has engaged the Court with regard to the role of race in law and political representation both implicitly (via legislative hearings) and explicitly (via amicus briefs). Extending the CBC's position, this book argues that the VRA and thus minority political power are caught in institutional, legal, and ideological cross fires over race and representation, especially those triggered by the use of race in redistricting. Consequently I argue that despite its purportedly egalitarian motivation, the Court majority's exclusively color-blind voting rights jurisprudence risks harming minority political power. By blinding itself to color, it blinds itself to subtly invidious uses of race, thus defeating the core purpose of the VRA and the Equal Protection Clause. Such jurisprudence is "false to the original vision of Fourteenth Amendment" and the VRA because it compromises the protections that were originally intended to protect minority voting rights against white dominance.[13]

Contrary to prevailing perceptions that color blindness and race consciousness are mutually exclusive, this book contends that they are better framed as complementary and potentially interdependent paths to equality. My use of the term *race conscious* draws from the legal school of critical race theory, particularly Gary Peller's argument that race must be seen "in the particular context of American history," in which racial identity has been a central basis for "comprehending the significance of various social relations."[14] For Peller, race is a significant element of what goes into the construction of America's social and political relations.[15] Consequently, it is essential to examine the relationship of race and representation from minority as well as mainstream perspectives.

At first glance, a race-conscious approach to equality may sound counterintuitive, particularly to advocates of a color-blind or "postracial" vision of America. However, it is useful for several reasons. First, as subsequent chapters show, race consciousness lies at the core of the CBC's approach as well as that of many black leaders preceding the caucus. Second, to idealize a color-blind or postracial polity is often to ignore the persistent double helix of racial and political inequality. Third, race consciousness allows for the recognition that racial hierarchies have not disappeared from the American polity; to the extent that such hierarchies are intertwined with others involving class and gender, they cannot simply be idealized out of existence.[16] A race-conscious perspective ultimately offers a realistic and collaborative resolution of debates over minority voting rights.

Central Questions

Race and Representation

What are the ramifications of institutional cross fires on black representation? The answer to this question is premised on the argument that the CBC is central to the battles over race, law, and representation. In its legislative capacity, the caucus has contributed to strengthening and extending the VRA. In particular, U.S. representatives Barbara Jordan, John Conyers, Harold Washington, Melvin Watt, and Robert Scott have been powerful voices in House committee hearings on the VRA in 1975, 1982, and 2006. Thanks in large part to their efforts, the number of blacks elected to Congress has grown dramatically. For example, in the first congressional election after the 1982 amendments, the number of blacks in Congress expanded from twenty-nine to forty. In addition to its primary legislative capacity, the caucus has taken on the role of civil rights organization by representing blacks' interests to the judicial branch as and amicus curiae advocating a race-conscious approach to minority voting rights cases.

Two chapters of this book are thus devoted to an examination of how the Court and the CBC have debated each other, again implicitly, about the meaning of equal protection in the context of black political power. Some readers may find such emphasis on the CBC to be misguided. As chapter 3 discusses, many studies of the CBC conclude that beyond its role as symbolic or descriptive representative of African Americans, it is marginally effective at best and illegitimate at worst.[17] Other observers, including me, see more utility in the caucus, not only in the symbolic and political senses but in the substantive sense as well.[18] Accordingly, this book challenges conclusions that the CBC is ineffective, at least in the area of minority voting rights. In particular, the caucus has assiduously sought to preserve and enhance minority voting rights in two important ways. It has thrice played an active role in strengthening the VRA, each time in the face of significant ideological and partisan resistance. These are not small accomplishments. Moreover, the caucus has been in dialog with the Supreme Court as amicus curiae, advocating an interpretation of the Equal Protection Clause that allows for race-based remedies to race-based discrimination.

The answer to the question about ramifications also exposes a troubling dilemma: While the VRA has enhanced black political power, the Court has rendered decisions that weaken the act and thus potentially that power. The CBC's advocacy of minority voting rights in Congress therefore demonstrates that success can breed retrenchment. In other words, it appears that the CBC's involvement in amending the VRA to accommodate both race-based and outcomes-oriented electoral measures has goaded the Court majority into ratcheting up its color-blind approach to jurisprudence in redistricting cases. The result has been a series of cramped and often confusing decisions that undermine Congress's intent for the VRA more broadly and African Americans' political interests more specifically. Paradoxically, as black political power gets caught between conflicting interpretations of the Fourteenth Amendment and the VRA, the Supreme Court has effectively hoisted the CBC on its own voting rights petard.

I am well aware of the contradiction here. On the one hand, I argue that the CBC has lobbied the Court with respect to the use of race in districting and other areas having to do with affirmative action policies. On the other, I contend that the caucus's legislative successes with the VRA have prompted the Court to render decisions that are inimical to the act's goals and potentially to black political power. Ultimately, I believe that both outcomes are true. But this book does not simply describe how the CBC may have influenced the Court's decisions. Rather, I demonstrate that the caucus has attempted to engage the Court majority in discussions of race that the latter might otherwise have avoided. If one believes that true objectivity where race is concerned is indeed as rare as a necklace of Hope diamonds, then the CBC's exercises in legislative and constitutional consciousness-raising are crucial in the long run, and despite shorter-run judicial setbacks.[19]

Constitutional Interpretation

Did the Radical Reconstruction Congress intend the Fourteenth Amendment to be interpreted solely in a color-blind manner? With respect to minority voting rights, the Supreme Court has been waging a pitched battle with itself over this question since the early 1990s, and the battle has yielded idealistic yet problematic decisions. With its landmark decision in *Brown v. Board of Education,* the Court solidified its foundation for color-blind constitutionalism. Subsequent decisions such as *City of Richmond v. U.S.* (hiring), *Arlington Heights v. Metropolitan Housing Development Corporation* (housing), *Regents of the University of California v. Bakke* (graduate school admissions), *Milliken v. Bradley,* the *Missouri v. Jenkins* trilogy, and most recently *Parents Involved in Community Schools v. Seattle School District Number 1 et al.* (all involving school desegregation) have laid the groundwork for the current Court majority's presumptive suspicion of all racial classifications.

In applying the Equal Protection Clause to minority voting rights, the Court now routinely equates remedial uses of race with racism. Beginning with *Shaw v. Reno,* the court held that "bizarrely" drawn districts with slightly more than a 50 percent black majority were tantamount to the Jim Crow–era "uncouth" district in *Gomillion v. Lightfoot* that excluded more than 95 percent of the municipality's black voters. The Court did not declare the districting at issue in *Shaw* unconstitutional in and of itself. In interpreting Equal Protection Clause to guarantee the right to a color-blind districting process, it simply gave standing to challenges to oddly shaped minority safe districts. To be sure, the districts in *Shaw* were racial gerrymanders in that they were oddly shaped and were drawn with the express intent of benefitting a specific race. However in *Gomillion,* the state's intent was to suppress as much of the black vote as possible. By contrast, in *Shaw,* the state's intent was to fortify African American political strength against the effects of *Gomillion*-type gerrymanders and other forms of political suppression.

In 1995, in *Miller v. Johnson,* the Court reaffirmed that the use of race as a primary factor in districting violates the Equal Protection Clause regardless of whether the intent was egregious or benign and regardless of whether such districting was done to comply with the VRA. In *Shaw v. Hunt* (essentially a remand of *Shaw v. Reno*), the Court raised the bar for states attempting to demonstrate that their interests in complying with the VRA compelled them to include race as a key factor when districting. Currently, an unusually shaped majority-minority district, if challenged, is almost sure to violate the Equal Protection Clause, regardless of whether a state's intent was invidious or benign or of whether any racial group suffered harm from the districting. Although they have not been challenged, the Court has been silent on the issue of bizarrely shaped majority-white districts.[20]

As the Court began restricting the scope of the Equal Protection Clause, it also began chipping away at the VRA's key provisions. Section 2 prohibits minority vote dilution, defined as the "process whereby election laws or practices, either singly or in concert, combine with systematic bloc voting among an identifiable group to diminish the voting strength of at least one other group [and where] one group, voting cohesively for its pre-ferred candidates, is systematically outvoted by a larger group that is also cohesive."[21] Section 5 prohibits minority vote retrogression, defined as an electoral plan that "would . . . diminish minority voting strength from what it had been."[22] In *Holder v. Hall*, the Court held in part that because of a lack of measurement standards, a paucity of racial minorities on a governing body is not sufficient to prove vote dilution. Inherent in the Court's rationale was the view that protection against vote dilution is not a guarantee of proportional representation. (As chapter 3 demonstrates, Congress made the same stipulation when it amended Section 2 in 1982.) Justice Clarence Thomas's lengthy concurrence in *Holder,* itself an elabo-ration of the *Shaw* opinion, laid much of the groundwork for the decision rendered in *Georgia v. Ashcroft* ten years later.[23] In the latter case, the Court interpreted Section 2 to allow minority "influence" districts to substitute for safer majority-minority districts. (An influence district is one in which there is a "cohesive quantitative minority of voters" who are not able to elect a candidate of their choice "but can still be expected . . . to influence the legislative behavior of the person who is elected" to represent them.)[24] By the late 1990s in *Reno v. Bossier Parish School Board et al. I* and *II,* the Court upheld a Louisiana districting plan that yielded a nearly all-white school board. In both cases, the majority applied a relative rather than an absolute measure of minority representation. In the process, it separated Section 2 from Section 5, thus contradicting Congress's intent for these provisions to function interdependently. Taken together, these decisions illustrate that the Rehnquist Court departed significantly from (1) the original intent of the Fourteenth Amendment, (2) the Supreme Court's initial interpretations of it, and (3) the VRA's original intent.

Separation of Powers

How has the battle between the Court and Congress, specifically the CBC, affected constitutional and statutory provisions intended to mitigate past and continuing racial discrimination at the polls? As noted previously, since the early 1990s the Court majority has undermined Congress's intent for the VRA. In particular, the justices' insistence on color blindness as the sole path to racial equality puts it at odds with Congress's and particularly the CBC's intent for the act to allow for remedially race-based electoral and districting measures. Unlike the Court majority, the CBC envisions color blindness more as a concept than as a concrete mechanism. Drawing from the caucus's comments during hearings and from its amicus briefs, color blindness is one—but not the only—legitimate criterion by which to measure racial equality. For the CBC, color blindness is more of a means toward equality rather than an end in and of itself. Hence, it endorses color blindness in addition to but not at the expense of race-conscious remedies to race-based electoral discrimination.

Congress and the Supreme Court are engaged in corollary skirmishes about whether the VRA should promote egalitarian processes or outcomes. For example, in 1981, in *Mobile v. Bolden,* the Court held that the VRA protected minority voters only against intentional (as opposed to effective) racial discrimination. The following year, Congress expressly rejected that decision and revised the act to prohibit electoral plans that have discriminatory effects regardless of intent. By the 1990 reapportionment cycle, due in part to these amendments to the VRA, several states drew majority-minority districts such as the one at issue in *Shaw v. Reno.* Between 1993 and 2003, the Court rendered decisions that restricted states' ability to create such districts. In addition to limiting the use of remedial racial gerrymanders, in *Reno v. Bossier Parish School Board I* and *II* as well as *Georgia v. Ashcroft,* the Court narrowed the VRA's scope.

Not surprisingly, Congress sought again to address what it saw as incorrect decisions when it reauthorized the act in 2006. Given the conservative inclinations of two of the last four appointees to the Supreme Court (John Roberts and Samuel Alito), an even sharper conflict between judicial and legislative interpretations of the VRA can be expected. The first challenge to the most recent reauthorization came from a tiny electoral district with a grand ambition in a case that essentially invited the Court to strike down Section 5 of the VRA. Although the Court declined to exercise its power of judicial review in *Northwest Austin Municipal Utility District Number 1 v. Holder,* it did suggest that Congress reconsider its intent for the act. Two justices, Sonia Sotomayor and Elena Kagan, have joined the Court since that decision was handed down, both more liberal than Roberts and Alito. For example, Kagan made an unusually pointed dissent from the Court's decision to strike down Arizona's public campaign financing law in *Arizona Free Enterprise Club v. Bennett.* Her vigorous critique of that decision as antiegalitarian suggests that she might advocate for the CBC's intent for the VRA.[25] While it is reasonable to expect that Sotomayor and Kagan will function as counterweights against the Court majority's stance, it is doubtful that they and their liberal colleagues will have enough momentum to shift the Court's current minority voting rights jurisprudence from where it currently stands.

Checks and Balances and Federalism

What implications does the Court's color-blind minority voting rights jurisprudence have on the system of checks and balances and on federalism? With respect to the former, the Court majority has said not simply what the VRA is but also what the justices think it should be. Regarding the latter, the Court has constrained states' traditional latitude in managing electoral processes. To be sure, the VRA has done the same (as have other federal laws, including the Motor Voter Act and the Help America Vote Act). Initial concerns about the VRA's effect on state autonomy led one Supreme Court justice to lament that the law would diminish states covered by Section 5 to the status of "conquered provinces" akin to the former Confederacy during the Reconstruction era.[26] Yet since the act's passage, most states have protected minority electoral power while staving off provincial status. That they have done so is especially commendable given that they are caught among competing legal, institutional, and jurisdictional forces: Under Sections 5 and 2, Congress and the Department of Justice obligate states to enact electoral plans that do not erode or dilute minority political power; under *Shaw,* the Court compels states to carry out these obligations within a narrower reading of the act.

Battles over the meaning of equal protection of minority voting rights have created a similar bind. Several decades before the passage of the VRA, the Court began enforcing the Fourteenth and Fifteenth Amendments to limit states' rights to discriminate against black voters by striking down grandfather clauses and whites-only primaries and political parties. Three decades after the passage of the VRA, the Court began interpreting the Equal Protection Clause to limit states' rights to use race-conscious measures to prevent ongoing and/or remedy historical discrimination. In other words, by limiting the Equal Protection Clause to color-blind electoral processes, the Court limits the use of race-conscious measures to remedy *racist* abuses of state power. In this respect, both states and black (and other minority voters) are caught in the cross fire of disputes over legislative intent, interpretation, and enforcement of laws written to protect the rights of those voters.

Structure of the Book

Chapter 1 examines the origins and changing nature of color blindness in American law and politics. Again, this examination extends the CBC's position that the Supreme Court's color-blind voting rights jurisprudence is an ahistorical and thus inaccurate approach to the VRA. This chapter also explores the CBC's more implicit claims that concept of color blindness is best understood in the context of Justice Harlan's initial invocation of it in his *Plessy v. Ferguson* dissent rather than the Warren Court's validation of it in *Brown v. Board of Education.* In light of persisting racial and ethnic inequities, this chapter concludes that the Rehnquist and now Roberts Court majority's color-blind voting rights jurisprudence risks perpetuating the inegalitarian status quo—and thus precisely what it purports to combat.

Chapter 2 illuminates an overshadowed but central aspect of contemporary debates over race, redistricting, and representation: the foundations of African American politics and political thought. This chapter has three goals. First, it introduces readers to nineteenth-century black activists and elected officials, thereby providing readers with a fuller context from which to examine the CBC and contemporary black politics more generally. Second, it demonstrates that the caucus emerged from an activist tradition that long preceded the civil rights movement, the New Deal, and even the Jim Crow era. Third, this chapter suggests that taken as a whole, African American political thought bridges the divide between color-blind and race-conscious approaches to racial inequality. In so doing, I demonstrate that although (or perhaps because) black politics has long been marginalized or associated with radicalism, most black leaders have advocated the core American principles of liberty, equality, and democracy as well as individualism and self-help. The tradition of black protest and resistance thus falls squarely within the American tradition of dissent.

Chapter 3 reviews the founding and growth of the CBC and then delves into its role in amending the VRA. By insisting on shifting the act from an opportunity to an outcomes orientation and on retaining federal oversight of targeted states and jurisdictions, the caucus helped transform the VRA into a more effective law. Its efforts helped trigger what has generally been lauded as a "quiet revolution" of political power in the South.[27] In turn, the increase in majority black districting that resulted from those amendments triggered a series of challenges by white voters on equal protection grounds. The Court has upheld virtually all of these challenges. This chapter concludes that paradoxically, the caucus's successful legislative efforts to amend the VRA to be more open to remedially race-conscious measures triggered the Court's retrenchment against such measures.

Chapter 4 focuses on the CBC's function as amicus curiae in challenges to majority-black districts drawn after 1990 and in compliance with the revised VRA. Turning from the preceding chapter's focus on the caucus's legislative advocacy of the VRA, this chapter sheds light on the CBC's little-known extralegislative role in the legal debates regarding race and redistricting. I emphasize the CBC's position that race-based districting falls squarely within the framers' intent for both the Fourteenth Amendment and the VRA and the idea that its position in these briefs reflects its mission as "the conscience of Congress."[28] This chapter features a content analysis of the briefs submitted by the CBC in *Rodgers v. Lodge, Miller v. Johnson, U.S. v. Hays, Shaw v. Hunt,* and *Northwest Austin Municipal Utility District Number 1 v. Holder. Rodgers* is notable as the first amicus curiae brief submitted by the caucus to the Supreme Court and thus as the starting point of the CBC's engagement with the Court in voting rights cases. *Miller, Hays,* and *Hunt* are the districting cases for which the Caucus submitted amicus briefs. They also demonstrate the CBC's increasingly forceful arguments about the salience of race to the districting process and to minority political power. *Northwest Austin* is the most recent voting rights brief submitted by the CBC and reveals a rhetorical shift back to a tone that is more typical for amicus briefs. Chapter 4 suggests that the CBC's increasingly race-conscious appeals to the Court made the latter more hostile to uses of race in districting and other electoral plans. Taken together, chapters 3 and 4 illustrate both the benefits and the costs of the CBC's "discourse-forcing" methods with respect to race, representation, and law.[29]

Chapter 5 examines these cases from the angle of the Supreme Court majority. The chief argument in this chapter is that through a color-blind interpretation of the VRA and the Fourteenth Amendment, the Court checked Congress in general and the CBC in particular. Chapters 4 and 5 also combine to illustrate the disputes between the legislative and judicial branches regarding the role of race in political representation. Chapter 5 concludes that these institutional and ideological battles endanger those for whom the institutions are ostensibly fighting: black and other historically suppressed minority voters.

Chapter 6 proposes that contemporary tensions about race, law, and redistricting can be informed and perhaps somewhat eased by lessons from the past. It first revisits the *Slaughter-House Cases* and *Strauder v. West Virginia,* two of the Court's earliest interpretations of the Fourteenth Amendment. The former decision has generally been emphasized for the Court's nullification of the amendment's Privileges or Immunities Clause. This analysis emphasizes the Court's narrow and unambiguously race-conscious interpretation of the amendment's Equal Protection and Due

Process Clauses in both cases. This chapter argues that both decisions still serve as appropriate precedents for remedial uses of race in the districting and other electoral processes. The chapter then suggests that because black political thought has embraced both traditional and modern approaches to equality, it offers a complementary and perhaps even transformative approach to considerations of race and equality today. Incorporating rather than continuing to marginalize this body of thought could ease this particular dilemma of pluralism.

Overall, this book examines perennial debates regarding race, law, and representation from perspectives that are typically overlooked or dismissed. Chapter 1 invites us to reconsider contemporary assumptions of color blindness as inevitably objective and egalitarian along with the primacy of color blindness over alternative approaches to eradicating racial inequality and discrimination at the polls.

1 | Competing Approaches to Law and Voting Minority Rights

"Whatever law protects the white man shall afford equal protection to the black man. Whatever means of redress is afforded to one shall be afforded to all."
— Senator Thaddeus Stevens

"Why not come out plainly and frankly to all the world and say what we mean? . . . Give us, then, the colored man, for that and that only is the object that is now before us."
— Senator Jacob Howard

Introduction

The central premise of this book is that black voting rights and political representation are caught between conflicting approaches to the Constitution and the Voting Rights Act (VRA). These conflicts are illustrated by the contrast between the race-conscious advocacy of the Congressional Black Caucus (CBC) and the Supreme Court majority's color-blind jurisprudence. Extending the caucus's position, the central claim in this chapter is that an exclusively color-blind approach to minority voting rights greatly oversimplifies the dynamics of race, representation, and political power. Moreover, it overlooks the race-conscious framing and original intent of the Fourteenth Amendment, along with the Court's initial and race-conscious interpretations of it. Of course the Court long ago declared itself the ultimate interpreter of constitutional and statutory law.[1] The founding fathers also charged the Court, implicitly at least, with balancing minority and majority interests. What is less clear is whether America's founding fathers intended for the Court to trump legislative intent in the process of striking such a balance. In today's context, a color-blind voting rights jurisprudence risks perpetuating persistent inequities between whites and racial minorities. For example, abundant evidence shows that blacks running for Congress still have great difficulty winning elections in anything but majority-black districts.[2] In this respect, minority voters *and* candidates are trapped between conflicting interpretations of the law.

The Court majority's presumptive suspicion of benign race consciousness in the face of continued racial discrimination resembles the concept of cognitive dissonance: "the feeling of psychological discomfort produced by the combined presence of two thoughts that do not follow from one another, in which the greater the discomfort over them, the greater the desire to reduce the dissonance between them."[3] The Court exhibited this condition in the 1990s districting cases when it asserted that minority officials elected by majority-minority districts would not sufficiently represent their white constituents, despite evidence to the contrary and without considering the long tradition of white nonresponsiveness to black constituents. Such dissonance also recurred ten years later in the realm of higher education admissions. While the Court upheld Michigan's use of race as a factor in its graduate admissions policy on the grounds that the state's interest in a diverse student body remained compelling, it also drafted a sunset clause of sorts by holding that "the use of racial preferences will no longer be necessary to further the interest" of racial diversity in higher education after twenty-five years.[4]

This chapter frames the debate between the CBC and the Supreme Court over how to protect black political power from subordination by majority political interests. While the Court majority has staunchly espoused color blindness since the early 1990s, the CBC has advocated a race-conscious approach in the amicus curiae briefs it has submitted in a series of cases involving redistricting and minority voting rights. In so doing, the caucus is continuing a tradition established by black leaders dating back to at least the revolutionary era. In pursuing its mission as the "conscience of Congress," the CBC attempts "honestly to state what [its] opponents and [its] opinions really are" and to engage "in the real morality of public discussion."[5] In this manner, the caucus has sought to expose gritty truths about race and representation despite the political dangers of doing so.

The Court has exchanged a good deal of cross fire across its own turf as well, particularly over the majority's assumptions about color blindness and representation in the 1990s districting cases. The Court as a whole acknowledges that the VRA, including various amendments to it, has fostered racial diversity among elected officials in Congress and elsewhere.

Yet the majority's perception of substantive, descriptive, and symbolic modes of representation is that they are mutually exclusive. Moreover, a racial-group approach to representation offends the majority's traditional individualist notion of equality. Conversely, the Court minority tends to be more open to group ascriptions and to the idea that the various modes of representation can be mutually reinforcing. From these divergent approaches emerge parallel dichotomies: The majority is committed to equalizing electoral processes via individualist color-blind measures, while the minority is more open to equalizing electoral outcomes via group-oriented race-based measures.

One explanation for this internal debate (a reason that is central to the CBC's position) is that viewing the Fourteenth Amendment solely through a color-blind lens distorts its meaning and intent. This point is controversial—which makes it all the more worthy of consideration. Speaking very generally, liberal advocates of minority voting rights tend to interpret the Equal Protection Clause in a way that allows for race-conscious measures to prevent or remedy racial discrimination at the polls. Conservatives, conversely, tend to interpret that clause literally, or by what they perceive as the framers' color-blind intent for it. However, the framing of the Fourteenth Amendment was far from a universal manifestation of color blindness or of racial equality. Moreover, contemporary understandings of racial equality were essentially foreign notions during the Reconstruction era. The following section sheds light on the amendment's framing context, thereby illuminating the paradoxes that have emerged from contemporary color-blind voting rights jurisprudence. This discussion does not intend to "denigrate [the] aspiration" of color blindness.[6] Rather, it intends to demonstrate that as constitutional principles are applied to an evolving society, the line between color blindness and blindness to persisting inequalities based on color can be difficult to discern, leading to confusing and at times retrogressive voting rights decisions.[7]

Racial Classifications in the Constitution

The tendency of voters to engage in racial bloc or other types of factional behavior is a core characteristic of American democracy. Despite Justice Sandra Day O'Connor's condemnation of the practice in *Shaw v. Reno*, racial bloc voting is not always or necessarily egregious. Some observers even consider it part and parcel of American democracy. Indeed, a crucial but forgotten (or ignored?) aspect of Martin Luther King Jr.'s dream of racial equality calls for blacks to "attain bloc-voting importance." Acknowledging that some people might "shudder" at the thought, King maintained that such blocs "are not unique in American life, nor are they inherently evil." On the contrary, because black bloc voting would allow a silenced minority to make its voice heard, such behavior is "a wholesome force on the political scene."[8] In assessing the dilemmas of democratic pluralism, Robert Dahl acknowledged that diversity is "precious" and that identity is tantamount to equality. For Dahl, the dilemma was balancing equality and diversity with uniformity and control.[9]

Another dilemma of racial bloc voting is when it rises (or descends) to the level of rigid and discriminatory racial polarization, i.e., to the level of racism. Specifically, a serious problem arises when a majority group consistently votes as a bloc with the goal of submerging the electoral power of the minority group and thus consistently negates the minority group's political power and preferences. In such situations, color-blind electoral processes do little to level the electoral playing field; worse, they may even perpetuate precisely the inequities that the Court is committed to eradicating. Both because of and despite the Court's deep suspicion of race-conscious electoral measures, the caucus has redoubled its efforts to advocate for race-consciousness measures to offset the effect of majority racial polarization on minority political power. Accordingly, the CBC advocates on behalf of group rights as well. In particular, the 1990s districting cases illustrate that in redistricting, there is no individual alternative "because political representation really pertains to the representation of *groups*, not individuals."[10]

That American politics and law tend to center on groups or racial classifications is not a recent development: The Constitution has deeply embedded racial and group dimensions.[11] Reflecting Enlightenment-era philosophies, America's founding fathers ostensibly sought to protect the liberties of individuals rather than classes of people. However, they did not frame the Constitution as a purely individualist document. Several provisions implicitly but very effectively subordinated blacks both as individuals and as a class. Such provisions include Article I's Three-Fifths Clause, which classified individuals in several ways: It separated whites from blacks, Indians and freedmen from slaves and indentured servants, and relegated "all other persons"—that is, black slaves—as entities to be partially counted for the purposes of apportioning congressional representatives. Article I, Section 9 protected the right to import slaves until 1808, thus classifying individuals by both racial group and servitude status. Article II, Section 1 extended the Three-Fifths Clause to the apportionment of members of the electoral college. The result was most ironic: The representation of slave interests in electoral politics by slaves who, because they had no legal personhood status, had neither the right to vote nor a right to representation. This "slave power" protected the institution of chattel slavery by maintaining the political dominance of proslavery interests until the Civil War.[12] Article IV, Section 2—essentially a fugitive slave clause—classified also by racial group and servitude status by mandating the return of escaped slaves to their masters. Finally, Article V prevented legislation that "in any manner" would affect Article I, Section 9's safeguards on the slave trade before 1808. In sum, while the terms *group, black, race,* and *slave* do not appear in the Constitution, as initially ratified, its subordination of individuals by racial and group classifications is undeniable.

According to the Supreme Court's voting rights decisions since *Shaw v. Reno,* the Fourteenth Amendment is a race-neutral, individualist, and procedural guarantee of equal protection. What tends to be overlooked is that it was framed in a very race- and group-conscious context. Although the Civil War had ended, conflicts over race continued on the legislative battlefield. While all three Reconstruction amendments are commonly viewed as pillars of egalitarianism, newly freed blacks found themselves fettered by what has been characterized as "the knot of Reconstruction": southern Democrat recalcitrance, northern and midwestern prejudice, and radical abolitionist egalitarianism.[13] Not surprisingly, congressional debates over the Fourteenth Amendment were "shot through with Negrophobia," reflected "the prevailing racist policy tacitly accepted by both parties and the general public," and were described by various legislators as "almost ineradicable," "morbid," "nearly insurmountable," and "iron-cased."[14] The Fourteenth Amendment's framers also drew a sharp distinction between comprehensive racial equality and equal protection of the law. Compared to contemporary understandings of it, the amendment was not intended to foster racial integration. Indeed, legislators did not seek to desegregate schools or other public facilities for fear that doing so would endanger the amendment's ratification. At that time, the idea of black children attending the same schools as whites (or schools of the same quality) was not considered a civil right. Indeed, a nondiscrimination clause was removed from the 1866 Civil Rights Act to make it "less objectionable."[15]

The Fourteenth Amendment thus fell far short of Radical Republican senator Thaddeus Stevens's "bright dream" of a mechanism that would erase "every vestige" of inequality, or of Republican senator John Bingham's almost utopian hope that the amendment would not only ensure blacks' civil rights but also purify the Constitution of the evils of its earlier compromises regarding slavery.[16] The amendment also fell short of mandating color blindness as either a means toward equality or an end in and of itself. With respect to civil rights, the Republicans' primary intent was to prevent states from denying people of African descent only the most basic of such rights. Aside from protecting these basic rights, the Republican Party was motivated to pass the Fourteenth and Fifteenth Amendments to add new citizens and voters to their existing coalition and thus shore itself up against the Democrats.[17] Such motivations readily explain characterizations of the initially "uneasy alliance" between blacks and the Republican Party. They also exemplify the theory of "interest convergence," which posits that whites in power do not concede to blacks' demands for civil rights out of altruism or on principle, but only when such concessions serve white interests as well.[18] At the very least, the racially "ambiguous" nature of the Constitution promises ongoing controversies over the meaning and scope of its Fourteenth Amendment.[19]

From Plessy v. Ferguson (1897) to Brown v. Board of Education (1954)

A core argument of this book, which draws from the CBC's amicus briefs, is that the *Shaw* majority's color-blind approach application of the Equal Protection Clause to the redistricting process has its roots in *Brown v. Board of Education*. However, and as the CBC has argued in its briefs, the majority's interpretation of that clause in *Shaw* is ahistorical and thus flawed.[20] The Warren Court's reliance on Justice John Marshall Harlan's *Plessy* dissent to invalidate the Jim Crow concept of separate but equal is itself historically problematic.[21] Examining both of these claims requires confronting difficult truths about Harlan's dissent as well as the context in which he made it. Although *Brown* transformed color blindness from a dissent to a constitutional doctrine, significant differences exist between color blindness as a concept and as a practice. These differences lead to two more difficult considerations: (1) whether color blindness is more appropriate as a means to racial equality or as the actual end and (2) whether color blindness should promote equality or fairness. The second question is particularly challenging, given that equality and fairness are not synonymous and may in fact be at odds with each other. For example, equal treatment of unequally situated actors will likely perpetuate inequality. Egalitarian processes that foster and/or maintain unequal outcomes thus become unfair.

Harlan is legendary for declaring against a majority on the Court and in America that "in view of the constitution, in the eye of the law there is in this country no superior, dominant, ruling class of citizens. . . . Our Constitution is color-blind."[22] Based on this declaration, a half century later, Chief Justice Earl Warren established his equally legendary repudiation of *Plessy*. What tends to be overlooked, however, is that Harlan's dissent was as much a realistic confirmation of America's racially regressive social climate of that era as it was an idealistic expression of racial equality. In raising the concept of color blindness, Harlan challenged the only concept of race consciousness that existed up to his time, a concept rooted in and generated by precepts of white supremacy.[23] For example, Harlan observed,

> The white race deems itself to be the dominant race in this country. And so it is, in prestige, in achievements, in education, in wealth and in power. So, I doubt not, it will continue to be for all time, if it remains true to its great heritage and holds fast to the principles of constitutional liberty.[24]

This aspect of Harlan's dissent is overshadowed, if not willfully ignored, by those who advance it as an embrace of color blindness in American society. Here, Harlan reveals an affirmation of racial pride and hierarchy and reinforces rather than rejects the prevailing racial paternalism of that era.[25] This passage also reflects a group-oriented concept of social order that is at odds with individualist approaches to constitutional law, particularly the Fourteenth Amendment. Harlan speaks of the dominance of one "race" over another, not simply of white individuals discriminating against Homer Plessy. In fact, Harlan's point here comports with another overlooked but perhaps even more crucial aspect of the Court majority's holding in *Plessy*:

> It is claimed by [Plessy] that, in any mixed community, the reputation of belonging to the dominant race, in this instance the white race, is property, in the same sense that a right of action, or of inheritance, is property. *Conceding this to be so,* for the purposes of this case, we are unable to see how this statute deprives him of, or in any way affects his right to, such property. If he be a white man and assigned to a colored coach, he may have his action for damages against the company for being deprived of his so called property. Upon the other hand, if he be *a colored man* and be so assigned, he has been deprived of no property, since he *is not lawfully entitled to the reputation of being a white man.*[26]

It is thus misleading to construe Harlan's statement that the Constitution is color-blind to mean that American society was or even should be racially equal. It is more likely that Harlan was challenging Americans to adhere to a color-blind rule of law. His dissent thus was less concerned with a racially ordered society than with state subordination of one racial group by another.[27]

Understood in this light, Harlan's dissent in *Plessy* illuminates an understated irony of *Brown*: In key respects, the Court's rationale promoted whiteness as the norm. Consequently, the decision reinforced precisely the racial hierarchy that Chief Justice Warren sought to condemn. For example, he made no mention of the harmful impact of racial segregation on whites or on society as a whole. Warren emphasized powerfully the importance of giving black children equal access to white children and superior white schools. But he did not mention the importance of giving white and black children equal access to each other. While the former approach was certainly justifiable in the short term, the holding that black *schools* are inferior to white ones did little to counter long-held perceptions that black *people* are inferior as well. In this way, the *Brown* Court implicitly affirmed the holding in *Plessy* that laws cannot force interracial social equality. The Court repeated such an affirmation in *Brown v. Board of Education II,* with its anemic command that southern states desegregate their schools "with all deliberate speed."[28] It is likely that the Court sought in that decision to balance national and state power during a watershed moment in racial relations and the system of federalism. Yet as the CBC has pointed out repeatedly in its amicus briefs, overlooking the crucial distinctions between color-blind law and a racially hierarchical society risks confusing rather than rather than clarifying contemporary assessments of racial equality.

The Court's rationale in *Brown* is historically inaccurate as well. In condemning racial segregation in public schools, the Warren Court obliquely referred to the "inconclusive nature" of the framing of the Fourteenth Amendment. Declining to "turn the clock back to 1868 when the Amendment was adopted," the justices looked only at the role of public education "in the light of its . . . present place in American life."[29] The intent of the Fourteenth Amendment's framers unquestionably defies easy categorization and reveals a great degree of ambivalence. Moreover, the Court was obviously mindful of burgeoning civil rights activism and the increasing awareness, both in the United States and abroad, of the contradictions between de jure segregation and America's core values.[30] Yet in declining to consider the context of the amendment's framing, the *Brown*

Court "drained [its] institutional memory" of what were clear and important racial aspects of the amendment.[31] In superimposing a color-blind ideal onto the remedially race-conscious origins of the Equal Protection Clause without acknowledging those origins, the Court read out of that clause what many of its framers might readily have accepted: race-based approaches to ending racial inequality.[32]

Such an ahistorical understanding of the Fourteenth Amendment is not unique to the Warren Court, to that era, or to a particular ideology. Liberal and conservative justices alike overlooked the race-conscious aspect of the Fourteenth Amendment in the Court's most recent decision involving pupil placement plans in public schools.[33] And as subsequent chapters demonstrate, beginning in the 1990s, the Rehnquist majority overlooked this aspect of the amendment in key minority voting rights cases.

The Limitations of Contemporary Color-Blind Approaches to Minority Voting Rights

Despite the Court's commitment to color blindness for over a generation, American society bears out Justice Harlan's anticipation of continued white dominance. Compared to whites, African Americans remain overwhelmingly disadvantaged both politically and economically. Between 1973, when the Joint Center for Political and Economic Studies first gathered data, and 2000, the total number of African American elected officials has grown from approximately 1,500 to 9,000.[34] However, African Americans still account for less than 2 percent of all elected officials in the United States.[35] At the end of 2010, the national government was headed by the first African American president, Barack Obama, and the 535 members of Congress included 42 African Americans.[36]

According to the U.S. Census Bureau, the median 2009 household income for blacks was $32,584, compared to $51,861 for whites, while the median per capita income was $18,135 for blacks and $28,034 for for whites. The rate for those living in poverty was 12.3 percent for whites and 25.8 percent for blacks.[37] The vast majority of public schools remain racially isolated and homogeneous (in practice rather than by law), and predominantly minority schools remain inferior in terms of funds, resources, and student outcomes. Thus despite the *Brown* decision and state and local commitments to desegregation, Court opposition to race-based policies designed to mitigate political and educational inequality has intensified in the past fifteen or so years.[38] These realities suggest that color blindness may be viewed at best "as aspiration rather than as description of reality"[39] or as more placebo than panacea: those who believe in color blindness may feel better for it, but color blindness alone has done little to ease the symptoms, much less cure the disease of racism.

Nevertheless, African Americans and other racial minorities have greatly benefited from the *Brown* decision and the commitment to color blindness on the Court and elsewhere. Contemporary race relations are no longer constrained by the invidious legal mechanisms that Homer Plessy and so many before and after him sought to dismantle; nor are they characterized by the systemically brutal racist hierarchy that once characterized the South. Despite these improvements, however, the overall status of blacks in America continues to lag far behind that of whites.

So is the glass of African Americans' political power half full or half empty? In an absolute sense, the past forty years have afforded African Americans the greatest opportunities to advance politically since the Reconstruction era. Not only are blacks again free to vote, they are free to run for and be elected to office and thus to participate fully in the American political system. In addition to the gains in elected office, African Americans have been appointed to increasingly powerful positions in the federal executive and judicial branches. Yet this progress has not been complete. In a relative sense, black political power and influence remain limited, especially in the legislative branch. The CBC's legislative influence in the House tends to be focused on a small cluster of successes, and for now at least, there are no blacks in the Senate.

Can such divergent assessments simultaneously apply to the current status of black political power in the United States? This question leads to another, equally important question that the CBC routinely albeit implicitly poses in its legislative and amicus role: *From whose perspective is the glass of black political power half full or half empty?* The context in which the Supreme Court assesses minority voting rights is crucial to any measurement of the overall strength of black political power. From the perspective of the Court majority since the early 1990s, the glass of black political power appears quite full. Yet because the majority blinds itself to alternative perspectives on the relationship of race to representation, it imperils the CBC's power in particular and the black political power more generally.[40] If, as black leaders have claimed for generations, racial equality is an indicator of the quality and scope of democracy in America, then racial inequality in the political arena undermines democracy.[41] For now, black voters and candidates face new challenges in asserting racial interests in what has now been proclaimed a postracial era that continues to emphasize individual rather than group preferences. Many expressions of the concept of postracialism—itself a vague and arguably premature concept—tend to evade the reality of persisting racial inequality along with the reality that color-blind and/or equal treatment do not necessarily equalize outcomes. To the extent that postracial politics is thus far characterized by minority candidates who present themselves as racially neutral to appeal to white voters, it (1) subordinates minority political interests to those of the majority and (2) is thus quite racialized.[42]

Again, these observations are not meant to condemn color blindness altogether or to suggest that it be replaced by race consciousness. This book posits that both concepts are complementary rather than competing approaches to racial equality. An exclusively color-blind perspective can blind its advocates to the complexity of the dynamics among race, identity, and representation. For example, Abigail Thernstrom has long theorized that "categorizing individuals for political purposes" by race and "sanctioning group membership" would impede political integration.[43] The Court majority relied heavily on this argument in its *Shaw* opinion. However, in its amicus brief in *Miller v. Johnson,* the CBC presented data indicating that blacks elected by majority black districts represented all of their constituents regardless of their race. David Canon and Katherine Tate have also found that blacks elected from districts drawn in a race-conscious manner are well integrated into the congressional mainstream, including party and committee leadership.[44] These findings verify that race-conscious districting does not foster racially exclusive representation; moreover, it can foster more inclusive and egalitarian outcomes. These conflicts between theory and facts inform the CBC's legislative and amicus arguments that for the most part, the choice is not so much between color blindness and race consciousness but between different forms of race consciousness.[45]

The Court majority conceded in 2003 that race remains a salient factor in American life despite decades of both race-conscious and color-blind remedies. Holding that fostering diverse leadership remains a compelling justification for using race as a factor in law school admissions, the justices nonetheless anticipated that there would be no need for such uses of race twenty-five years in the future. Four years later, in a challenge to the use of race in public school pupil placements, the Court seemed to obviate the need for both time lines and diversity, as evidenced by Chief Justice John Roberts's rather specious conclusion that "the way to stop discrimination on the basis of race is to stop discriminating on the basis of race."[46] Roberts's stance reveals how far the Court has departed from its 1977 observation that "in order to get beyond racism we must first take account of race," a view that more closely aligns with the CBC's approach to law and voting rights.[47]

The Shallow Roots of Color-Blind Originalism

A key source of the debate between the CBC and the Court majority over race and voting rights is their divergent approach to constitutional interpretation: Where the former takes a more flexible reading, the latter adheres to a more strictly originalist one. Generally speaking, originalism is the practice of interpreting constitutional provisions as closely to the actual text as possible and, in the absence of specific text, according to the original intent of those who drafted and adopted the Constitution.[48] The question of how closely original intent should bind subsequent generations has long been debated. Starting with the 1990s districting cases, the Court majority has taken what is generally considered an originalist approach to the Fourteenth Amendment, concluding that the Equal Protection Clause guarantees a color-blind districting process.

A distinguishing feature of the CBC's position with respect to race-based districting and its intent for the VRA is the challenge of the Court majority's originalism. The caucus's challenge is intensified by its call for the majority to make a more fully historical application of the Equal Protection Clause to race and representation. In the caucus's view, an originalist reading of the Fourteenth Amendment does not mandate color blindness. This view reflects the provocative claim that there is "no plausible originalist argument that the Constitution proscribes" federal enactment of either benign or invidious race-conscious laws.[49] This claim is grounded in a close reading of the Reconstruction amendments as well as founding-era federal and state laws. In addition to the Constitution's original provisions that protected chattel slavery and promoted racial inequality, the antebellum Congress passed several statutes that were both explicitly and invidiously race-conscious. The Naturalization Act of 1790 limited naturalization to immigrants of white descent. The Militia Act of 1792 compelled states to exclude blacks from military service. (Ironically, an earlier version of that act was race-neutral.) The Judiciary Act of 1789 was racially discriminatory as a consequence of its incorporation of state-level laws excluding free blacks from jury duty and from testifying against whites. Congress also enacted several laws that were racially benign with respect to blacks—most notably, an extension of prohibitions against kidnapping free blacks and taking them into newly admitted slave states and territories.[50]

At the state level, race-conscious laws protected slavery, denied blacks the right to vote or hold office, limited blacks in state militia to unarmed duties, denied or restricted blacks' ability to own property or enter into a contract negotiations, restricted the entry of manumitted blacks into free states, created two-tiered criminal codes, and denied blacks' rights to bear witness against whites or to own weapons, congregate publicly, or consume alcohol in taverns. Laws prohibiting interracial marriage and miscegenation and imposing residency limitations on blacks were also common. Many laws (particularly those banning interracial marriages and miscegenation or assigning servitude status to children based on their race or the status of their mothers) were extensions of colonial-era provisions.[51] As with federal laws, some states had benign race-conscious laws that, for example, mandated black literacy, guaranteed blacks' rights to jury trials, limited the length of time that blacks could be indentured as servants, and penalized the capture and sale of free blacks in slave states.

The race-conscious aspects of the ensuing Reconstruction amendments also contradict contemporary originalists' claims that the amendments were intended to be color-blind. While the state- and local-based institution of Jim Crow is common knowledge, less is known about invidious federal laws enacted during and after the Reconstruction. Many of these measures called for the segregation of schools and the armed forces, while others put limits on nonwhites' ability to naturalize as citizens. (Although Congress extended basic citizenship rights to all with the Fourteenth Amendment, the Naturalization Act of 1790 continued to prevent immigrants not deemed white from naturalizing.)[52] Conversely, the Reconstruction-era Congress enacted a great deal of laws treating blacks preferentially, most notably the Civil Rights Act of 1866. Although the statute was weak, poorly enforced, and ultimately overruled by the Court in 1875, its remedially race-conscious intent is significant. The Freedmen's Bureau, while notoriously poorly administered, was explicitly and benignly race-conscious. Congress also passed other laws that provided educational benefits exclusively for black Civil War veterans, regulated the fees for agents collecting war bounties for black veterans, and regulated charity payments directed to institutions servicing former slaves. The existence of such laws suggests that contemporary policies such as remedial race-based districting and affirmative action, at least at the federal level, do not violate the Constitution.[53]

As with legislative intent, the early record of the Supreme Court's interpretation of the Fourteenth Amendment defies simplification. In its initial readings, the Court took a decidedly race-conscious perspective, holding that the Reconstruction amendments were primarily for the benefit of blacks (see chapter 6). At the same time, the Court did not establish a racially egalitarian or exclusively color-blind doctrine. Reflecting the distinctions of that time between higher-order social equality and more basic civil equality, the Court cobbled together an equal protection jurisprudence that rejected challenges to segregated public accommodations while protecting (albeit incompletely) blacks' physical and property security. Such ambivalence during this time also reflected the Republican Party's waning commitment to the Reconstruction's civil rights goals.[54]

In light of these considerations, it is clear that the Reconstruction amendments "as understood by those who enacted them" allow for remedial race-conscious laws and grant the legislature and the executive "near plenary power to enact invidious, as well as benign, color-conscious laws."[55] That last point is admittedly an unsettling one. However, the CBC would argue that given persistent racially polarized voting, minority vote dilution, and other discriminatory electoral challenges that have emerged despite the Fourteenth and Fifteenth Amendments and the VRA, fear of invidious federal uses of race is not a sufficient reason to prohibit preventive uses of race. Take for example Mark Graber's claim that condemnations of the *Dred Scott* decision obscure the view that as a matter of law, it was correct.[56] In other words, fears of such invidious uses constrain the search for truth in John Stuart Mill's sense. They also ignore historical justifications for race-conscious federal enforcement of blacks' voting rights.[57] Such fears foreclose difficult but necessary discussions about the Fourteenth Amendment's significance in American law and politics and discourage efforts to discern the intent and meaning behind contemporary uses of race.[58] This discernment includes the recognition that (1) the dichotomy between color-blind originalism and race-conscious interpretivism can be false and distracting and (2) strict adherence to the Constitution's text is not always "right," nor is a flexible reading of it always "wrong."[59] As the CBC has pointed out to the Court, such all-or-nothing approaches betray the Constitution if taken at the expense of those whom the Fourteenth Amendment was originally intended to protect.

Conclusion

Since the 1970s, the CBC has played a key role in the debate regarding competing approaches to the role of race in law and representation. Its race-conscious activism in Congress and with the Supreme Court will remain crucial as long as blacks struggle to maintain meaningful political presence and power, especially in Congress. Again, African Americans have certainly enjoyed substantial political gains since the passage of the VRA. African Americans are present at all levels of government. Yet while Obama's pathbreaking election as U.S. president is monumental, it is so far an exceptional occurrence. It is too soon to gauge the putative "Obama effect" on established or future black representation.[60] Nor has his presidency automatically advanced blacks' political and policy interests.[61]

Here, it is crucial to note that black political advancement since the passage of the VRA is significant because such a large portion of the black electorate was starting virtually from zero. In other words, gains in African American electoral power appear far more striking when evaluated in an absolute rather than a relative sense. But when compared to the inroads made by other racial and ethnic minority groups into American politics, African Americans' gains appear less striking. Black political power continues to be challenged by lags in education and income levels, felon disfranchisement laws, instances of voter suppression and "caging,"[62] distrust of authority, frustration with the electoral process, perceptions of an insufficiently responsive Democratic Party, and skepticism of an unconcerned if not hostile Republican Party. When Republican Party chair Michael Steele was asked after a lecture he had delivered why any black person should vote for a GOP candidate, his response—that the party currently does not offer sufficient reason to do so—was particularly illuminating.[63]

Several years ago, Girardeau Spann concluded that African Americans' traditional reliance on legal strategies to enforce civil rights is misguided. Framing the Warren Court and its civil rights jurisprudence as an exception, Spann argued that the Supreme Court is on the whole an "inherently conservative" body that is "consigned to operate as little more than a covert agent of the majority." For Spann, the problem is that the Court is generally "unable to protect minorities from the tyranny of the majority" even when it is willing to do so. Thus, the constitutional provisions intended to insulate the judiciary from political pressures and maximize its objectivity— life tenure and guaranteed salaries—are generally insufficient to counter the pull toward majoritarian decision making and preservation of the status quo.[64] More recently, Michael Klarman has argued that because legal meaning lies in the eye of the beholder, constitutional interpretation is inevitably bound up with political and personal considerations. Taking Spann's argument further, Klarman concludes that the justices have "little inclination and limited power to resist" dominant public opinion. Ironically, therefore, a minority group most in need of judicial protection is often "least likely to receive it."[65] Similarly, Graber contends that constitutional law itself "is structurally incapable of yielding consensually just ... or right answers to constitutional controversies," in part because "an ambivalent polity generates ambivalent constitutional arguments."[66]

From these perspectives, the CBC's advocacy of a jurisprudence that allows for race-conscious remedies to race-based problems such as vote dilution becomes even more compelling. As a friend of the Court, the caucus has endorsed contemporary "redemptive constitutionalism": a "great American tradition" that approaches the Constitution as a work in progress and that necessitates ongoing amendment to promote the great American traditions of liberty, equality, and democracy.[67] African American voters are of course responsible for enhancing their political power via increased mobilization and participation. Similarly, the CBC's success depends on its ability to coalesce with other interests in Congress while promoting Democratic Party imperatives. As chapter 3 demonstrates, without coalitional politics, the CBC could not have been as instrumental in strengthening and extending the VRA in 1975, 1982, and 2006. Yet for the moment, African Americans still depend heavily on judicial receptiveness to race-based efforts to level the political playing field and to prevent the weakening or retrogression of those gains in political power that have come about with the help of the VRA.

So, as Martin Luther King Jr. asked near the end of his life, Where do we go from here as far as black political power is concerned? What is to be done to keep African American political power from being whittled back down by a Court majority that blinds itself to the effects of residual and ongoing racial discrimination? Must black folk again hurry up and wait for the Court to adopt a more inclusive ideology, this time geared toward parity of political outcomes as opposed to equal opportunities alone? How can blacks increase their political power given (1) judicial hostility to racial- and group-oriented electoral remedies, (2) judicial and political hostility to electoral alternatives such as proportional representation or voting,[68] and (3) the constraints of America's two-party system?

A preliminary response is more of a challenge than an answer. As the CBC has suggested in its amicus briefs, if the Court is truly interested in protecting blacks' voting rights and in enhancing the overall quality of democracy, it must be open to race- and group-based approaches to combating persistent racial discrimination at the polls. To do so, the Court must adopt a more historically and racially contextualized jurisprudence. For its part, the CBC and minority voters must be patient. In the words of one observer, "taming Court opposition takes time, energy, and requires living uncertainly" with possible judicial retrenchments.[69] The CBC and its allies must also continue to be architects of an expanded vision of political representation. Such actions include promoting frank, substantive discussions of how color-blind processes can yield racially unequal outcomes, with the goal of holding color-blind constitutionalists more accountable for their "ambivalent" attitudes toward matters of race and power.[70] In so doing, perhaps Americans can rise to one of King's final challenges:

> Let us . . . not think of the [civil rights] movement as one that seeks to integrate [blacks] into all existing values of American society. Let us [instead] be those creative dissenters who will call our . . . nation to a higher destiny, to a new plateau of compassion, to a more noble expression of humaneness.[71]

Chapter 2 will explore the calls of several creative but largely forgotten dissenters who laid much of the substantive and rhetorical groundwork for King's challenge and for the CBC's agenda.

2 | Foundations of Black Political Activism: Pushing Idealist Boundaries

> "The macro-historical perspective seems to me to be eminently sound. . . . There are certain 'realities' of developments over time that should not be overlooked. The courts have faced these matters head-on and . . . were not blind to the historical purpose of continuing racial *exclusion*. . . . Today . . . we should not be blind to the need to take race into account for the ultimate purpose of *inclusion*."
> —Charles Hamilton, 1994

This chapter offers an essential context for any analysis of contemporary African American politics and for this particular analysis of the approach taken by the Congressional Black Caucus (CBC) to the Voting Rights Act (VRA) and the Fourteenth Amendment: nineteenth-century black political thought. With respect to contemporary work on African American politics, this chapter attempts to fill in the gaps of what has been termed the "political context variable"—that is, an approach to representative politics from a black, or race-conscious, perspective.[1] This chapter also illustrates how African Americans' "quest for universal freedom" has consistently sought to expand the scope of the core American values of liberty, equality, and democracy.[2] Moreover, since its inception in 1971, the CBC has advanced a race-conscious quest for universal freedom to its fellow legislators at each renewal of the VRA. It has had considerably less success with the Supreme Court in cases involving minority voting rights. However, simply because the caucus's perspective troubles the majority on the Court does not rob that perspective of its value. The caucus, like the black leadership that preceded it, has often provoked difficult but necessary discussions of the centrality of race in American democracy. Such discussions are all the more crucial now, as America attempts to untangle persisting knots of racial tension and inequality while crossing the threshold into a putatively postracial era.

The goal of this chapter is to remedy ahistorical approaches to American politics that "warp and distort" contemporary studies of race and politics.[3] Such distortions include the misperceptions that black politics were nonexistent prior to the 1960s and that African Americans were politically "awakened" during the 1950s–60s. Another misperception is that because the civil rights movement accomplished so many of its goals, racial discrimination has been all but eradicated from American society and that moments of racism are rare and isolated and the related view that contemporary racial inequality results from blacks' failure to avail themselves of the opportunities that emerged out of the civil rights movement. Overall, these misperceptions make it easy to believe that America is indeed color-blind and that remedial or preventive race-conscious laws such as the VRA are now obsolete.[4] Such conclusions not only marginalize blacks' participation in America's political development but reflect a disturbing disconnection from reality.

By no means does this chapter attempt to cover the entire body of nineteenth-century black political thought. It is impossible for one chapter or even one book to do justice to this rich literature. This chapter emphasizes the political contributions of black leaders, particularly of the antebellum era, who have been overlooked in political science or overshadowed by luminaries such as Frederick Douglass, Sojourner Truth, Booker T. Washington, W. E. B. Du Bois, and Ida B. Wells. It also situates these larger figures in context with other lesser-known but equally significant black leaders of their time. Finally, this chapter will show that the CBC's substantive and rhetorical roots reach far deeper than the civil rights movement or the twentieth century. This chapter also corrects the misperception that because blacks during the antebellum and early Jim Crow eras were largely disenfranchised, they were politically disengaged as well. Such misperceptions are fueled in part by the dearth of early black voices in the canon of American political thought and development. Because nineteenth-century blacks had virtually no formal political presence except during the brief Reconstruction era, they tend not to be studied as political actors. Until the past fifteen or so years, scholarship on black leadership and political thought has been classified under African American studies, history, or similar disciplines. Indeed, a particularly thorough and illuminating analysis of black political thought appears in a volume on the history and influence of African American art on American history.[5] While the interdisciplinary nature of black political thought is one of its strengths, this body of thought needs to be more fully incorporated into political science. For example, students encountering these thinkers in my courses routinely express frustration at having previously learned little or nothing about these men and women. This chapter thus introduces young scholars of American politics to this vital body of thought.

Finally, this chapter illuminates the relevance of blacks' dual outsider/insider perspectives on the American polity to contemporary debates regarding race and representation.[6] Even when they were completely marginalized from politics, African Americans (like many other marginalized groups) had a great deal at stake in and a great deal to say about the American political system. Nineteenth-century leaders offered multiple approaches to resolving the legal and political tensions between race and representation in America. Borrowing Hannah Pitkin's description of the various concepts of representation, early black political thought contributes an embarrassment of ideological riches to the canon of American political thought.[7] Consequently, and as chapter 6 discusses in more detail, the arguments of early black political leaders provide a useful fulcrum on which to balance contemporary conflicts about race and representation.

One of the hallmarks of nineteenth-century black political thought is its "creative conflict" of voices and ideas.[8] Black leadership drew from slaves, free persons, ministers, entrepreneurs, journalists, laborers, educators, and politicians. And although nineteenth-century women were relegated to the "private sphere," black women participated in abolition and suffrage movements. The immediate goals of black leaders during this century varied as circumstances changed. Objectives included abolition, emigration, suffrage, civil rights, land and labor rights, and integration. Despite the diversity of voices and circumstances, early black political thought of this era was consistent in its overarching goals. Virtually every black leader in this century advanced America's core principles of liberty, democracy, and equality, including a racially inclusive concept of them. What at times appears to be a conflicted body of thought reflects in part the debate among whites over blacks' position in the American polity. Conversely, the disagreements among early black leaders more often involved means rather than than ends. This chapter explores blacks' early expressions of liberty and democracy, all of which had equality at their core.

Liberty and the Battles to Abolish Chattel Slavery

Black leaders of the nineteenth-century universally embraced the concept of liberty.[9] However, blacks and whites had profoundly different concepts of it. As expressed by American revolutionaries and founding fathers, liberty centered on individual autonomy and freedom of action from the state. In other words, liberty meant freedom to *do*. For African Americans, liberty was premised on physical freedom, both as individuals and as a class, from a system of involuntary servitude that deprived blacks of autonomy, legal personhood, and humanity. For them, liberty was first and foremost about freedom to *be*. This aspect of liberty, which even indentured whites took for granted as a natural and inevitable right, was for blacks a prerequisite to all other aspects of liberty.

David Walker's expressions of this concept of liberty were audacious, pushing for an expansion of limited visions of liberty and equality, and his rhetoric resonates far beyond his time. Born of free status 1785 in North Carolina, Walker spent most of his life in Boston, supporting himself as a clothing merchant. With the release of his 1829 *Appeal to the Coloured Citizens of the World*, Walker became America's first widely published black abolitionist.[10] He was widely known in Boston abolitionist circles and worked closely with William Lloyd Garrison. Garrison initially endorsed Walker in *The Liberator* and lent Walker the use of his presses to print the *Appeal*.[11] Yet Walker's militance conflicted with Garrison's commitment to pacifism and the politics of moral suasion (the belief that slavery must be abolished not by armed resistance but by moral example). Walker's firsthand observations of chattel slavery were limited to his early childhood and to his adult travels to South Carolina. The atrocities of that institution, his routine experiences with discrimination in Boston, his commitment to racial solidarity, and his belief in the American revolutionary concept of citizenship and autonomy motivated him to write the *Appeal*. In this regard, the title of his treatise is inaccurate. Walker in fact appealed to at least four primary audiences: enslaved blacks, free blacks, whites involved in slavery, and whites who were not directly involved in but tolerated the institution.

The roots of the contemporary concept of Black Power clearly trace back to Walker, making him one of the chief "creat[ors of] Black nationalist ideology."[12] Proudly black and Afrocentric, he celebrated Africa's contributions to world history. Yet Walker also professed a love of America's ideals and put the nation to the test with respect to its professions of liberty and equality. Indeed, the *Appeal* resonates with the Declaration of Independence and America's founding fathers, particularly Thomas Jefferson. Rather than wait for whites to abolish slavery, Walker sought to "awaken in the breasts of afflicted, degraded and slumbering brethren a spirit of inquiry . . . respecting [blacks'] miseries and wretchedness in this

Republican Land of Liberty." For him, free blacks had no moral or practical choice but to pursue abolition and self-determination; their "glory and happiness . . . shall never be fully consummated but with the entire emancipation of their enslaved brethren."[13] Here and in general, Walker endorsed both individual and collective forms of resistance that relied on the assets of free blacks. This prescription was reintroduced several decades later by Alexander Crummell and was reshaped by Du Bois's "Talented Tenth" approach to uplifting the black race.

Walker's *Appeal* was also a religious crusade against an institution that he condemned as a "curse to nations," "hell upon earth," and "barbarous cruelty."[14] He was influenced by black Christian leaders such as Robert Allen and Absalom Jones, founders of the African Methodist Episcopal Church, and by Protestantism more generally. Like his colleagues Maria Stewart and Henry Highland Garnet, Walker believed that religion and social justice were too interdependent for one to be properly served without a clear commitment to the other.[15] Walker's dual commitment amplified his abolitionism: Because "God almighty is the sole proprietor or master of the whole human family . . . the man who will stand still and let another murder [or enslave] him is worse than an infidel."[16] Walker predicted (or threatened, depending on one's perspective) that chattel slavery, being "ten thousand times more injurious to this country than all the other evils put together," would be "the final overthrow of this government." He thus cautioned those who complied with it "to repent and reform, or [be] ruined."[17] This prediction may sound purely vengeful, especially to contemporary ears that have become sensitized to religious zealotry and violence in recent years. Yet given the centrality of chattel slavery in antebellum America, this prediction was not implausible. Nor was it unique to abolitionists. Walker was clearly responding to Thomas Jefferson's reflections on slavery as a "great political and moral evil" and his trepidations that with respect to slavery, God's "justice cannot sleep for ever. . . . The Almighty has no attribute which can take side with us in such a contest" between slave owners and slaves.[18]

Walker is accurately described as militant and radical. However, such characterizations are incomplete. To the extent that he reflected the spirit of the American revolution, his motivation is quite conventional, if not patriotic. While he argued that blacks were obligated by America's founding principles to overthrow the institution of chattel slavery, he challenged whites to compare "their own" Declaration of Independence to the "cruelties and murders inflicted" on blacks. He closed the *Appeal* with the preamble with the Declaration, daring blacks to "throw off [their] murderous government and provide new guards for [their] future security."[19] Walker invoked American ideals to justify extending them to African Americans. In this respect, he sought to complete the American Revolution in a more inclusive manner.

Walker was equally adamant that blacks needed to be self-sufficient and they had more than earned the right to pursue happiness in America, having "enriched it with [their] blood and tears." He also believed that whites were obligated to help "raise [blacks] from the condition of brutes to that of respectable men, and to make a national acknowledgement . . . for the wrongs they have inflicted." Here, Walker almost scripts later calls for slavery reparations. Ultimately though, he held blacks responsible for earning respect as human beings by "prov[ing] to the Americans and the world that [they] are men, and not brutes." He was keenly aware of why blacks were kept "in the lowest state of degradation and ignorance," noting that "for coloured people to acquire learning in this country makes tyrants quake and tremble." This was all the more reason to push for an education that went beyond "pretenses" and involved "the substance of learning."[20] Walker's emphasis here previews the debates between Booker T. Washington and W. E. B. Du Bois. It also previews class divisions on this issue as reflected in more recent debates among African Americans over vouchers, charter schools, and the role of "ebonics" and Afrocentrism in the curriculum.

Walker's belief that blacks had earned the right to pursue happiness in America made him particularly scornful of emigration to Liberia or other countries. Like many of his peers, he was well aware that the American Colonization Society, instrumental in establishing the colony and eventually the state of Liberia, was comprised of white elites whose economic stakes in maintaining the institution of slavery prompted them to establish a place to which to remove black abolitionists from the United States.[21] In a rare conciliatory moment, Walker acknowledged that blacks and whites "are all in this world together," entreating whites to "throw away [their] fears and prejudices" and treat blacks like men so that Americans "will all live in peace and happiness together." This is one of several ways that Walker challenged Jefferson's assertions of black inferiority. Recognizing that Jefferson was "as great a characters [sic] as ever lived amongst the whites," Walker commended the former president for his "public labours for the United States of America" and lauded him as a "great [a] philosopher as the world never [sic] afforded." Walker also believed that Jefferson's stature meant that his pejorative views of African Americans would not likely "pass away into oblivion unobserved by his people," thus rendering him "as great a barrier to [black] emancipation as anything that has ever been advanced against" the race. Walker's commendations of Jefferson's principles underscore his belief that Jefferson had betrayed those principles and thus America. In his typically race-conscious manner, Walker declared that Jefferson's misperceptions of blackness must be "refuted by the blacks themselves"; otherwise, blacks risked confirming those misperceptions.[22]

Walker's race consciousness was perhaps most evident in his militant approach to the abolition of slavery. For him, the black man "who would not fight . . . to be delivered from the most wretched, abject and servile slavery . . . ought to be kept with all his children or family, in slavery."[23] To those who hesitated at opportunities to resist or escape slavery he proclaimed,

> Whites have had us under them for more than three centuries. . . . [T]here is an unconquerable disposition in the breasts of blacks which, when it is fully awakened . . . will be subdued only with the destruction of [their] animal existence. . . . [T]herefore, if there is an attempt [to escape] made by us, kill or be killed.[24]

Walker reserved his harshest criticism for slaves who betrayed escape efforts. In his view, any collaboration with slave owners or overseers was unforgivable; for slaves motivated to prevent the murder of white slave owners or overseers, death was a just compensation.[25] Walker's wrath at such complicity may seem justifiable; however, it is likely that his vantage point as a free man in Boston impeded his appreciation of the difficulties slaves faced in openly challenging slavery. He may also not have been aware of slaves' myriad and subtle acts of resistance disguised by appearances of ignorance and servility.[26] That point aside, it is clear that Walker did not advocate abolition merely for its own sake but also to redeem the nation.

Not surprisingly, the *Appeal* was banned in the South. Some states levied fines of one thousand dollars against anyone caught smuggling the piece into the South. Georgia offered a ten-thousand-dollar bounty for Walker's live capture, and the mayor of Savannah implored his counterpart in Boston to punish Walker. The governors of Georgia and Virginia also wrote to Boston's mayor expressing their trepidations about the presence of the *Appeal* in their states. Such reactions were not born merely of paranoia. Not only did Walker's essay call for armed rebellion, it may have helped incite Nat Turner to launch his bloody 1831 insurrection.[27] Walker may have paid the ultimate price for his militancy. Shortly after the third edition of the *Appeal* was published, the thirty-five-year-old Walker was found dead near his home. Rumors that he was poisoned have been neither confirmed nor put to rest, although recent research suggests that he died of tuberculosis or natural causes.[28]

It is easy to compare Walker's militant and race-conscious approach to liberation to that of Malcolm X. Yet Walker's faith in Christianity and America's core values is clearly echoed by Martin Luther King Jr.'s approach to racial equality. King was committed to nonviolent resistance, whereas Walker, like Malcolm X, viewed violence as a necessary evil. All three men, however, shared a redemptive and universal approach to liberty and equality in that they were not solely concerned with blacks' interests but were also committed to enhancing the integrity of the state and ultimately humanity. Walker has also been credited with laying the groundwork for modern expressions of Black Power and nationalism. With a rhetorical force rivaling that of Malcolm X, Fred Hampton, and Kwamé Touré (Stokely Carmichael), Walker pioneered the pursuit of liberty and equality "by any means necessary." Yet to the degree that Walker's *Appeal* was grounded in America's revolutionary principles, he is as much a patriot as a pariah. In his view, slavery constituted the ultimate betrayal of the American people and state. Like so many black leaders who succeeded him, Walker challenged America to redeem itself by holding itself accountable to its values and by granting blacks full and equal membership in the polity.[29]

Given that the vast majority of African Americans had no access to formal political processes during the antebellum era, they were compelled to pursue political and economic autonomy through nonelectoral means. Some sought opportunities in Canada and Liberia as well as in Mexico, South and Central America, and the Caribbean. For the most part, however, blacks opposed emigration on three grounds. First was the principled conviction that all blacks born in the United States were first and foremost humans and thus entitled to full U.S. citizenship. Second was the pragmatic argument that blacks both free and enslaved had earned their citizenship rights as an overworked but undercompensated group. The third reason stemmed from suspicion of the motives of the American Colonization Society. As one skeptic summed it up, if society members were "real friends to Africa, let them expend the money which they collect in erecting a college to educate her injured sons in this land of gospel, light and liberty."[30]

Given the dearth of opportunities for blacks, interest in emigration peaked twice during the nineteenth century, first in the late antebellum era (in response to the Fugitive Slave Act of 1850 and the *Dred Scott* decision of 1857) and later as the Republican Reconstruction efforts were dismantled by southern Democratic Redeemers and the Jim Crow regime. Black support of emigration tended to diverge in two key ways: (1) between religious and secular approaches; (2) whether to establish a colony or an independent nation. Much of the research on emigration focuses on its sociological, cultural, and economic aspects, especially with regard to Marcus Garvey's entrepreneurial vision, which swept through northern black communities in the early 1900s. Far less attention has been paid to the political aspects of nineteenth-century black emigration. The proslavery aspect of Liberia's founding is routinely overlooked as well, and it is still commonly mischaracterized as a country created by and for the benefit of freed slaves, with little mention that many blacks who emigrated were not slaves but members of the educated elite. Such depictions also omit the African Civilization Society, an alternative to the American Colonization Society that was largely founded by blacks and sought to create a black-run and autonomous West Africa.

One founder of this latter organization was Henry Highland Garnet, a protégé of Walker who picked up the mantle of radical black abolitionism after Walker's death. Born in 1815 as a slave, Garnet escaped with his family to New York City. He was spurred to activism in his teens after witnessing his father's narrow escape from bounty hunters.[31] Garnet received a year of liberal education at the Noyes Academy in Canaan, New Hampshire (an experimental school integrated by race and sex), before the school was demolished by local whites who opposed it. As an adult, he quickly ascended in the abolition movement and by the late 1830s was second in influence only to Frederick Douglass. Garnet initially took a racially integrated approach to abolition and, like Douglass and Walker, worked with William Lloyd Garrison. Over time he turned more toward Walker's aggressive and race-conscious views and split from Douglass and Garrison.[32] Although Garnet never completely abandoned the goal of racial integration, he emphasized black autonomy as the foundation of black resistance and empowerment. This shift in trajectory likely resulted in part from his upbringing in a self-sufficient, Afrocentric community.[33] Garnet became most renowned for his race-conscious approach to abolition, particularly his 1840s address to blacks to "let [their] motto be resistance!" as well as his view that "no oppressed people have ever secured their liberty without resist[ing]" their oppression actively. To amplify his points, when Garnet published his address in 1848, he included the entire text of Walker's *Appeal* as an appendix.[34]

Around that time, Douglass began to wield his enormous influence in a way that discredited Garnet within the mainstream and more pacifist abolitionist community.[35] Although he was eventually overshadowed by Douglass, Garnet did not waver from his activism. Like Walker (and as a Presbyterian minister), Garnet's abolitionism was imbued with Christian morality. He believed that it was "sinful in the extreme for [blacks] to make voluntary submission" to slavery and that it was their "solemn and imperative duty to use every means, both moral, intellectual and physical," to achieve liberation. Similarly, he implored blacks in bondage to appeal to whites' "sense of justice, and [to i]nform them that all you desire is freedom, and that nothing else will suffice." Also like Walker, Garnet grounded his resistance in American revolutionary terms. Echoing Patrick Henry's famous declaration, Garnet asserted that it was better for blacks to "die freemen than live to be slaves" and that there was simply no debate "whether it is better to choose liberty or death."[36]

Over time, Garnet developed a sophisticated three-pronged theory of black liberation, some of which resonates in the writings and goals of the National Association for the Advancement of Colored People, the civil rights and Black Power movements, the Black Panther Party, and eventually the CBC. On the issue of black citizenship and civil rights, he stated that the "discerning political economist" had no more right than the "untutored African . . . to the full enjoyment of his freedom" and that the "history of the human race is but one continued struggle for rights."[37] Second, primarily as a result of his "growing disillusionment with racial conditions in America," Garnet became convinced that emigration from America was the only viable option for black liberation and self-sufficiency. Mere colonization, however, was not an option. Rather, he advocated the establishment of a politically and economically independent, black-led nation in Liberia, at which point he became involved in the African Colonization Society. Third, and most presciently, Garnet addressed the crippling effects on both blacks and whites of chattel slavery in the context of capitalism and wage labor. He contended that both races shared interests around which to unite and that blacks "could [not] be completely free as long as whites were under the control of monopolists."[38] Making this point in 1841, he foreshadowed by more than two decades Karl Marx's converse axiom that "labour cannot emancipate itself in the white skin where in the black it is branded."[39] Garnet also laid a plank in the foundation of the alternative budget that the CBC has advanced every year, seeking "to preserve a national commitment to fair treatment for urban and rural America, the elderly, students, small businessmen and women, middle and low income wage earners, the economically disadvantaged and a new world order."[40]

In sum, Garnet stands out for his appeals for an integrated effort to overthrow the oppressive aspects of both slave and wage labor. He endeavored to maximize the possibilities for interracial cooperation and advancement without sacrificing blacks' autonomy in the process. He also sought to reconfigure the relationship between black nationalism and liberty, equality, and patriotism. Garnet's fusion of self-determination with integration reappeared in the modern civil rights era, as echoed by Martin Luther King's observation that disputes over communism increased his concern about social justice" and the hardships of the underprivileged.[41] Garnet's economic theories have also been reflected in the work of post–civil rights era black economic theorists such as Robert Allen and Manning Marable.[42]

Working with Garnet, especially with respect to emigration, was Martin Delany. Delany wore several hats from the 1840s through the 1880s, including abolitionist, emigrationist, Union Army officer, politician, party activist, and political writer. Fiercely race-conscious, Delany has also been credited as a founding father of black nationalism. Later in his life, perhaps as a response to slavery and entrenched white resistance to black activism, he came to hail blacks, particularly those of "pure" African descent, as a superior people. Overall however, Delany advanced "eloquent espousal[s] of purely American ideals purged of racism and racial subjugation."[43] He attacked prevailing theories of race science that buttressed notions of white supremacy, asserting that "white is simply a negative, having no color at all," and that the "coloring matter [of the] blackest African is . . . identically the same" as for the "most delicately beautiful white lady." Delany also theorized that because Africa "stands in the centre" of the five major global divisions, Africans were in fact "the centre and propagators of the highest civilization."[44] Yet while his Afrocentrism unabashedly rejected white supremacy as well as the color caste bias pervasive among blacks and whites, it was shot through with elitism. Delany's class bias likely reflects that he was born free, was formally educated, and had married into Pittsburgh's black elite. He was admitted to Harvard University's medical school but remained there only briefly before Dean Oliver Wendell Holmes asked Delany and his black classmates to leave because their presence "distracted" their white colleagues.[45] Delany's prescription for racial "elevation" reflected fellow emigrationist Alexander Crummell's theory that black elites were obligated to commit their talent and resources to the uplift of the entire race. This view would later be adapted by Crummell's protégé, Du Bois, into the more familiar "Talented Tenth" approach. Delany also extolled the value of industrial education; in that respect, he presaged Booker T. Washington's emphasis on practical rather than theoretical learning.

In 1852, Delany published *The Condition, Elevation, Emigration, and Destiny of the Colored People of the United States, Politically Considered.* This treatise appeared shortly after the enactment of the 1850 Fugitive Slave Law, which strengthened and expanded slave owners' constitutional right to reclaim their escaped chattel.[46] The new law also increased the risk of free blacks being kidnaped and taken South to be sold as slaves, obligating them to provide proof of their free status.[47] Although Delany extolled the virtues of hard work, thrift, education, and honesty in the *Condition,* he was no accommodationist of white supremacy. Rather, he emphasized the importance of black liberty and self-determination. Delany also differed from Washington in emphasizing black suffrage. In this regard, the *Condition* functioned as a primer for black political citizenship and can be compared to Du Bois's and others' efforts to develop a politically informed and active black electorate—a goal that remains a priority for the CBC.

As with Garnet and Walker, many of Delany's positions in the *Condition* were ahead of their time. Under the specter of the Fugitive Slave Act, the seeming intractability of chattel slavery, and the *Dred Scott* decision, he turned to emigration as the most feasible path to black uplift. Denouncing the American Colonization Society as a "scheme to remove free blacks . . . so as to make slavery more secure," Delany nonetheless conceded that "according to the economy that regulates the policy of nations . . . it may be necessary to take another view" of blacks' existence in America.[48] Although he did not work directly with the alternative African Civilization Society, he embraced its goals of a black-run and autonomous Liberia. He later contended that the West Indies and Central and South America were the "ultimate destination and future home of the colored race" and that the benefits "to be derived from emigration to [those regions] are incomparably greater than that of any other parts of the world at present." (While he correctly assessed the dismal state of race relations in the United States, he profoundly underestimated the racism present in Caribbean and South and Central American colonial societies.)[49]

On the whole, Delany's concept of emigration reflected his own elitism as well as the paternalism associated with European colonization. He intended for black American elites to civilize and manage Africa in keeping with a Western model, with indigenous Africans supplying the labor; he did not envision Africans ruling themselves. From another perspective, Delany's vision of emigration resembles late-nineteenth-century Zionist rhetoric, particularly in his belief that the redemption of an oppressed group necessitated the establishment of a strong, independent homeland for and by that group.[50] In the end, Delany appears to have been an emigrationist by default. In that role, he was less motivated by politics or nationalism than by the economic elevation of blacks: "Let us have but one object—to become men and women, worthy of freedom. . . . Go not with an anxiety of political aspirations; but go with the fixed intention . . . to become the producers of the country instead of the consumers."[51]

Throughout his exploration of emigration, Delany never retreated from his belief that American blacks' rightful country was the United States and that they had "a birthright citizenship—natural claims upon the country . . . common to all others of our fellow citizens." The *Condition* was in many ways a prescription for black political empowerment in America (the booklet's full title indicates a study of black elevation "*politically* considered"). When southern Reconstruction afforded Delany the opportunity to exercise political leadership, he became active in the Republican Party. However, by the early 1870s he became disillusioned with what he perceived as the corrupting aspects of the party. He blamed northern carpetbaggers in particular for fomenting racial divisions and thus arresting the development of black political power. He also accused carpetbaggers of turning rank-and-file blacks against the black elites, which included him.[52]

As the Hayes Compromise of 1877 ushered in the demise of Republican dominance in the South, Delany threw in his lot with the reemerging Democrat Party, preferring to work with the local power structure. Recognizing the interdependence between black workers and white elites, he speculated that the New South formula would be more conducive to racial cooperation than what had been imposed by Republicans, and that the restoration of Democratic rule would offer more potential for the "elevation" of blacks. He was wrong in both respects. At the same time, Delany's political leadership was too ambivalent to have elevated the race. On the one hand, he scorned intraracial discrimination by lighter-skinned blacks against darker-hued ones. While his willingness to work with southern Democrats resembles Washington's accommodationist politics, Delany fiercely affirmed black pride in a region that was hostile, to say the least, to such a mind-set. On the other, he displayed little actual affinity for the masses of poor blacks he purported to serve.[53] More broadly, Delany's fluctuating political leadership reflects the challenges southern black leaders faced in advancing blacks' interests in the face of overwhelming racial and political odds.

The pro-black militancy of Walker, Garnet, and Delany was bold. It was also perilous. Along with a moral commitment to the peaceful abolition of slavery, the risks of black militancy explain Frederick Douglass's more restrained approach. He could deliver scathing condemnations of slavery as an institution, yet be quite generous to whites involved in or tolerating it. Such racial diplomacy was a likely reason for his preeminence among white abolitionists. For example, Douglass argued that "the slaveholder, as well as the slave, is the victim of the slave system" and that the inhumane treatment he received was "a part of the system rather than a part of the man." His reserve, however, went far beyond diplomacy. Echoing Garnet's multifaceted liberation theory, Douglass articulated deeply introspective and humanitarian condemnations of what he called the "hydra-headed monster" of slavery, racism, and labor exploitation.[54]

Douglass's more militant moments, especially those coming after the passage of the Fugitive Slave Act, are as worthy of consideration as his trademark equanimity. At times he sounded almost like Walker in terms of both anger and patriotism. For example, in 1850, he closed a speech on "The Inhumanity of Slavery" with the words,

> In the spirit of genuine patriotism, I warn the American people, by all that is just and honorable, to beware! . . . [F]or in an evil hour, those sable arms that have, for the last two centuries, been engaged in cultivating and adorning the fair fields of our country, may yet become the instruments of terror, desolation, and death, throughout our borders.[55]

In 1852, Douglass assessed Independence Day from a different perspective:

> Scorching irony, not convincing argument is needed. . . . What to the American slave is the Fourth of July? . . . To [the slave] your celebration is a sham, your boasted liberty an unholy license . . . your shouts of liberty and equality, hollow mockery. . . . For revolting barbarity and shameless hypocrisy, America reigns without rival.[56]

Douglass must have known that his denouncements of slavery as "the sin and the shame of the American people" would provoke defenses of slavery. His response was to "invoke the spirit of patriotism . . . not to cover up our national sins, but to inspire within us sincere repentance . . . to unite all our energies in the grand effort to remedy" the wrong of slavery. Like Walker, Douglass's criticism of slavery drew as much from his love of America's core values as his hatred of slavery (and those involved in it) for compromising those values. In his view, the Constitution "not only contain[s] no guarantees in favor of slavery but is, in its letter and spirit, an anti-slavery instrument."[57] This interpretation was entirely at odds with the views of those who understood the Constitution and its intent as protecting the institution, as Chief Justice Roger Brooke Taney articulated in *Dred Scott v. Sandford*.[58] Indeed, such conflicting interpretations illustrate the conflict between African Americans' concepts of universal freedom and equality and the selective application of those principles.

Liberty and Gender

Despite the fact that all women were excluded from the "public sphere" of discourse, some of the most resonant antebellum voices were female. Many black women took to heart abolitionist Maria Stewart's challenge to do more than "sit with [their] hands folded, hanging [their] heads like bulrushes, lamenting [their] wretched condition" of racial and gender subordination.[59] Like their white counterparts, free black women in the North began organizing for abolition through feminized activities such as sewing circles and literary societies. By 1833, the Philadelphia Female Anti-Slavery Society had splintered off from the male-only American Anti-Slavery Society, and began to hold interracial meetings. Two years later, as members of the Boston Female Anti-Slavery Society were forced out of a meeting where William Lloyd Garrison was being swarmed by opposing mobs, each white woman took a "colored sister by the hand, and . . . walked calmly down the stairs and out [of] the building . . . their eyes busily identifying the genteel leaders of the mob." The Grimké sisters, abolitionist daughters of a slave owning father, vowed that "abolitionist women are turning the world upside down"; they were ostracized not only for their antislavery efforts but for intruding into the public sphere as well.[60] Black women who attempted to turn things around were stymied by the double helix of racism and paternalism. Then as now, they faced the challenge of voicing black and female perspectives, both of which were marginalized. This challenge was even more daunting when the intersectional concept of a black woman's perspective was virtually alien.[61]

Maria Stewart was the first American woman of any race to deliver a public address. Born of free status in 1803 in Hartford, Connecticut, she was orphaned as a young child. Bound out to a clergyman's family until she reached her teens, she worked as a domestic prior to her marriage in 1826. She lived quietly until she was widowed and essentially swindled out of a rather sizable inheritance. She initially became acquainted with David Walker through her husband, a shipping agent, and joined Walker's abolition movement after her husband's death. Her activism was also rooted in her church, which was a major hub of abolitionism in Boston's black community. Publicly active in abolitionism for only three years, Stewart spent the rest of her life as a teacher in New York, Baltimore, and Washington, D.C. During those three years, however, she proved herself a gifted orator, grounding much of her substance and style in the Bible as well the arguments of Walker and English women's historian John Adams.[62]

The intensity of Stewart's delivery along with her sometimes strident emphasis on black—particularly male—accountability was at times off-putting. Predominantly male audiences struggled with the propriety of a woman speaking in public, much less a woman who so effectively appropriated the patriarchal language of the Bible. Stewart challenged black men to seek more than whites' approval as "clever negroes" and "good creatures," imploring them to "flee from the gambling board and the dance hall" and "contend for the cause of God and the rights of man." In her view, "distinguished [black] men have not made themselves more influential . . . because they fear that the strong current of [white] opposition through which they must pass would cause their downfall and prove their overthrow." She questioned how long the "daughters of Africa [should] be compelled to bury their minds and talents beneath a load of pots and kettles" and how long "a mean set of men [should] flatter [women] with their smiles and enrich themselves with [women's] hard earnings." She also implored women to "possess the spirit of independence." Stewart's farewell address featured a defiant query that encapsulates her view of abolition and racial uplift: "What if I am a woman?"[63]

Stewart's role in abolition and women's rights has long been overshadowed by that of Sojourner Truth, who is widely renowned for her query, in many ways the converse of Stewart's: "Ain't I a woman?" Along with promoting abolition, Truth fought for women's rights, including suffrage. She captivated white audiences throughout the North and Midwest with her egalitarian plain talk.[64] Truth's striking physical presence and simple demeanor may well have made her, and thus her message, less threatening to whites. She did not, however, resonate nearly as well with her fellow black abolitionists, perhaps because blacks perceived her as more of a champion of women's rights than of blacks' rights despite her obvious commitment to abolition. It is also possible that precisely the characteristics that appealed to white abolitionists may have had the reverse effect on middle-class black audiences, many of whom had elitist tendencies and who may have preferred to distinguish themselves from former slaves such as Truth. And yet appearances ultimately may not have mattered. Both Truth and Stewart were stepping much further out of the constraints of the private sphere than most people at that time were willing to accept.

Truth and Stewart were not the last black women to take a public role in abolition. Mary Ann Shadd Cary, born free in Delaware in 1823, used her journalistic skills to promote abolition, racial, and gender equality. After her family fled to Canada in 1852, following the passage of the Fugitive Slave Act, she published *A Plea for Emigration: or, Notes of Canada West,* a pamphlet encouraging escaped slaves and free blacks to find refuge in Canada. Two years later, she established the *Provincial Freeman,* making her the first black woman in North America to establish and edit a newspaper. Cary also took to the public speaking circuit to promote emigration to Canada. Like Stewart, Cary was known for her hard-hitting rhetoric and unwillingness to defer to male leadership. Her motto, "Self-reliance is the fine road to independence," reinforced the centrality of racial autonomy among antebellum black leaders. She was particularly opposed to abolition efforts that portrayed blacks as incapable of taking care of themselves.[65]

Echoing Walker, Stewart, and Delany, Cary cautioned against "the folly of black imitation of white conspicuous materialism" that, in her view, undermined the pursuit of self-reliance. Rather than racial emulation, she advocated racial integration, along with gender equality, as essential steps to universal equality. She fought an uphill battle on both fronts. In the first area, Cary was criticized by her colleagues on the *Freeman* as "deluded" for her commitment to racial integration, and she was condemned for providing "aid and comfort" to white oppressors. On the second front, she was eventually pressured to relinquish editorial control of her newspaper to a male colleague. Though she lamented that her colleagues succumbed to their misgivings about her as a female editor, she still encouraged women to pursue journalism. Cary's dilemma exemplifies the conflict between gender and racial priorities that have yet to be fully reconciled (if anything these conflicts have been exacerbated by the Supreme Court's application of different levels of scrutiny to racial and gender classifications that make it nearly impossible for women facing discrimination on both fronts to press both claims).[66]

Democracy and Battles for Suffrage

Although the Fifteenth Amendment offered blacks their first opportunity to establish a formal political presence, many had been preparing for that moment since before there was realistic hope for it. Fifteen years prior to the amendment's passage, Delany was setting a standard for black political participation. In the *Condition,* he urged African Americans to prepare for citizenship by proving they could "equal the whites . . . in acting, doing, and carrying out practically, the measures of equality" and to "understand the political economy and domestic policy of nations [and be] the practical demonstrators of equal rights and self-government." For Delany, a strong black political and civic identity was crucial to freed blacks both individually and as a race, and failure to prepare for voting and self-government made it merely "idle to talk about [such] rights."[67] He was particularly adamant that meaningful black political participation required more than simply casting a ballot. In Delany's view, "the *elective franchise* makes the enfranchised *eligible* to any position attainable; but [blacks] may exercise the right of *voting* only, which . . . is but poor satisfaction." In other words, there was no use in blacks' "cherish[ing] the privilege of voting" into office other people who would in turn pass laws to degrade blacks.[68] Delany's ultimate political goal was black participation in setting public agendas and in making the laws that governed everyone.

The Fifteenth Amendment gave African Americans the chance, at least in theory, to do just that, and they entered the political sphere with vigor. A total of 268 African Americans participated in southern state constitutional conventions. From 1870 to 1901, 1,510 blacks—all but approximately 15 of them Republicans—were elected or appointed to office in every part of the former Confederacy. African Americans served at various levels of office, including 112 as state senators and 682 as state representatives. With the exception of Pinckney Pinchback's monthlong tenure as governor of Louisiana as a result of his predecessor's impeachment proceedings, however, no black ever served as governor. While the majority of black officeholders were from the South, roughly 140 of them were either born in the North or had moved there prior to the Civil War.

Southern whites and Democrats and even some northern whites condemned black officeholders as buffoons, dishonest, opportunistic, or pawns of Republican carpetbaggers and scalawags. Characteristic of such perceptions is a newspaper account that one black South Carolina state representative would be "more in his place if he were in his native jungles munching the shin-bone of a Wesleyan missionary."[69] In reality, the majority of black officeholders were literate and entered office with solid occupational backgrounds, having worked as artisans, entrepreneurs and small business owners, professionals, ministers, and skilled laborers.[70] In sum, black Reconstruction officeholders were not, as many southern whites feared, out for revenge against them, nor were they interested in "Africanizing" American society or government.[71] Most black politicians promoted legislation that would benefit blacks along with other groups such as laborers, children, and the poor. Most also avoided the notion of reparations, recognizing the futility and even the danger of holding Congress true to its promise of "forty acres and a mule." As one black Georgia state legislator told his colleagues, "Do we ask [whites] for compensation? . . . We ask it not. We are willing to let the dead past bury its dead; but we ask [whites] now, for our rights."[72]

At the national level, twenty-two African Americans served in the U.S. Congress, including two in the U.S. Senate. Approximately nine of these men were born free, ten were born into slavery, ten were of mixed race, and ten were considered fully black. Ninety-eight percent of these men were literate. The majority of black Reconstruction congressmen were conscientious and astute political negotiators.[73] Their legislative approach reflected a mixture of pragmatism, egalitarianism, and affirmative race consciousness. Their modes of representation ranged from compliant to pragmatic to defiant. Aside from Republican Party imperatives, the chief influences on their representational styles were the racial demographic and racial climate of their districts, their class/caste status, their expressions of race consciousness, and at times their oratorical skills.

Hiram Revels of Mississippi was the first black U.S. senator. Born free of mixed-race parents, he served a partial term in Congress in 1871. He was technically Confederate president Jefferson Davis's replacement, a circumstance that compelled him to devote his first address to Georgia's recent ouster of the thirty-two blacks elected to its legislature (four of mixed race were later readmitted). A civil rights activist before the war and after Reconstruction but wary of white resentment of black political advancement, Revels sought in this address to reassure southern whites while mobilizing southern blacks. To fears in Georgia's legislature that black representatives would wield their newfound power against whites, Revels responded that blacks had "a true and conscientious desire to further the interests of the whole South," emphasizing that blacks had not taken advantage of chances to reverse racial fortunes during the Civil War. Revels also endorsed amnesty for former members of the Confederacy. Revels's speech exemplifies some black legislators' view that a conciliatory approach was best in preparation for the inevitable return of the southern Democratic presence.[74]

Senator Blanche K. Bruce, also of Mississippi, served a full term in the Senate. The son of an enslaved woman and her master, he also exemplified the conciliatory and at times accommodationist approach to Reconstruction. At the same time, he pursued policies with universal benefits. A light-skinned, well-educated, and landowning son of a plantation owner, his political ascent may have resulted as much from his perception by whites as a nonthreatening candidate with little affinity for the black masses as from black support on the basis of race and regardless of class and caste differences.[75] Described as a "decent" man by Mississippi's white establishment, Bruce's politics were both moderate and humane. In keeping with the aforementioned black "quest for universal freedom," Bruce opposed Native American extermination policies and racially restrictive legislation such as the Chinese Exclusionary Act of 1882. He also called for federal coordination of the flood-prone Mississippi Delta region, a policy that would benefit all who lived there.[76] Although not aggressively race conscious, he was proud of his race and asserted that African Americans deserved full rights "given by the Constitution and laws," asking of "white fellow-citizens only the consideration and fairness that [blacks] so willingly extend to them." With respect to Senator Pinchback's contested election to Congress, Bruce lamented that black voters went from physical bondage to political enslavement by the Republican Party and threatened to resign from "a body which presents this spectacle of asinine conduct."[77]

U.S. Representative Robert Elliott of South Carolina exemplified a more forceful brand of politics characterized by racial militancy and his alliance with the Radical wing of the Republican Party. Unlike most of his black peers, he was not born or reared in the South. Though he claimed Boston as his home, other accounts suggest that he was born and educated in England, joined the Royal Navy, deserted while stationed in the United States, and settled here in the late 1860s. Elliott's political appeal was in his self-confidence, his strong analytical and oratorical skills. His dark complexion, which radical whites presented as a refutation of prevailing theories of black inferiority, at times worked to his advantage. Elliott was an aggressive advocate of blacks' civil and voting rights, and he vigorously opposed amnesty for secessionists.[78] His oratorical acumen prompted his colleagues to choose him to rebut Georgia representative (and former Confederate vice president) Alexander Stephens in debates over a bill to suppress the Ku Klux Klan. Elliott framed his rebuttal in the context of the Fourteenth Amendment, declaring that it protected blacks' civil rights at both the federal and state levels. Framing his arguments in a universal manner, Elliott contended that the amendment protected any class of citizens who felt discriminated against. He then juxtaposed this universal concept of equality against more limited concepts of it, suggesting that Stephens

> would better befit his station if, instead of throwing himself in the way of the progress of the nation that had so magnanimously pardoned him for conspiring to overthrow the Republic, he would lay his shoulder to the wheel and help it on to a better and more glorious future.[79]

Elliott's rhetorical skills led one Republican colleague to remark that black representatives were better parliamentary speakers than were white representatives; for its part, one Democratic newspaper described him as "as big a rascal as can be found . . . supremely insolent, arrogant and arbitrary." Eventually, Elliott was charged by others in Congress with corruption. Though the charges were never proven, they took momentum from his congressional career. Convinced that he could be more effective in local politics, he served in South Carolina's general assembly (including a stint as Speaker of the House) and as the state's attorney general. By 1876, as southern Democrats intensified their purge of blacks and Republicans from office, Elliott returned to private law practice. He and his wife survived several financial and health crises, but he ultimately succumbed to malaria at the age of forty-two.[80]

The diversity in rhetorical and policy approaches among Reconstruction-era black legislators is comparable to members of the CBC. Although today's African American legislators are no longer fettered by caste concerns, profound educational and economic disadvantage, or abject racism, they bring distinct policy concerns to Congress. As with their Reconstruction predecessors, they must also negotiate partisan conflicts while striving to improve blacks' political, economic, and educational outcomes. In the process, and like their predecessors, they squarely address the salience of African American interests to the well-being of all Americans.

As opportunities for black political participation became more restricted, Henry McNeal Turner became a strong advocate of blacks' rights in the South. Continuing the tradition of politicized religious leadership, he described himself as a "minister of the gospel and a kind of politician—both."[81] Born free in Georgia in 1834, his parents hired him out in his childhood to work on local plantations. In his adolescence, he ran away to become a minister in the African Methodist Episcopal church and eventually rose to the level of bishop. During the Civil War, Turner recruited blacks into the Union Army. As a result, he was appointed as its first black chaplain. Turner's political career began as a delegate in the Georgia Constitutional Convention.[82] Like many politically active freedmen during this time, he was conciliatory, tending to accommodate whites' interests in anticipation of receiving reciprocal support. For example, as a delegate to the Georgia Constitutional Convention, he supported poll taxes and educational qualifications for voting and opposed highly controversial proposals for land reform.[83] Turner was elected to Georgia's state assembly in 1867 but was among those black legislators whom whites refused to seat. Continuing black leaders' tradition of asserting black humanity, Turner protested to his fellow legislators, "I am a member of this body. . . . I shall neither fawn nor cringe before any party, nor stoop to beg them for my rights. . . . I claim the rights of a man," including citizenship, the right to vote, and the right to hold office. Advancing a universal concept of liberty, he vowed, "Never, so help me God, shall I be a political slave. . . . Congress . . . did not intend to put me and my race into political slavery. If they did, let them take away my ballot. . . . I don't want to be a mere tool of that sort."[84]

After Turner and three of his ejected colleagues were reinstated under federal auspices, his racially conciliatory approach took on a more aggressively race-conscious dimension. He introduced bills to subsidize black higher education, establish black cooperative stock companies, assist sharecroppers, establish eight-hour workdays, abolish the convict-lease system, and to create a black militia to defend blacks against white violence.[85] Likely dejected by his experience in the Georgia Assembly and by the demise of the Reconstruction, Turner withdrew from politics after just one term in office. Nonetheless, he retained faith in the American concept of democracy, and he remained a public commentator about race and politics for the rest of his life. Like Walker, he could be a harsh critic of

American government. He castigated the Supreme Court for what he saw as its "prostitution" of itself to party politics. He was particularly scornful of its *Civil Rights Cases* decision, which invalidated the Civil Rights Act of 1875, and which, in his view, was so "barbarous" and "death dealing" as to absolve "the negro's allegiance to the general government." Similarly, he condemned blacks' loyalty to a racist, exclusionary nation, asserting that anyone "who loves a country that hates him, is a . . . dog and not a man." Echoing Douglass's deconstruction of Independence Day, Turner observed in 1906 that while he "used to love the grand old flag . . . to the Negro in this country the American flag is a dirty and contemptible rag." Drawing from such criticisms, Turner's key contribution to contemporary African American political thought was his conviction that black political power first required allegiance to the race. His advice that blacks should strive for political autonomy is as fitting now as it was in his time: "Neither the Republican nor Democratic party can do for the colored race what they can do for themselves. *Respect black.*"[86]

Turner's assertions of black political power were the antithesis of his more influential and conciliatory contemporary, Booker T. Washington. However, Turner tempered his criticisms of Washington out of a reluctance to expose or exacerbate intraracial antagonisms.[87] Turner's race-conscious political rhetoric is clearly an extension of the ideas of Walker, Garnet, and Delany. It also presages W. E. B. Du Bois's theory of dualism, which held that blacks have a "second sight" that yields one "no true self-consciousness but only lets [one] see [one]self through the revelation of the other world . . . two warring ideals in one dark body."[88] Here, Du Bois describes the painful challenge of embracing one's blackness in a larger environment that reviles it. For Turner, reconciling these warring ideals first required a strong sense of one's worth as a black person. The collective, self-sufficiency aspects of Turner's political thinking resounded nearly a century later in the expressions of Malcolm X and other black nationalists, in Martin Luther King Jr.'s commitment to black pride and collective political action in the form of racial bloc voting, and in the CBC's advocacy of pluralism in its amicus briefs.[89]

Although the preceding discussion is far too short and selective to do justice to nascent black politics in America, it illustrates several key points. First the vast majority of black Reconstruction politicians were, contrary to much lore about them, intelligent, strategic, and well qualified to govern. Contrary to fears of black revenge, most of these leaders practiced a politics of conciliation and egalitarianism rather than of conflict. Then as now, their leadership was not monolithic, nor were the interests of their black constituency they fought to serve. Black Reconstruction officeholders found themselves hamstrung by race (at times even complexion), insufficient finances and other resources, and by tenuous connections to the political and economic powerhouses. Then as now, African Americans were "agenda-rich but resource poor."[90] The fact that no blacks served as governors also limited their effectiveness at state and local levels. Then as now, the majority of black elected officials pursued racial advancement in the context of liberty, equality, and democracy and strove in the process to convince others that their goals were fully compatible with America's values.

Democracy and Gender

As with abolition, black women did not sit passively on the sidelines of blacks' mass entry onto the electoral playing field. Many were active in political meetings, convention activities, and the mobilization of male voters. In words characteristic of the era, one northern observer of an 1867 Republican convention in Richmond, Virginia, reported that "not only had Sambo gone to the convention, but Dinah was there also."[91] Newly freed black women in the South lacked the opportunity to fight for their own suffrage, however. First, the woman suffrage movement did not have a serious presence in the region because the patriarchal southern social structure had such little tolerance for it. Of the southerners who endorsed woman suffrage, most were motivated to ensure white supremacy by doubling the white vote. Moreover, the mainstream woman suffrage movement had never been very hospitable to northern black suffragists and made few calls for the enfranchisement of black women.[92]

Consequently, black women in the North and the South saw the vote as a communal right exercised by men on behalf of family and community. Northern suffragist Anna Julia Cooper extolled the efforts of southern black women who "left their husbands' homes and repudiated their support for what was understood by the wife to be race disloyalty, or voting away . . . the privileges of herself and [her] little ones."[93] For these women, "the fact that only men had been granted the vote did not mean that only men should exercise that vote." In addition, some women assumed they had an equal right to participate as party delegates. Others ran interference between black men and unscrupulous white party organizers, physically challenging violent "redshirt" forces by escorting black male voters— at times with barely concealed weapons—to the polls.[94]

Frederick Douglass initially worked to enfranchise both women and blacks as a key step toward universal equality. However, by the late 1860s, the Republican Party had foreclosed the possibility of universal suffrage. At that point, he shifted his priorities to the "'immediate, unconditional and universal' enfranchisement of the black man."[95] Douglass never abandoned his belief "that women, as well as men, have the right to vote," but felt driven to make this choice by partisan limitations and increasing acts of violence against black men. For Douglass, the right to vote was becoming a question of life and death for black men: "When women, because they are women, are hunted down . . . dragged from their houses and hung from lamp-posts . . . they will have an urgency to obtain the ballot equal to [black men]."[96]

Excluded from the Fifteenth Amendment, black women such as Cooper, Mary Church Terrell, Frances E. W. Harper, and Josephine St. Pierre Ruffin relied increasingly on their own suffrage groups for political empowerment. Many of them were well educated or were married to prominent men, often civil rights activists as well. As with their abolitionist predecessors, they pursued suffrage via other feminized issue areas such as temperance, train desegregation, antilynching activism, and community service programs. The tradition of black women's club activism, most of which was regional, intensified as black women were increasingly excluded by white suffragists, many of whom were by this time mobilizing "from the position of expediency rather than justice."[97] Anna Julia Cooper thus wrote in 1892 of the "unique position" of black women who were confronted by both race and gender challenges and who were limited by those black men "for whose opinion [they care] most." Her justification for suffrage reflected the common practice in that era of converting the reasons for denying woman suffrage into justifications for suffrage. Because "American politics is hardly a school for great minds," women's management of the private sphere uniquely qualified them to conserve the deeper moral forces that "make for the happiness of homes and the righteousness of the country."[98]

The exclusion of black women from the mainstream suffrage organizations reflects the racial hierarchy that permeated American society and prevented unity with regard to gender inequality. Some black women allied with mainstream suffrage groups, but with limited success. Terrell was a long-term member of the majority white National Woman Suffrage Association and gained considerable stature in it. However, neither it nor the more racially egalitarian American Woman Suffrage Association ever fully incorporated black women into its membership or governance.[99] Black suffragists participated in the 1913 suffragist march in Washington, D.C. But they were not invited to do so by mainstream suffrage groups and were made to march separately from their white counterparts.[100] Black women remained on the margins of women's political organizations even after the passage of the Nineteenth Amendment. For example, northern white women protested little against southern efforts to disenfranchise blacks during the 1920s and 1930s, even though such efforts robbed black women of a right that they had only recently possessed.[101]

Given these limitations on black suffrage activism, black female leaders put their efforts toward other pressing issues such as racial equality and racist violence. Journalism and public speaking were by this time somewhat more viable paths to women's activism. The writings of Ida B. Wells-Barnett were as forceful as those of her male peers and predecessors. She was fearlessly defiant and was known for, among other things, biting a railway conductor who attempted to eject her from a ladies' train car.[102] Like Douglass and Du Bois, Wells-Barnett supported universal suffrage and was closely involved in the Niagara Movement, a precursor to the National Association for the Advancement of Colored People. However, her priorities in the late nineteenth century were focused more on racial than gender equality. Reflecting Douglass's concern about violence against black men, Wells-Barnett combated lynching through journalism and as a public speaker.[103]

Known in black journalistic circles as the "Princess of the Press," Wells-Barnett took advantage of her position as editor of the newspaper *Free Speech* to gather and publish data on the rate of and purported justifications for lynching. She also challenged official justifications for it as spurious and arbitrary. In exposing the racist motivations behind lynching, Wells-Barnett directly confronted white southerners with their fears and taboos about interracial sexuality. For a black woman to challenge white authority by confronting such topics was risky in many ways. But she was undaunted. In 1895 Wells-Barnett published the data she had compiled on lynching in a one-hundred-page pamphlet, the *Red Record*, and she spent the rest of her life fighting for a federal antilynching law.

Wells-Barnett saw the issue of suffrage as having less to do with gender equality than with democracy as a whole. In her view, the principles behind a woman's right to vote "were inseparable from those promoting black suffrage." Like several of her male peers, she presumed that suffrage in the hands of white women would impede racial reform. She once told venerable suffragist Susan B. Anthony that she doubted that female suffrage would "change women's nature or the political situation." Wells-Barnett's wording here is crucial, demonstrating a dilemma that has long bedeviled the broader feminist movement: Though black women face both racial and gender discrimination, the nature of race relations in America has generally compelled them to identify more with race than with gender. Wells-Barnett's political thinking was further complicated by her views on partisanship, which resembled those of her contemporary, Turner. On the one hand, she criticized black voters for their unquestioning loyalty to the "party of Lincoln." On the other, she dismissed the Democratic Party for its legacy of slavery and racism, and the Republicans for embracing black voters and then forsaking them with the Hayes Compromise. Nonetheless, her race-first attitude and partisan ambivalence did not completely shut her out of suffrage efforts and local politics. After moving to Chicago, she became active in the Illinois Equal Suffrage Association. She was also involved in the city's politics by mobilizing the black vote and serving as an intermediary between the political establishment and the black community.[104]

Equality and Battles for Citizenship

As the Republican Reconstruction gave way to the reconstruction of white and Democratic supremacy in the South, the debate between accommodation and integration dominated black political discourse both there and in the North. This debate is most strongly associated with Booker T. Washington and W. E. B. Du Bois. Volumes have been written on both men, and Du Bois was a prolific writer over seven decades, covering such issues as slavery, Jim Crow, dualism, integrationism, capitalism, socialism, war, decolonization, intraracial antagonisms, nationalism, and pan-Africanism. Having reevaluated these topics in light of major social, political, and economic upheavals over nearly seventy years, it is impossible to briefly summarize all of his positions here. This discussion of the Washington–Du Bois debate is instead intended to illuminate some of the lesser-known contours of that debate.

Du Bois was born in 1868 in Great Barrington, Massachusetts. Raised in modest circumstances, his educational accomplishments and intellectual prowess quickly catapulted him to academic and political leadership. Du Bois earned a bachelor's degree in history from historically black Fisk University in 1888. He then matriculated to Harvard University, where he earned a master's degree in history in 1892. He continued studies at Harvard and for two years in Germany, and in 1895 he became the first African American to earn a doctorate from Harvard.[105] Du Bois taught at the University of Pennsylvania and at historically black Wilberforce University and Atlanta University. Du Bois had a seventy-year-long career—

illustrious and often contentious—as a scholar, political activist, and public intellectual.

Continuing in Douglass's footsteps, Du Bois was an unrelenting universal suffragist and racial egalitarian. In his view, racial segregation and the concept of separate-but-equal facilities branded blacks with a badge of inferiority that violated the spirit of America's core values as well as the Fourteenth Amendment. Racial integration, to be achieved and maintained through universal suffrage, was the ultimate confirmation of an egalitarian society. In other words, Du Bois saw racial integration not as an end in and of itself; it was a necessary but not sole precursor to racial equality. Similarly, his theory of dualism and the dilemma that it presented to blacks and whites in America was a call not for color blindness but for the recognition of race without being perverted by hierarchical concepts of it. These distinctions are as critical to black politics now as they were in Du Bois's time.

Du Bois's intellectual and political approach to black uplift conflicted sharply with that of Booker T. Washington. Washington was born a slave in 1856 in Virginia. In his youth he worked as a laborer before putting himself through what is now Hampton University. He eventually taught there before moving on to head Alabama's Tuskegee Institute in 1881. Both Hampton and Tuskegee offered blacks industrial education and skills, in contrast to Du Bois's liberal arts education at Fisk and Harvard. This difference in educational goals was central to the two men's debates regarding black uplift. Washington was most renowned for his politics of "accommodation"—the belief that blacks could prosper within the system of Jim Crow and eventually lift themselves out of it through industry and good citizenship. Some observers considered this approach tantamount to defeatism or a slave mentality; others, however, saw it as practical and self-sufficient, and he earned a substantial following among blacks in the South as well as the North.

Washington's emphasis on black self-help and autonomy was inevitably and positively race-conscious. Even though Du Bois was also positively race-conscious, Washington's approach, combined with his personal history of being born into slavery and raising himself up by his own bootstraps, resonated with many blacks, especially those who were poor and working class. Moreover, he and his "Bookerites" were willing to admit what many northern black activists were loath to admit: Pushing the issues of social or political equality, especially as the South was "redeeming" itself, was "the extremest folly" if not downright dangerous. Hence, Washington sought to appease the southern white elite, as evidenced in his declaration that "in all things purely social [the races] can be as separate as the fingers, yet one as the hand in all things essential to mutual progress." Given his appeal to the black masses (and many black elites) as well as the white political establishment, Washington generated more support, including money. He consequently became far more powerful than Du Bois and his followers.[106]

Although Washington's accommodation of racial segregation has always been controversial, he was motivated by pragmatism rather than a belief in or loyalty to white hegemony. He neither argued nor believed that blacks were inferior to whites.[107] Instead, he advocated accommodation as the path of least resistance and as the safest option for southern blacks living under the specter of Jim Crow racism. In advising southern blacks to "cast down their buckets" and remain where they were, he sought to maintain blacks' numerical advantage in some regions and ultimately to translate that advantage into economic, political, and social strength. He thus sought to reassure whites that blacks "have proved our loyalty to you in the past . . . so in the future . . . we shall stand with you . . . ready to lay down our lives, if need be, in defense of yours." In a twist on white paternalism, Washington condemned Jim Crow not simply out of principle but because a "segregated Negro community is a terrible temptation to many *white* people. . . . [It] invariably provides certain types of white men with hiding places . . . from the law . . . decent people of their own race . . . [and] their wives and daughters."[108]

Washington's logic here represented an extension of abolitionist arguments that slavery was as morally destructive to whites as it was to blacks. It also constituted an intriguing reversal of the theory of the "white man's burden," suggesting that the key to blacks' well-being lay in their ability to keep whites happy. In sum, accommodationism was not simply a palliative for whites but was a survival strategy designed to protect even incremental black progress from violent white reprisal. On the whole, Washington's politics were far more nuanced than what appeared to be blind fealty to the southern white establishment. He sought to convince that establishment—in the type of language its members most wanted to hear—that freed blacks were no threat to the southern way of life. In hindsight, Washington's rhetoric can be seen as an example of the slave tradition of shucking and jiving: feigned compliance that conceals resistance to or challenges of authority. In fact, several decades after Washington's death, scholars learned that he had anonymously funded efforts to prevent black disfranchisement in the South and to promote full citizenship for blacks.[109]

Conclusion: Black Militants or Radical Conformists?

Again, this chapter gives but a cursory overview of early black political thought and activism. Yet from it, one arrives at two seemingly contradictory conclusions. First, this body of thought reflects and often amplifies America's core principles of liberty, equality, and democracy. In particular, it reveals that blacks have struggled for the full and equal right to pursue happiness—both as individuals and as a class—far more than they have attempted to change or subvert the American political system. In this sense, early black political thought fully comports with traditional American values. Conversely, nineteenth-century black political thought is both race- and group-conscious. Moreover, it tends to gauge equality by outcomes as well as processes. At times, it has urged blacks to resist or break laws that discriminate against them, meaning that it has a revolutionary component. In this sense, African American political thought is truly radical in the sense that it digs deeply to eradicate the roots of inequality.

I argue that these conclusions are as complementary as they are contradictory. The race- and group-conscious aspects of nineteenth-century black political thought reflect the race- and group-conscious aspects of the American polity. What can be seen as militancy is the same spirit that pervaded the Declaration of Independence and the American Revolution. Nineteenth-century political thought is thus classically revolutionary. To paraphrase Martin Luther King Jr., the black revolution has largely been about getting into, as opposed to overthrowing, the American political system.[110] As a central "political context variable," early black political thought offers a useful fulcrum on which to balance race-conscious and color-blind approaches to race and representation. Since its inception, the CBC has been a contemporary extension of blacks' historical efforts to push the boundaries of America's core values. The next two chapters explore the presence of early black political thinking and activism in the caucus's efforts to protect minority voting rights in its legislative capacity and as amicus curiae.

3 | The Congressional Black Caucus: Pushing Legislative Boundaries

"The elective franchise makes the enfranchised, eligible to any position attainable; but we may exercise the right of voting only, which to us, is but poor satisfaction; and we by no means care to cherish the privilege of voting somebody into office to help to make laws to degrade us."

—Martin Delany, 1852

"If Congress has simply given me merely sufficient civil and political rights to make me a mere political slave for Democrats, or anybody else . . . I do not thank Congress for it . . . I don't want to be a mere tool of that sort. I have been a slave long enough already."

—Henry McNeal Turner, 1868

Origins, Goals, and Current Status of the Congressional Black Caucus

This chapter explores the position of the Congressional Black Caucus (CBC) in the institutional battles over contemporary minority voting rights. The caucus extends in important ways the traditions and efforts of early African American political leaders in general and of black Reconstruction-era legislators in particular. It also embodies the long history of blacks' civil rights activism in Congress; in this respect, it functions as an internal civil rights lobbying group on behalf of black and other minority voters. The CBC's symbolic and descriptive modes of representation are thus central to its substantive representation of its black constituents. In particular, the caucus's commitment to reinforcing the Voting Rights Act (VRA) demonstrates how these three modes of representation converge.

This chapter focuses on the CBC in its legislative role in amending the VRA. Given that "the VRA is a number one priority" for the caucus, it has consistently and "aggressively [sought] to protect the integrity of this Act."[1] This chapter also contextualizes chapter 4's examination of the CBC in a role that garners scant attention from political scientists: that of an amicus curiae, effectively lobbying the Supreme Court on behalf of black voters in cases involving race-based districting and vote dilution. Taken together, chapters 3 and 4 demonstrate that whether the CBC appeals internally to Congress or externally to the Court, it has consistently advocated race-conscious measures to mitigate past and continuing racial discrimination in the electoral arena.

This chapter begins by reviewing the caucus's founding. I then turn to the caucus's role in amending the VRA in 1975, 1982, and 2006 and in triggering what has been widely commended as a "quiet revolution" of minority political power in the South.[2] This analysis features the CBC's efforts to shift the act's focus from electoral opportunities to electoral outcomes and to allow for remedial race-conscious districting in areas with a long history of discrimination at the polls. The chapter concludes with a paradox: The CBC's race-conscious approach to the VRA, particularly in 1982, provoked the Supreme Court to check Congress by restricting the act's scope in cases involving race and redistricting. The Court's minority voting rights retrenchment not only checks congressional power but also threatens the CBC's legislative and political influence. This retrenchment also limits the power of the Department of Justice (DOJ) and thus the executive branch to administer the VRA as Congress intended. More important, the Court's actions threaten to erode the political gains that the VRA has afforded minority voters.

Congressional caucuses are formally known as "legislative service organizations" or "congressional member organizations" and are defined as influential bodies of legislators that make independent policy judgments and win support for their policies and proposals in the Congress. They intersect with, but are autonomous from, formal congressional committee and party systems.[3] A significant aspect of congressional caucuses is their function as tools of the trade with which lawmakers advance their legislative goals and policy agendas within Congress. Although the caucus system is relatively stable, it has very fluid dynamics, reflecting the fluidity of constituent and electoral imperatives.[4] For these reasons, it is difficult to determine exactly how many caucuses officially exist at any given moment. Nonetheless, congressional caucuses clearly have grown in number and scope. The first official congressional caucus, formed in 1959, was the House's Democratic Study Group. Current estimates show that Congress has roughly 225 caucuses, most of which have been established since the 1970s. Caucuses target a wide variety of interests, including domestic and international geographic matters, labor, trade, industry, agriculture, technology, environment, health and specific diseases, race, ethnicity, gender, and ideology.[5]

Most caucuses have emerged from "groups created by party factions and organizations representing the interests of ethnic groups, women and regional constituencies."[6] One explanation for the recent proliferation of caucuses is that members of Congress "are trying to expand their representational portfolios beyond" the traditional avenue of committee membership. Having said that, caucus members are increasingly garnering appointments to major congressional committees and task forces, likely because caucuses offer additional opportunities for legislators, especially those with less seniority, to develop expertise on particular issues. Although each caucus has its own legislative and policy agenda, as a whole, they "collectively help shape the congressional agenda." Congressional caucuses have thus evolved over time into "powerful lobbying forces" that have in turn "fundamentally change[d]" how external interest groups pursue their legislative agendas in Congress.[7]

Unless affiliated or closely aligned with political parties, congressional caucuses typically do not coordinate their agendas with the parties. In fact, many caucuses emerged because of their perception that party leaders failed to sufficiently or correctly address a particular issue. Over time, however, as caucuses have grown in number and influence, party leaders have had to adapt to and support the caucus system as legitimate actors in law- and policymaking.[8] Incumbency concerns present particular challenges to legislators' involvement in congressional caucuses. For example, to win reelection, candidates may sidestep sensitive issues that may be germane to a caucus on which they serve but could alienate voters. Indeed, the degree to which a caucus can garner legislative support for an issue depends on factors such as party agendas, congressional organization, legislative scheduling, and incumbency. These factors in turn compete with or are at least complicated by the controversy a particular issue may generate. Consequently, an incumbent candidate might decline membership in a caucus that is associated with an issue that could cost her votes. Representatives opting to participate in caucuses that generate controversy may find themselves under heightened scrutiny from their constituents as well as their opponents.

Such is often the case for members of a caucus based on racial issues, such as the CBC. To the extent that racial issues in America are "too salient to elicit indifference, too controversial to allow neutrality, and too divisive to produce [sufficient] white support," controversy tends to accompany the CBC.[9] To be sure, more African Americans are representing racially diverse districts than in the past. But they remain exceptions rather than the rule. In general, representatives of racially diverse districts (and less senior members of the caucus) are more likely to engage in the relatively conciliatory "politics of new pragmatism" than the "politics of confrontation" associated with their more senior colleagues.[10] Indeed, some of the more centrist CBC members have been accused of practicing a modern-day "politics of accommodation."[11]

For the most part, the CBC tends to balance the "politics of commonality" with "the politics of difference" rather than taking one approach alone.[12] And while it brings a unique perspective to and has a distinct mission in Congress, its members, like other legislators, must respond to the core and at times competing demands of representation, legislation, party discipline, and reelection.[13] That today's African American representatives engage in such a representational balancing act is nothing new. As demonstrated in chapter 2, this approach was developed more than a century ago by black Reconstruction-era legislators. Then and now, however, black legislators' overarching political concerns remain deeply rooted in racial concerns that include the historical and contemporary challenges that accompany being black in America. Thus, the CBC's commitment to racial uplift motivates it to take a race-conscious approach to these challenges.

The CBC was established in 1969. It is reminiscent of the Reconstruction-era black delegation in that it emerged from a sudden increase in the number of blacks elected to Congress—in this case, as a result of the civil rights movement and the passage of the VRA. Unlike black Reconstruction congressmen, the caucus distinguished itself as a formal organization working within the legislature rather than as individuals that were marginalized by most of Congress and the political leadership in general. The CBC established itself to present an organized black front in Congress and to garner better partisan and national recognition of blacks' political interests.[14] Initially calling itself the Democratic Select Committee, it began with thirteen black representatives. Reflecting its race-conscious approach to political equality, the committee changed its name to the Congressional Black Caucus in 1971. The CBC at first sought to "positively influence the course of events pertinent to African Americans and others of similar experience and situation, and to achieve greater equity for persons of African descent in the design and content of domestic and international programs and services."[15] In this respect, it exemplifies the emergence of a caucus from party factions and organizations with the goal of advancing the interests of historically underrepresented racial and ethnic groups.[16]

Broadly speaking, the CBC works to aggregate priorities, introduce proposals, and act as a power broker on behalf of African Americans in the legislative arena.[17] Asserting itself as the "conscience of the Congress," it strives to promote the public welfare as a whole through legislation that is also designed to meet the needs of America's neglected minority citizens.[18] Here as well, the caucus reflects Reconstruction-era black legislators' pursuit of policies that helped others in the process of helping blacks. It also reflects Martin Luther King Jr.'s approach to racial inequality, which included class inequality. In addition to its efforts with the VRA, the CBC

> has been involved in legislative initiatives ranging from full employment to welfare reform, South African apartheid and international human rights, from minority business development to expanded educational opportunities. Most noteworthy is the CBC alternative budget which the Caucus has produced continually for over 16 years. Historically, the CBC alternative budget policies depart significantly from administration budget recommendations as the Caucus seeks to preserve a national commitment to fair treatment for urban and rural America, the elderly, students, small businessmen and women, middle and low income wage earners, the economically disadvantaged and a new world order.[19]

Here, the CBC demonstrates how caucuses form in response to the juxtaposition of external interests and internal factors, particularly when party leaders do not sufficiently address the policy concerns advocated by a caucus.[20] Although race is not explicitly mentioned in its mission and policy statements, the CBC provides an African American context for national law- and policymaking in ways that are clearly intended to benefit blacks' political interests. These efforts include political outreach and empowerment programs targeting youth, increasing Internet access in black areas, enhancing the caucus's visibility on the Internet, and an energy task force that seeks to enhance African Americans' role in energy and environmental policies and investigate the negative impact of environmental discrimination on black and poor communities.[21]

The CBC initially modeled itself after traditional civil rights organizations such as the National Association for the Advancement of Colored People (NAACP) and the National Urban League. Some early caucus members even suggested that "as the highest body of black elected officials," the CBC's members were the most legitimate representatives of the entire black community. In addition to advancing the mainstream civil rights agenda, the caucus initially envisioned itself as a legislative extension of regional and at times more militant civil rights organizations such as the Congress of Racial Equality and the Student Nonviolent Coordinating Committee, both of whose influence and effectiveness had begun to wane by the time the caucus was formed. By the early 1980s, however, civil rights groups and some CBC members argued that replicating the efforts of civil rights leadership was obscuring the caucus's core legislative and representational mission. In response to these assessments, the CBC tightened its focus on the legislative process while continuing as a voice of civil rights in Congress.[22] As one caucus member put it,

> Many of the senior Black caucus members came out of the heat of the civil rights struggle. . . . We ha[d] a group of new members whose strategies were shaped in the post civil rights movement— who use leverage within the system. We [saw] ourselves not as civil rights leaders but as legislators. . . . [T]he [civil rights] pioneers made it possible for us to be the technicians.[23]

In 1976, the private Congressional Black Caucus Foundation (CBCF) was established to assist the caucus, particularly with programming, fundraising, and public relations. The CBC has increasingly relied on this ancillary organization, especially after it and several other congressional caucuses were defunded in 1995. Throughout its existence, the CBCF has performed the role of political steward by promoting political leadership initiatives among African Americans in and out of Congress. Describing itself as "a nonprofit, nonpartisan public policy, research and educational institute that aims to help improve the socioeconomic circumstances of African Americans and other underserved communities," the CBCF "envisions a world in which the black community is free of all disparities and able to contribute to fully advancing the common good . . . and to advanc[ing] the global black community by developing leaders, informing policy and educating the public." As with other ancillary arms of congressional caucuses, the CBCF facilitates the exchange of ideas and information to address critical issues affecting black communities; develops strategic research and historical resources for the public; provides leadership development and scholarship opportunities, particularly for students; develops programs and research to address social, economic and health disparities; and coordinates the CBC's legislative conference, held every September in Washington, D.C.[24]

Whether the CBC functions, in Hannah Pitkin's terms, as an autonomous trustee for or as a delegated agent of its black constituents is not as important as the fact that it has consistently advocated a descriptive, race-conscious approach to representation and to achieving democracy and equality in America.[25] Despite the obligations of partisanship and legislative norms premised on seniority and specialization, the CBC promotes an Afrocentric approach to politics and attempts to express to African Americans that it is fighting for them in the legislature and elsewhere.[26] In this endeavor, the CBC assumes the role of legislative gadfly, pricking the consciences of its fellow legislators.[27] In so doing, the caucus echoes the assertiveness of earlier legislators such as Henry McNeal Turner and Robert Elliott and abolitionists such as Maria Stewart, Henry Highland Garnet, and Martin Delany.

As implied in its mission statement and despite its overwhelmingly Democratic membership,[28] the CBC's partisanship has been more ambivalent than is generally acknowledged. The caucus does not hesitate to reach across the aisle to gain support on issue, an approach expressed by another of its credos: "No permanent friends, no permanent enemies—only permanent interests."[29] Similarly, Bill Clay (D-MO) once proclaimed that "Democrat or Republican, [the CBC] will challenge anybody who seeks to undermine the basic interests of [black] people." Both declarations invoke Turner's approach to balancing racial and partisan interests: "Neither the Republican nor Democratic party can do for the colored race what they can do for themselves. Respect black."[30] This is not to suggest that the caucus refuses to toe the Democratic Party line. However, since both parties have been known to marginalize and undermine African Americans' political interests, it is logical for the CBC to keep blacks' concerns at the forefront.[31] As more blacks in Congress are representing racially and politically diverse constituencies, and as two black Republicans were recently elected to Congress, this element of the CBC's partisan ambivalence will likely continue.[32]

As of the 112th Congress, there were forty-three members of the CBC (including nonvoting delegates from Washington, D.C., and the U.S. Virgin Islands).[33] At this level, the caucus has come close to achieving proportional representation of blacks in the House. This growth has largely resulted from the reapportionment that followed the 1990 census, after which several southern state legislatures drew majority-black districts. Several related factors have caused this increase in the number of majority black districts. First, the 1990 census generated a more accurate count of blacks than the preceding census. Second, the 1982 amendments to the VRA allowed states with long histories of racial discrimination at the polls to draw more majority-minority districts. Consequently—and most crucial to the arguments advanced in this book—the 1990 reapportionments were done in a remedially race-conscious manner, with the goal of enabling blacks to elect representatives of their choice to Congress in states where racial discrimination had prevented such outcomes for nearly a century.

However, the momentum of the 1992 elections was soon stymied by the intersection of racial, regional, and partisan politics. By this point, the southern white electorate was completing a massive shift toward the Republican Party. Where most black voters in the South had remained Democrats since the 1960s, the region's white Democrats who felt betrayed by the party's liberal wing began to shift over to the Republican Party.[34] This shift included white Democrats who had been drawn out of majority-black districts after the 1990 redistricting. The result was an overwhelming Republican victory in the House of Representatives in 1994 that in turn placed major constraints on House Democrats, including Democratic-leaning caucuses. For example, in 1995, the House passed a measure to curb caucus influence by cutting off their funding and by ejecting them from their quarters in the House office buildings.[35] House Speaker Newt Gingrich is commonly believed to have felt threatened by some of these caucuses, particularly the recently expanded CBC. In what appeared to be a mutual sentiment, CBC members swiftly attacked what they saw as a racially motivated defunding measure. Outgoing CBC chair Kweisi Mfume accused Republicans of waging an assault on legislative diversity and attempting to disempower minority communities "through congressional ethnic and philosophical cleansing." Incoming CBC chair Donald Payne contended that the measure represented not so much an attempt at legislative reform as "a blatant move to put a gag on minorities and others who may differ in opinion from the new majority party."[36] Since the defunding, the CBC has had to scale back its activities and rely increasingly on the ancillary CBCF.

Despite periodic setbacks, the CBC has enjoyed significant legislative triumphs. On the international front, these triumphs include pressuring the U.S. government to divest from and sanction South Africa's apartheid government, advocating for the political and human rights interests of undocumented Haitian detainees in the 1990s, calling for investigations into the Rwandan genocide and more recently into the humanitarian crises in the Darfur region of the Sudan, and calling for U.S. assistance to

Haiti after the 2010 earthquake. The caucus has also pushed to ease federal restrictions on travel and financial remittances to Cuba, with members of the caucus recently traveling there to discuss these issues with both Fidel and Raul Castro. Such actions demonstrate that the caucus responds to domestic as well as international constituencies when the interests of latter affect or intersect with those of the former.[37] On the domestic front, the CBC also cosponsored the Humphrey-Hawkins Act[38] for full employment and enhanced economic growth, advocated a national holiday to commemorate the birth of Martin Luther King Jr., and helped fortify the VRA. Most recently, it has launched the "Jobs For the People" initiative, featuring job fairs and town hall meetings around the country. It has also greatly increased its presence in the mainstream media and on social networking sites such as Facebook.[39]

The CBC has also lost numerous legislative battles. Some of the more notable losses include the "Constructive Alternative Budget," which it proposed in 1981 and has submitted to every Congress since then. The caucus has never expected this budget to be adopted. A largely symbolic endeavor, it may "better [be] viewed as a relatively sophisticated response by the CBC to its limited resources . . . influence, and increasing internal pressures," allowing the caucus to express its social justice agenda to the national level of government. The CBC has also been relatively unsuccessful in expanding gun control policies, increasing federal school spending, using statistical sampling methods for the census, opposing the movement to add a biracial category to the census, and enhancing welfare provisions.[40] With respect to the latter objective, the caucus's social services agenda was sharply curtailed by President Clinton's welfare reforms.

The caucus has at times disagreed sharply with the African American rank and file. For example, most members oppose the death penalty, despite significant black support for it. The caucus also vigorously objected to the nomination of Clarence Thomas to the Supreme Court despite the strong support of most African Americans (at least before the confirmation hearings and before his stance on race-based policies became more clear). Based in part on Democratic Party imperatives, the CBC also tends to take a more liberal stance on gay rights, reproductive choice, and immigration than many of its black constituents. During the 2008 presidential campaigns, some members of the caucus initially backed Hillary Clinton rather than Barack Obama. Those initially supporting Clinton may have been driven more by political expediency than by aversion to Obama's candidacy. In particular, the more seasoned Clinton posed a formidable challenge to perceptions of Obama as an inexperienced political upstart. Internal divisions within the caucus about Obama's candidacy were mitigated by his strong showing in the Iowa primary and were put to rest by his victory in the South Carolina primary.[41]

Like many caucuses of its size and focus, the CBC typically sponsors hundreds of bills and cosponsors even more during each Congress. Like most other legislators in general, caucus members devote much of their energy to symbolic and noncontroversial issues. And even when the CBC does not succeed with its important substantive proposals, it has nonetheless demonstrated that it—and often the Democratic Party leadership—is on the "right side" of issues that are important to its constituents.[42] Most notably for the purposes of this book, the CBC played a central role in strengthening and extending the VRA in 1975, 1982, and 2006.

Amending the Voting Rights Act

Protecting African Americans' right to vote has always been the core of the CBC's agenda. The VRA has two primary provisions. Section 2 is intended to prevent racially discriminatory electoral plans and covers the entire country. In particular, Section 2 stipulates that "no qualification or prerequisite to voting, or standard, practice or procedure shall be imposed or applied by any State or political subdivision to deny or abridge the right of any citizen of the United states to vote on account of race or color."[43] Section 5 targets the former Confederacy, along with jurisdictions in the West, Northwest, and Northeast with a history of suppressing minority political power.[44] This provision seeks primarily to prevent the erosion of gains in minority political power. States and jurisdictions covered by Section 5 must submit any electoral changes for approval, or "pre-clearance," by the Department of Justice before those plans can be carried out. Section 2 was enacted as a permanent provision. Given the unprecedented implications of Section 5 for federalism and states' rights, the provision was initially enacted for a period of five years.

Amending the VRA in 1975

The VRA was first revised in 1970. Minimal changes were made to it at that time; most notably, Section 5 was extended for another five years. By the 1975, pressure was mounting to strengthen the act and to extend Section 5 for at least ten years. The chief justification for a longer extension was that racial and electoral discrimination had been too deeply etched into the southern political landscape to be significantly mitigated in relatively short five-year increments.[45] In 1975 congressional hearings on the VRA, Civil Rights Commission chair Arthur Flemming testified that progress had been too modest to conclude that Congress's goals for the act were fulfilled. In his view, letting Section 5 lapse would halt that progress and thus "betray the solemn national commitment embodied in the Voting Rights Act." CBC chair Charles Rangel (D-NY) asserted that the VRA needed to be extended because the intended results had not yet been completed: Although "ten years . . . sounds like a long time . . . it is far from excessively long when viewed in the light of the voting rights abuses that were allowed to grow up in the nearly 100 years that elapsed between the ratification of the Fifteenth Amendment . . . and the enactment of the Voting Rights Act."[46]

By 1975, there was also increasing evidence of and attention to language-based electoral discrimination, particularly against Spanish-speakers in the Southwest.[47] In light of Texas's history of discriminating against black and Latino voters, Texas representative and CBC member Barbara Jordan sought to extend Section 5's coverage to Texas.[48] She noted such obstructions as insufficient or no access to private voting booths in majority black and Latino precincts; clerks filling out absentee ballots for whites over the phone while failing to similarly assist minority voters; election officials identifying and tracking votes via numbered stubs; local laws that allowed clerks to begin opening ballots after only ten people had voted; and the rejection of voter registration forms containing visibly corrected errors.[49] Jordan also recognized the pressing need to protect Texas's large Spanish-speaking minority from language discrimination at the polls. According to Jordan, the "same discriminatory practices which moved the Congress to pass the Voting Rights Act in 1965, and renew it in 1970, are practiced in Texas today" against its Mexican American populace.[50] In turn, this discrimination suppressed the presence of Latinos in elected office.

Some members of Congress did not perceive language-based electoral discrimination to be sufficiently widespread or acute to merit VRA coverage. For example, the Republican Policy Committee issued a statement criticizing language-based amendments as "punitive 'reconstruction'-type federal intervention in southern states" and as a "spotty approach that will augment the voting strength of some, but not all, groups in the electorate."[51] Robert McClory (R-IL) argued that amending the VRA to protect language minorities "goes far beyond what is needed, wanted or desired in our [electoral] system" and that doing so would constitute an unjustifiably "far departure" from the act's original scope.[52] Others opposed extending the VRA on federalism principles. Representatives Henry Hyde (R-IL), Walter Flowers (D-AL), and M. Caldwell Butler (R-VA) argued that the act was no longer needed at all, much less on a linguistic basis. Referring to Section 5, Flowers argued that on federalist grounds he "long opposed the act in its [existing] form" because it was "wrong" to "require . . . only seven states . . . to do certain things that no other state in the union has to do." Hyde and others proposed several alternatives to extending and broadening the VRA, most of them grounded in the concepts of dual federalism and states' rights. Hyde spearheaded the position that Section 5 should apply to all fifty states rather than selectively. Edward Hutchinson (R-MI), and McClory proposed extending Section 5 for five rather than ten years and rejected Jordan's language-based proposals altogether.[53]

Countering these arguments and corroborating Jordan's observations, fellow CBC member Andrew Young (D-GA) likened the obstacles encountered by Spanish-speaking minorities to those encountered by blacks in the South. Young called attention to inadequate numbers of Spanish-speaking registration personnel; uncooperative registrars; purging of Spanish surnames from voter registration lists; intimidation by election officials; failure to locate voters' names on precinct lists; lack of bilingual materials; and difficulties with the use of absentee ballots.[54] In Young's view, these practices "operated to effectively deny Mexican-Americans access to the political processes in Texas for even longer than the blacks were formally denied access by the white primary."[55] Young concluded that the VRA could and should serve as "an instrument of progress for all people in those areas where there are Spanish-speaking communities" in the same manner in which the law was serving black voters.[56]

For Jordan, the only means available for language minorities— specifically Mexican Americans in Texas—to gain equal access to the franchise was by extending the protections of the VRA to them.[57] She thus urged legislators "to make it very clear that they want the VRA to cover those minorities who are discriminated against" on the basis of the fact that English is not their primary language.[58] In proposing the extension of the VRA's protections to protect Spanish-speaking language minorities in the Southwest from electoral discrimination, Jordan argued that "the VRA may have overcome blatant discriminatory practices, but it has yet to overcome subtle discriminatory practices" against both black and Spanish-speaking voters. Therefore, Congress should "extend the provisions of the act to Texas, New Mexico, Arizona and parts of California [to] guarantee to Mexican Americans and blacks residing these jurisdictions the same special attention to their voting rights now afforded blacks in the South."[59]

A key challenge for Jordan was convincing the CBC and black civil rights leaders of the broader merits of preventing language-based electoral discrimination. Her proposal initially troubled black civil rights groups. Although they wholly supported the principle that all minorities deserved protection from electoral discrimination, some feared that adding language-based protections would endanger the chances that Congress would approve the VRA with both the new language provisions and an extension of Section 5. And even if Congress passed such a bill, they worried that President Ronald Reagan would veto it. The NAACP also expressed concern that adding language protections might invite the Supreme Court to overturn the act as overly broad.[60] These concerns were eventually resolved by adding a clause separating the language-based proposals from the main provisions of the act.[61]

In response to contentions that Section 5 had outlived its utility, Jordan emphasized the persistence of voting rights infractions, noting that "for conclusive proof that the act is still needed one need only look to the DOJ's own records," which revealed a rise in problematic Section 5 preclearance requests. For example, despite decreases in voting rights infractions in the South, the DOJ objected to fifty requests for pre-clearance of new electoral or redistricting plans in 1971, thirty in 1972, twenty-seven in 1973, and thirty again in 1974 because those plans violated Section 5.[62] Flemming echoed Jordan's position, noting that the number of objections justified the continued need for the legislation, especially in regions where compliance with Section 5 was slow or had stagnated. In Flemming's view, "The continuing high level of Section Five objections is evidence of the persistence with which some jurisdictions covered by the act continue to resist fulfillment of its purposes."[63] Congressman Rangel echoed Jordan's claims, concurring that "malevolent local government must not be exposed to any temptation to take back the political rights and powers that have so recently come to southern blacks" and other historically disfranchised minorities.[64]

On June 4, 1975, the House approved with a decisive 341–70 majority H.R. 6219, which extended Section 5 of the VRA for ten years and which included new protections for language minorities. The Senate followed suit by a 77–12 vote but added one significant amendment, introduced by Senator Robert Byrd (D-WV), that reduced the duration of Section 5 from ten to seven years. Byrd had preferred to reduce the extension to five years. Yielding to arguments that the VRA would be expiring just as states would be gearing up for the 1980 census and ensuing reapportionments, he conceded to a seven-year extension. Accepting this adjustment, the House passed the final version of the bill on July 18 by an even greater majority, 346–56.[65] Most notably, the 1975 amendments to the VRA

- added protection for language-based minorities in the Southwest and parts of the Northeast;
- extended Section 5 until 1982;
- extended Section 4's "bailout" provision for states proving compliance with Section 5 until 1982;
- made permanent the nationwide ban on literacy tests; and
- continued the protection of citizens of American Indian, Asian, and native Alaskan descent in the Northwest.[66]

Amending the VRA in 1982: The Problems of Noncompliance and Vote Dilution

Continuing its mission to broaden and elevate the influence of African Americans in the political, legislative, and public policy arenas, the CBC was at the forefront of the 1982 amendments to the VRA. As in 1975, there were several compelling reasons to extend and strengthen the VRA. Noncompliance with Section 5's pre-clearance requirement was still very much in evidence; it was becoming more clear that five- to ten-year increments were insufficient to allow Section 5 and other key provisions of the act to root out deeply entrenched discrimination at the polls. In addition, the phenomenon of minority vote dilution had begun to emerge. Minority vote dilution occurs when election processes systematically combine with racial bloc voting by the majority group to weaken the electoral strength of the minority group, which also tends to vote as a bloc. Unlike traditional voter disfranchisement, which blocks access to the polls, minority vote dilution can occur even when all voters have equal access to the polls and even when their votes are counted.[67] Consequently, whereas minority voter disfranchisement impairs electoral processes, minority vote dilution compromises electoral outcomes for those voters. Given vote dilution's propensity to "abridge" one's right to vote, it potentially violated Section 2 of the VRA.

By 1982, John Conyers (D-MI) and Harold Washington (D-IL) represented the CBC on the House Committee on the Judiciary. Washington was also a member of the committee's Subcommittee on Civil and Constitutional Rights. In his opening remarks for the 1981 hearings on the

VRA, Washington asserted that the law remained necessary given that the United States had yet to purge itself of the racial hierarchy around which the nation was framed:

> [It] may be unpleasant to hear, but it's a manifestly true reality [that Congress] has a history of denial or superficial acceptance of the reality of race relations in this country. I for one do not intend to indulge that non-reality, to do so would be a denial of . . . the history of my people. To kill or water down the Voting Rights Act at this time would be the wrong signal to send out to our own people and to a troubled world.[68]

Washington and Conyers relied heavily the support of other minority members of Congress and House Democrats as well as the continued support of Pete Rodino (D-NJ), chair of the House Judiciary Committee, and Don Edwards (D-CA), chair of the House Subcommittee on Civil and Constitutional Rights. The caucus again relied heavily on the testimony of civil rights and other leaders. Echoing the gist of Washington's opening declaration, National Urban League president Vernon Jordan noted that much more remained to be done to achieve the equality about which Americans have dreamed, while NAACP executive director Benjamin Hooks cautioned that although good progress had been made, America had not yet reached the voting rights millennium. AFL-CIO president Lane Kirkland cautioned Congress against resting prematurely on its laurels: despite the progress made by the VRA, "relative success does not mean that [America] has reached a state of grace" with regard to political equality.[69]

The caucus was particularly concerned that the expiration of Section 5 would lead to the retrogression of the minority vote. In an earlier hearing, Jordan recalled the negative effects of the Hayes Compromise on the Reconstruction amendments and blacks' civil rights. Noting that scores of southern jurisdictions continued to make ostensibly innocuous alterations in electoral systems that were in fact designed to dilute the black vote, he cautioned that "history [has told] us we can go back to where we were." Hooks reminded the subcommittee about how Black Codes and later Jim Crow policies eroded the progress made during the Reconstruction era, concluding, "But for the fact that there is a VRA . . . a number of innovative schemes and devices would [again] be used to deny blacks the opportunity" to vote. Finally, another veteran civil rights activist, the Reverend Ralph Abernathy, suggested that those who saw the VRA as obsolete failed to take into account "the potential deviousness of human nature and the likelihood of reverting to the outmoded political ways of governing."[70]

In a moment of candor, civil rights attorney Jack Greenberg hinted at the racist animus behind opposition to the VRA, suggesting that "the rush to scrap [it] is perhaps evidence of the fact that the law is . . . a deterrent to some things some people would like to do," such as enacting electoral plans that would discriminate against black voters or weaken their vote. Eddie Williams, president of the Joint Center for Political Studies, bluntly asserted that it "would be a very dangerous gamble" to assume that the inequities the VRA had begun to correct would not reappear in the absence of the act given that "racism persists and cannot be wished away." By the last days of the hearings, the chair of the CBC, D.C. delegate Walter Fauntroy, had repeated four times his concern that without the VRA, "the clock may be turned back as far as 1870" in the South.[71] Such concerns were more than racial or partisan hyperbole. Although the VRA helped uproot overtly discriminatory electoral laws and policies, new strains of discrimination began to emerge in their place. Such discrimination often took the form of subtly worded policies that were facially neutral but that yielded racially disparate results and that, in turn, strained Sections 2 and 5 of the act. In sum, the CBC was concerned about three types of electoral discrimination. One type was procedural, impeding minorities' attempts to register to vote, including

- insufficient availability of registrars at registration sites;
- limited registration times outside the standard workday schedule;
- relocating registrars in or near places historically hostile to blacks (such as private, all-white social clubs, sheriff's offices, and so forth); and
- reregistration requirements that effectively and disproportionately purged minorities from voter registration rolls.

A second type of discriminatory tactic, also procedural, impeded registered minority voters' access to ballots on Election Day:

- insufficient polling places, hours, and personnel;
- last-minute relocation of polling places to inconvenient or distant areas;
- last-minute closures of polling places; and
- inadequate publication of voting rules/procedures.

The third type, vote dilution, was particularly vexing in its scope and in terms of assessing both its scope and effect, and includes

- white racial bloc voting that submerged black votes;
- accepting/certifying absentee ballots from white nonresidents of a jurisdiction;
- changes from single-member to multimember districts;
- prohibition of "bullet" voting options in multimember district elections;
- annexation of white subdivisions into majority black districts;
- majority-vote runoff elections in areas with no districting;
- racial gerrymanders that excluded black voters;
- open primaries decided by majority rather than plurality decision rules; and
- increased campaign filing fees for candidates.[72]

Noncompliance with Section 5 turned out to be a particularly thorny problem. Many jurisdictions enacted new electoral procedures, many with potentially diluting or retrogressive effects, without first submitting the proposed changes to the DOJ for pre-clearance. This problem was exacerbated by the fact that the department lacked sufficient resources to keep current with the volume of pre-clearance requests and was thus minimally equipped to detect and address noncompliant jurisdictions. It was thus not unusual for the DOJ to learn of discriminatory plans that had existed for years only when an offending jurisdiction submitted pre-clearance requests to change those plans. In the interim, faulty electoral provisions remained in place, to the detriment of minority political power.[73]

In 1969 the Supreme Court invalidated in *Allen v. State Board of Education* electoral measures that resulted in "a dilution of [the] voting power" of African Americans.[74] The CBC relied on this precedent to justify the retention of Section 5 during the 1982 deliberations over reauthorizing that provision. The caucus also recognized that eliminating the problem of vote dilution required expanding legislators' focus to examine the outcomes of voting as well as opportunities to register and then vote. Congressional efforts to eliminate vote dilution called for a reevaluation of on whom the burden of proof should fall and who should bear the costs of that burden. The challenge was that proving discriminatory intent was becoming increasingly difficult given the disappearance of the traditional smoking guns of racist animus. Yet the CBC was emboldened by what promised to be an effects-oriented decision to be handed down by the Supreme Court in *Rodgers v. Lodge*, which was argued while Congress was revising the VRA. The Court was likely well aware of Congress's explicit intent to check the intent-oriented precedent handed down earlier that year in *Mobile v. Bolden.*

The Court's holding in *Mobile v. Bolden* signaled to the CBC that the neutral wording of electoral plans with discriminatory results made proving discriminatory intent difficult, if not impossible. Interpreting statutory language often necessitated researching the legislative history of suspicious electoral schemes, a task that is usually time-consuming and prohibitively expensive.[75] According to testimony provided during the VRA hearings, the time required to litigate alleged voting rights violations could exceed six thousand hours. As a consequence of the slow nature of these investigative processes, resolution often came after the election, thus cementing the political damage to minorities for several years until such processes might be invalidated. Ironically, efforts to remedy vote dilution could themselves impede black political power in regions covered by Section 5.[76]

The CBC thus sought to shift the burden of proof from the potential victims of discriminatory electoral plans to the jurisdiction/state responsible for enacting such plans. The burden of proof dilemma troubled the Supreme Court when it confronted the problem fifteen years earlier in *South Carolina v. Katzenbach.* In that case, the Court was struck not simply by the slow and arduous process of voting rights litigation but by the speed and facility with which states and jurisdictions enacted discriminatory electoral laws during that process. Consequently, the justices asserted that the burden of proof should fall on accused states and jurisdictions rather than on the plaintiffs: Sending an important signal to legislators, the Court held that "after enduring nearly a century of [states'] systematic resistance to the Fifteenth Amendment, Congress might well decide to shift the advantage of time and inertia from the perpetrators of the evil to its victims."[77]

Along with *Allen,* the CBC relied on *Katzenbach* to justify amending Section 5 in a way that would relieve minority plaintiffs of the burden of proving discriminatory intent in light of the increasing difficulty of finding explicit evidence of it. The debate over intended as opposed to effective discrimination intensified as House deliberations over Section 2 progressed. The issue spilled over into the Senate hearings as well, eventually dominating two months of that chamber's debate over the act.[78]

Extending Section 5 in 1982

In April 1981, Representative Rodino proposed extending Section 5 for ten more years. As in 1975, some members of Congress voiced strong objections to this proposal. Led again by Hyde, opponents of Rodino's proposal argued that the provision treated states unequally, in violation of the Tenth Amendment and the principle of dual federalism. Hyde objected in particular to the "selective application of pre-clearance" that put covered states in a "penalty box," unfairly targeted them as electoral scapegoats, and wrongly labeled "a handful of States as racists" while disregarding the fact that most southern states had improved their voting rights practices. Representative Billy Lee Evans (D-GA) suggested that it was unfair to apply Section 5 to the South alone simply because the region's history of overt racial discrimination made it an easy target. Accordingly, Hyde and others introduced proposals to weaken Section 5. Such proposals included shortening the duration of pre-clearance obligations, expanding Section 4's bailout provisions for states that proved compliance with Section 5, and settling disputes locally rather than through the District of Columbia Court of Appeals.[79]

As the hearings progressed, Hyde withdrew his opposition to the act's pre-clearance requirements, "largely because of testimony about voting abuses that he . . . heard during several weeks of hearings" convincing him "that there are still enormous difficulties with people getting the vote in the South and other areas."[80] Hyde later explained that he changed his mind following a tour in the South with members of the CBC, during which he heard directly from African American voters about the electoral challenges they still faced. Balancing his long-standing aversion to Section 5's effect on federalism and state autonomy with this newfound knowledge, Hyde ultimately sought to enhance the bailout mechanisms for covered states and regions that proved compliance with Section 5.[81] A recent interview with Republican representative Jim Sensenbrenner (WI) sheds additional light on this critical turn of events. He entered office in 1982 skeptical about Section 5, but the hearings on the VRA convinced him as well of the continued need for it. He has since concluded that much of the long-standing Republican opposition to the provision is "not necessarily based in fact or law" but arises out of their commitment to a states' rights concept of federalism. (Sensenbrenner has subsequently maintained this position on the VRA.)[82]

Transforming Section 2 in 1982

Where extending Section 5 rehashed perennial debates about federalism, the effects-oriented nature of vote dilution compelled legislators to take a drastically different perspective on representation. From the CBC's perspective, the outcomes of voting are as important as the opportunity to vote. In civil rights lawyer Greenberg's words, "An effect, after all, is what we're talking about."[83] Yet in contrast to the 1975 reauthorization, the CBC in 1982 operated in an era of renewed conservatism that dominated both Congress and the executive branch. This change in ideological climate, combined with the fact that the proposed amendments were far more expansive than their predecessors, made for much more intense deliberations than had occurred in 1975.

The CBC's preference for a results-oriented Section 2 was motivated in part by its response to the Supreme Court's decision in *Mobile v. Bolden*. At issue in that case was the claim by black voters in Mobile, Alabama, that the city's newly enacted at-large districting plan, combined with persistent white racial bloc voting, diluted blacks' votes to the point that they were unable to elect a candidate of their choice to the city council. In its holding, the Court departed from its 1973 precedent in *White v. Regester*, where it initiated an approach to determining racial discrimination by considering the "totality of the circumstances."[84] This approach entails verifying the existence of a politically cohesive black electorate and of white racial bloc voting that consistently overwhelms blacks' political preferences. In *Mobile*, the Court held that racially discriminatory results alone were insufficient to prove violation of the Equal Protection Clause of the Fourteenth Amendment. Instead, the justices required plaintiffs to prove discriminatory intent as well. In the CBC's view, the decision in *Mobile* threatened to erode the political progress brought on by the VRA. In order to prevent further erosion, the CBC and civil rights leaders sought to transform Section 2 into a provision that prohibited racially discriminatory intent *and* effects.

In his testimony supporting a results-oriented VRA, Urban League president Jordan asserted on Fifteenth Amendment grounds that the *Mobile* decision necessitated amending Section 2 to a results standard: the Fifteenth Amendment assumed "that the fact of denial [of the franchise] is evil enough, without inquiry into the minds and intents of the deniers." Jordan then noted that prior to *Mobile*, no one had seriously doubted that the VRA operated on the same basis. NAACP president Hooks asserted that Congress never intended that the difficult burden of proving intent to discriminate be placed on the persons affected by such discrimination. Former assistant attorney general and law professor Drew Days argued that the Court's decision in *Mobile* made proving intent to discriminate "not only overwhelming but almost impossible" and that proposals to amend Section 2 were "designed to return to the difficult but [more] workable standards of earlier cases."[85]

Opponents of an outcomes orientation, led also by Congressman Hyde, asserted that the Constitution was intended to ensure equal electoral opportunities rather than equal results. Of particular concern was that changing the law to a results standard would guarantee proportional representation.[86] Hyde thus proposed a rider stipulating that "proportional representation is not necessarily required as a result of statistical [racial] imbalance and [racially] polarized voting."[87] Responding for the civil rights community, Hooks emphasized that a results orientation had always been Congress's intent for Section 2. Indeed, because the Court had "confused the issue of standard of proof" in *Mobile v. Bolden*, it was imperative for "Congress to take the necessary action to amend Section 2 of the Act to restore the law as it stood before [that] decision." Hooks also reminded the opposition of the underrepresentation of blacks in political office and the corresponding overrepresentation of whites. On the one hand, the presence of five thousand African American elected officials in 1981 was proof of significant progress; on the other, that number amounted to fewer than 1 percent of all of the nation's elected officials.[88]

While the CBC desired an outcomes standard for Section 2, it also recognized that such a standard could endanger the passage of the VRA as a whole. As a result, the caucus distanced itself from the shibboleth of proportional representation. CBC chair Walter Fauntroy called a results-oriented Section 2 "a necessary tool to insure equal access, not a stick to mandate proportional representation." He also asserted that the caucus "totally reject[s] any statement which contends that it is anything more than that and . . . suggest[s] that such statements are merely attempts to discredit the true intent of the act—to ensure equal access for all Americans to the electoral process." Days sought to allay Hyde's concerns by clarifying the difference between a results-oriented Section 2 and proportional representation. Noting first that the Court's decisions prior to *Mobile* had made it clear that there is no right to a quota system or proportional representation, Days explained that "the proposed amendment to Section 2 simply clarifies that section's protection of the right to access to the political process, the right not only to cast a vote but to have that vote count." He also asserted that creating an outcomes standard would not predetermine the results of a particular election but rather would allow potential litigants realistically to challenge structural barriers to free and open electoral competition "without taking on the impossible task of reading the minds of those who erected those barriers."[89] The House Judiciary Committee ultimately compromised by incorporating a results orientation into the revised Section 2 along with a disclaimer that "the fact that members of a minority group have not been elected in numbers equal to the group's proportion of the population shall not, in and of itself, constitute a violation."[90]

The intent/outcomes debate was equally intense on the Senate Judiciary Committee. That committee was chaired by Senator Strom Thurmond (R-SC), whose hostility to civil rights legislation was legendary. Although he had softened over time on such legislation, Thurmond voted against the VRA in 1965 and against extending it in 1970 and 1975. Another detractor was Senator Orrin Hatch (R-UT). A relative newcomer, Hatch was soon perceived by the CBC and other Democrats as hostile to civil rights.[91] Moreover, the Senate committee as a whole was mindful of President Reagan's reservations about revising Section 2 toward a results orientation, especially given attorney general William French Smith's testimony before the committee that the executive branch strongly opposed any move toward proving discriminatory intent based on electoral outcomes or the totality of electoral circumstances.[92]

The Senate debate was resolved by an amendment proposed by Bob Dole (R-KS). The Dole amendment allowed Section 2 to have a results orientation, on the condition that "nothing in [Section 2] establishes a right to have members of a protected class elected in numbers equal to their proportion in the population."[93] Dole's motivations for proposing this compromise are difficult to determine. In one instance, he held that Section 2 was to be applied only "if a voting practice or structure operates to exclude members of a minority group from a fair *opportunity* to participate in the political process," thus clearly endorsing procedural equality. Yet he also contended that "citizens of all races ... are intended by Section 2 to have an equal chance of *electing* candidates of their choice"; here, Dole seems to promote the CBC's outcomes approach.[94]

The anti-proportional-representation riders in the House and Senate versions of the bill bridged the gap between the CBC and those who opposed the CBC's goal of a results-oriented Section 2. In October 1981, the House approved the bill by a 389–24 vote; the following June, after a brief filibuster by Jesse Helms (R-NC), the Senate followed suit by a vote of 85–8.[95] The amended Section 2 stipulated that

no qualification or prerequisite to voting or standard, practice, or procedure shall be imposed or applied by any State or political subdivision in a manner which results in a denial or abridgement of the right of any citizen of the United States to vote on account of race or color.... [N]othing in this section establishes a right to have members of a protected class elected in numbers equal to their proportion in the population.[96]

As amended in 1982, the VRA

- allowed plaintiffs to prove a Section 2 vote dilution violation with a showing of discriminatory results;
- stipulated that Section 2 does not guarantee the proportional representation of racial minorities;
- extended the pre-clearance provisions of Section 5 for twenty-five years and required nine states in their entirety and parts of thirteen others to obtain justice department approval of proposed electoral changes;
- provided a new mechanism for covered jurisdictions to "bail out" of Section 5 by allowing them to show to a three-judge panel in Washington, D.C., that they have had a clean voting rights record for ten years;
- extended until 1992 provisions requiring certain areas to provide bilingual election materials; and
- authorized blind, disabled, or illiterate voters to receive assistance in voting, provided that such assistance does not come from the voter's employer or a labor union officer.[97]

The 1982 amendments to the VRA, many of which initially faced energetic opposition, ultimately garnered widespread bipartisan support in both chambers of Congress. Congress's authorization of several controversial provisions was due in part to the CBC's efforts to protect minority political power from retrogression via dilution and other discriminatory procedures. That Section 5 was extended for an unprecedented period of twenty-five years—more than three times longer than previous extensions of it—is especially significant. Although the longer extension still represented a compromise between the CBC's desire to make Section 5 permanent and those who wanted to abolish it altogether, the extension clearly affirmed the interests of the caucus's chief stakeholders and the originally intended beneficiaries of the VRA.

Republicans agreed to the CBC's preferences for two reasons. With respect to Section 5, witness testimony and copious evidence of noncompliance and problematic electoral plans convinced skeptics such as Hyde and Sensenbrenner of the continuing need for the provision. With regard to Section 2, the CBC's push for an outcomes orientation to shore up minority political power offered an ironic windfall benefit to Republicans. Since the GOP was at the time a minority in the South, the party stood to benefit from an enhancement of the black vote; amending the VRA in a way that fostered majority-black districting in the South would likely provoke disaffected white Democrats in those districts to either vote Republican or switch parties. Motivated by these potential benefits to the GOP, Sensenbrenner appealed personally to the executive branch to support the proposed amendments and to convince President Reagan to sign the bill.[98]

The benefits of the 1982 revisions of the VRA to the GOP were remarkable. Ten years later, the party submitted an amicus curiae brief *endorsing* the majority-black districts at issue in *Shaw v. Reno.* Two years later, Republicans captured Congress and much of the southern white electorate. By 2000, state legislators in Georgia conceded that the creation of black supermajority districts in the state would "push the Senate more toward Republicans and correspondingly diminish the power of [Georgia's] African Americans."[99] At that point, however, not a single Republican state legislator approved the state's redistricting plan. By that time, the party may well have reaped most of the windfall benefits of white Democrat crossover voting or conversion. Whether as a result of the Republican Party's prescience, changing dynamics in both parties, the cyclical nature of critical elections, racial bloc voting among both blacks and whites, white disgruntlement, or some combination of all of these factors, enough southern whites either voted Republican or joined the party for it to regain control of Congress in 1994 and to dominate southern politics in a manner unprecedented before the 1982 amendments to the VRA.

The CBC's role in amending the VRA to promote the electoral power of black voters—as evidenced by significant increases in the number of blacks and other minorities elected to office in regions that had long suppressed such outcomes—was a major victory for the caucus. Conversely, these amendments also boosted the Republican presence in the South and triggered resistance on the Supreme Court, thus making the CBC's victory somewhat pyrrhic. Nevertheless, the gains in minority political power combined with continued evidence of the need for federal oversight of covered jurisdictions compelled the CBC to push even harder twenty-five years later to retain Section 5 of the act.

Reauthorizing the VRA in 2006: Continuing the Battle to Justify Section 5

With respect to race, the 1982 revisions of the VRA significantly altered the contours of the American political landscape in a way that greatly benefited minority voting and representation. By enabling (or, depending on one's point of view, compelling) states with a history of electoral discrimination to draw more minority safe districts, the numbers of black and other minority elected officials grew at a rate unprecedented since the Reconstruction era. In the South alone, the number of blacks elected to public office grew from 2,400 in 1980 to 9,100 in 2005.[100] Despite such accomplishments however, two conflicting problems loomed on America's political horizon. First, African Americans still comprised only about 3 percent of all elected officials nationwide. Second, the Supreme Court majority was increasingly hostile to the use of race in redistricting and other electoral processes, especially when such processes yielded majority-minority districts with irregular shapes. In *Shaw v. Reno,* one year after North Carolina elected its first two black members of Congress since 1901, the Court eased the process for white voters to challenge irregularly shaped minority electoral districts of the type that sent those two representatives to Congress. That decision was followed by a series of similar decisions that included *Miller v. Johnson* (1995), *Reno v. Bossier Parish School Board I* and *II* (1997 and 2000), and *Georgia v. Ashcroft* (2003).

In 2005, House Democrats and the CBC in particular sought again to rein in what they considered continued judicial erosion of the VRA. In 2005, however, Congress had to work with the Court's stipulation in *Boerne v. Flores* that legislators must establish a record showing "congruence and proportionality between the injury to be prevented or remedied and the means adopted to that end" when enacting remedial legislation under the Fourteenth Amendment.[101] Where the transformation of Section 2 from an intent to an outcomes standard was cause for much consternation in 1982, it barely raised a ripple in 2005. Section 5, however, continued to garner the same federalism opposition as it had in 1975 and 1982. For its part, the CBC justified Section 5 with the ongoing need to retain the electoral gains made by blacks and other minorities and with evidence of persisting noncompliance with that provision. By this time, the CBC had more than doubled its presence on the House Judiciary Committee, where it was represented by John Conyers (the ranking Democrat), Bobby Scott (D-VA), Sheila Jackson-Lee (D-TX), Maxine Waters (D-CA), and Mel Watt (D-NC), with Conyers, Scott, and Watt on the Committee's Civil and Constitutional Rights subcommittee. By this time, Walt was also the chair of the CBC.

Although Section 5 did not expire until 2007, Congress moved the reauthorization process up two years. According to Watt and Scott, the CBC sought to avoid revisiting the act after it expired and during the presidential election season; to reinstate an expired Section 5 during that time would involve far heavier political lifting, especially in the Senate, than extending it. Recognizing that the 2008 elections would likely bode better for Democrats, thus affording them an opportunity to amend the VRA beyond what Republicans envisioned, the GOP agreed to the expedited timeline.[102] According to Sensenbrenner, waiting until 2006 presented two challenges for supporters of the VRA. If Republicans took the House, Representaive Lamar Smith (TX), a certain opponent of Section 5, would chair the Judiciary Committee. If the Democrats kept control, Conyers would remain the committee's chair but would not have sufficient time during the lame-duck postelection session to, in keeping with *Boernes v. Flores,* document the continuing need for Section 5. Both scenarios left Section 5 hanging by a thread. Recognizing Sensenbrenner's commitment to the VRA and his pivotal role in the 1982 amendments, and on behalf of the CBC, Watt approached the Wisconsin representative to help coordinate an early, bipartisan effort to reauthorize the VRA. They agreed to prevent the left from adding provisions that fell outside the act's purview and to prevent the right from weakening it by weakening or omitting Section 5.[103]

From Watt's perspective, in addition to navigating around partisan opposition, it was essential to do "as little as possible" to the VRA that would run it afoul of the Supreme Court. On this point, he stood apart from those caucus members who preferred to strengthen Section 2 and those who hoped to address the problem of felon disfranchisement laws and the disproportionate impact of such laws on the black and Latino electorate. In Watt's view, because the Court majority had already expressed unease with the results orientation of the VRA, it would have been imprudent to draw attention to it in 2005. Watt also saw felon disfranchisement as a separate issue that called for its own legislation. Concurring with external civil rights organizations that the CBC was "operating in a very definitive box" that left it little room to expand the VRA, Watt coordinated a focused approach to reauthorizing the act.[104]

Scott emphasized his concerns over the retrogression of minority political power via discriminatory electoral plans that were enacted by jurisdictions that had failed to comply with the VRA's pre-clearance provisions. On the first day of the hearings, he asserted that allowing Section 5 to lapse would likely invite more discriminatory electoral plans and thus fraudulent elections. In his view, the victors in such elections

> get an advantage by cheating. . . . [T]he people who have perpetrated the fraud get to enjoy the fruits of their fraud while [Section 2] litigation goes on, as opposed to Section 5 where [they] never get

to enjoy the fruits of [their] fraud to begin with because [they] can't get it pre-cleared.[105]

Scott did not simply explain the need for Section 5's prophylactic function, he emphasized that the provision properly takes the burden of proof off of minority voters. Conyers called attention to persisting problems with minority access to the ballot, including instances "in which people have been discouraged, misdirected, [and] given improper information, sometimes from the electoral system locally itself." On behalf of the CBC, Watt called for Congress "to strengthen and expand the Voting Rights Act by addressing restrictive Supreme Court decisions."[106]

Once again, there was a push to extend Section 5 to all 50 states. Arguing against nationalizing Section 5, Watt noted that "covered jurisdictions, simply put, are covered because they have not only a history of discriminatory practices, but have a history of ongoing discrimination as well." CBC member David Scott (D-GA) was not a member of these committees but was an occasional participant in the hearings. In his view, Georgia was the "poster state" for and at the "epicenter" of the need for Section 5, and "there was no greater example" of the continued need for it than the law that Georgia had recently passed requiring voters to obtain voter identification cards before they could cast ballots. Scott and the caucus believed Georgia's law was unjustified, unduly burdensome to poor and elderly voters, and tantamount to a poll tax. Scott then expressed his concern that Georgia had the highest number of unapproved pre-clearance requests, which suggested a high number of discriminatory electoral plans. Scott also condemned the Court's decision in *Georgia v. Ashcroft* as potentially very retrogressive. Finally, Scott was attempting to counter the strong opposition to Section 5 of his fellow representative from Georgia, Republican Lynn Westmoreland.[107]

The 1982 amendments to the VRA intensified institutional tensions regarding the scope and intent of the act. Since the early 1990s, the Supreme Court has interpreted the Equal Protection Clause and the VRA in a way that undermines the power of both laws to protect minority voting rights. Effectively, the Court has checked Congress's intent for those laws. In *Shaw v. Reno,* Justice Sandra Day O'Connor applied the Equal Protection Clause in a way that chipped away at Congress's intent for Section 2 to prevent minority vote dilution and for Section 5 to prevent retrogression of the minority vote. In *Reno v. Bossier Parish School Board I,* O'Connor unyoked Section 2 from Section 5. Essentially, the majority held that it does not matter if an electoral plan has a discriminatory purpose as long as it has no discriminatory effect. In other words, because no minorities had served on the school board in the past as a result of intentional discrimination, an intentionally discriminatory plan in the present from which no minorities are elected is not retrogressive and thus does not violate the VRA. Citing the Senate Report on the 1982 VRA amendments but no House or other congressional record, O'Connor reasoned that "Congress has made it sufficiently clear that a violation of Section 2 is not grounds in and of itself for denying pre-clearance under Section 5" and left open the question of whether Section 5 prevents more than the retrogression of the minority vote.[108]

Picking this question up in *Bossier Parish II*, Justice Antonin Scalia wrote for the majority that Section 5 only prevents retrogressive vote dilution as opposed to other types of vote dilution. In so doing, not only did Scalia interpret Sections 2 and 5 in a way that elided Congress's explicit goals of preventing both effective and intentional abridgements of the right to vote, he criticized the DOJ for "refusing to accept the limited meaning that we [the Court] have said pre-clearance has in the vote dilution context."[109] With this pair of cases, the Court restricted both the scope and intent of Sections 2 and 5. In *Georgia v. Ashcroft*, the Court extended its truncation of Sections 2 and 5 in a way that permitted the DOJ to accept minority "influence" districts (those with a white majority but with a critical mass of minority voters) as proxies for actual majority-minority safe districts in states covered by Section 5.

Not surprisingly, the CBC and congressional Democrats explicitly sought in 2005 to check the Court's minority voting rights jurisprudence by restoring to the VRA what the justices had chipped away from it. Conyers contended that the *Bossier Parish* precedents "need[ed] remedying," reminding his colleagues that legislative checks on the Court's interpretation of statutory laws is "nothing particularly new." On this point, he emphasized that the Court's reading of the VRA was "certainly not the result that Congress contemplated when Section 5 was written" and that the *Shaw* rationale "substantially weakened the DOJ's power to protect minority voters from voting practices that are *intentionally* designed to diminish" their political power. Noting also that Congress had just "correct[ed]" the Court's decision in a Fifth Amendment eminent domain case, Conyers called for his colleagues to do the same with the *Bossier Parish* decisions by restoring the purpose prong of Section 5 and by strengthening the DOJ's power to enforce it. Watt characterized *Bossier Parish II* as "a radical departure from prior judicial interpretations of Section 5" and exhorted Congress to correct the "corrosive effect" of that decision on minority political participation. In his view, the decision meant that intentionally discriminatory electoral plans designed to keep a minority group "in its place" did not violate Section 5. Watt invoked *South Carolina v. Katzenbach,* arguing that this result "cannot be what Congress intended in 1965 when it resolved to shift the advantage of time and inertia from the perpetrators of [such] evil to its victims."[110]

Virginia's Bobby Scott argued that offsetting the *Bossier Parish II* decision called for more than simply extending Section 5. It called for strengthening the act's "traditional intent and purpose of disallowing voting changes with a discriminatory purpose as well as just effects." In his view, the Court majority "incorrectly interpreted congressional intent in crafting Section 5 by limiting its impact" to those cases where retrogression had occurred. Moreover, to render a decision that would compel the DOJ to pre-clear a plan that violated Section 2 because it did no worse harm than the preceding plan that violated Section 2 is an "absurd result that . . . eviscerates the very purpose of Section 5 preclearance." For Georgia's David Scott, *Bossier Parish II* was "like a cancer, eating away at the Voting Rights Act."[111]

The CBC members and their congressional colleagues were no less determined to remedy the *Georgia v. Ashcroft* decision. According to Conyers, the Court's ruling in that case made the question of retrogression "of paramount importance." Bobby Scott singled out the Court's redefinition of retrogression, the result of which undermined the ability of minority voters to elect the candidates of their choice.[112] Watt focused on judicial interpretations of the VRA that threatened its essential purposes. For example, by promoting the concept of influence districts, the *Ashcroft* Court "strayed" from Congress's intent for Section 5:

> To the extent that *Georgia v. Ashcroft* depreciates the role of minority groups' ability to elect plays in the retrogression analysis, it invites the potential for an erosion of the protections embodied by Section 5. To paraphrase . . . Professor Pamela Karlin [*sic*], there is a retrogression of the retrogression standard when you do that.[113]

The CBC was also concerned about the administrative difficulty of defining an influence district in the absence of clarification by the Court. Conyers emphasized the need to more clearly discern between influence and safe majority-minority districting:

Georgia v. Ashcroft: can it be made workable? In the Texas congressional redistricting plan, we packed in four [districts] and we dismantled four influence districts. We tried this. . . . And so what I'm here to suggest to you is that we're tossing around the standard way we've looked at this question, with opportunity districts, versus the new way that we're looking at it, with influence districts. And we're going to have to come to some conclusion here.[114]

According to Bobby Scott, minority political influence was an important measure of evaluating whether a plan should be pre-cleared under Section 5, but the "primary evaluation" should be the ability of minority voters in such districts to actually elect candidates of their choice.[115] In other words, both Congress and the Court need to clarify the difference between "arithmetic" and "functional" majorities of minority voters. For example, in areas with high degrees of racial polarization, a 60 percent minority population may be needed for that group to elect the candidate of its choice, while in areas with a history of coalitional voting, only between 40 and 45 percent may be needed. For Scott, redistricting (and adjudications of redistricting challenges) must take place on more of a case-by-case basis that acknowledges that, like politics, "all districting is local" and thus very specific.[116]

CBC member Representative John Lewis of Georgia played a unique role in the CBC's efforts to check the Court's decision in *Georgia v. Ashcroft.* Like his colleague, David Scott, Lewis was not a member of the committees that had jurisdiction over the VRA. He had, however, submitted an affidavit assessing the act in an early round of the *Ashcroft* litigation, on which the Supreme Court majority relied in its opinion. According to Lewis, the majority (and others since then) had willfully misinterpreted him as conceding that Section 5 was no longer necessary.[117] In the 2005 VRA hearings, Lewis sought to clarify that although the VRA has indeed advanced minority voting rights and political power, too much ground remained to be covered to allow Section 5 to expire. Echoing Bobby Scott's concerns, Lewis also contended that the *Ashcroft* decision suffered from "severe problems" of poorly defined standards for the opportunity to elect and did not address important questions about who speaks for a minority group when redistricting and how much weight to give to that voice.[118] Following Lewis's testimony, David Scott condemned the *Ashcroft* decision in the most caustic of terms and urged his colleagues to "excise [the decision] out of the law." In his view, the *Ashcroft* rationale shows clearly this schizophrenic, dichotomized mindset that this Nation has historically had in terms of extending voting rights, and then taking them back. . . . [T]he threat of this Act not being renewed, presents the height of hypocrisy of our country; especially when we have men and women dying on the battle fields of Iraq to bring democracy there; and we have these efforts to overturn one basic legislative instrument that guarantees and enforces our basic rights here.[119]

The CBC remained wary of attempts to nationalize Section 5 by extending it to all fifty states on the grounds that doing so would render it overbroad, thus putting it at risk of being overturned by the Court. In addition, nationalizing Section 5 would overtax the DOJ, effectively mooting the provision by rendering it unenforceable. Here, the caucus found unexpected allies in Republican representative Tom Feeney of Florida and J. C. Watts of Oklahoma. Given Feeney's opposition to pre-clearance as an extraordinary exercise of congressional power over states, his critique of the Court majority's voting rights jurisprudence was remarkable. Focusing on Justice O'Connor's swing position in voting rights decisions and on her case-by-case approach, Feeney characterized her centrality to "virtually every meaningful case that has been decided in the last fifteen years" as essentially creating "a Court of one" and as generating decisions with which states had increasing difficulty complying.[120] Feeney saw O'Connor's opinion in *Georgia v. Ashcroft* as "unenforceable because it is unintelligible." Echoing one of Bobby Scott's points, Feeney noted that in the absence of clearer stipulations from the Court, measures of minority influence could differ too greatly depending on the candidate and/or geographic area involved. Contending that electing a candidate perceived as the lesser of two evils (as opposed to a candidate of choice) might at times be a sufficient choice for African Americans, Feeney nonetheless implored Congress to "aspire to better than that" in reconsidering Section 5. In a frank discussion of the exceptional minority candidates elected from mostly white districts, Feeney noted,

Let's face it, there are minority voters in my community that will be very attractive in drawing White votes [but] there will be other minorities that are very highly acceptable and desirable in the minority community that may not be able to attract significant support from the White community.[121]

Feeney was particularly adamant that O'Connor's *Ashcroft* opinion further obscured already murky waters:

> Much as I love [Justice O'Connor], I have to tell you I'm amazed at the hairsplitting she can do in some of her written opinions. It brings the nano-science of hair-splitting to new levels. And I think that the *Georgia v. Ashcroft* case is an example of that, in which she really threw out the old retrogression standards as we knew them. . . . [S]he basically says that we can substitute now a certain number of coalition or influence districts, or even other considerations, in her opinion, that are added. . . . And what I said in the last hearing is that it is totally unintelligible, not only by the next Supreme Court who has to follow *Georgia v. Ashcroft*, but if you happen to be involved in the Justice Department or a lower Federal court, or if you happen to be drawing new district lines or deciding on an annexation case or any other policy-making decision, there is absolutely no standard whatsoever.[122]

Another unexpected ally regarding Section 5 was African American Republican congressman J. C. Watts of Oklahoma. Watts chose not to be a member of the CBC; likewise, he was not an advocate of descriptive representation or race consciousness. However, he provided a ringing endorsement of the VRA, particularly what he referred to as the "genius" of Section 5's remedial and deterrent provisions. In the statement he submitted for the hearing record, Watts noted the precedent of "overwhelming bipartisan support of the VRA" and affirmed President Reagan's characterization of the VRA as the "crown jewel in American liberties." He then observed that "equal opportunity in voting still does not exist in many places" and called attention to recent cases of "intentional" voter discrimination. In light of the persistence of such problems, Watts applauded legislators' efforts to restore and "clarif[y] the original intent of Congress" by rejecting "two recent Supreme Court decisions that have eroded the effectiveness of the Act"—*Boissier Parish II* and the "troubling holding" in *Georgia v. Ashcroft*—and urged Congress to "ensure that the VRA remains strong and effective in protecting the right to vote for all Americans."[123]

In a subsequent interview with Bobby Scott about the VRA's reauthorization, he elaborated on the complexity of the relationship between minority influence districts and minority political power. The conventional thinking among CBC members and those involved in the redistricting process is that majority-minority districts offer minority voters the best opportunity to overcome dilutive white racial bloc voting and to elect candidates of their choice. Scott, however, disagrees with his fellow CBC members on the utility of influence districts. His position is premised on the likelihood of coalition voting between black and other minority voters and/or white crossover voting for black or other minority candidates. Scott also emphasizes that influence districting should be carefully considered on a case-by-case basis, rather than applied across the board.[124] In Scott's view, "overpacking" districts with black voters well above the threshold needed to elect the candidate of their choice may guarantee their election of that candidate in one district. However, it may also reduce the chances of the election of a coalition candidate in an adjoining influence district. Rather than strive solely for majority-minority districts, Scott holds that "every effort should be made to both maximize the number of districts in which the black community can elect candidates of choice *and* at the same time create additional influence districts in which the black community can influence the outcome of the election."[125]

In Scott's view, striking such a balance might lead to more responsive representation overall. In theory, the choice is between minority influence districts versus minority safe districts; in practice, however, influence and potentially coalitional districts mean that incumbents will not be able to rely on supermajority black districts that are immune from challenge. Such incumbents would instead have to mount competitive campaigns and "earn" their election to office. The CBC's preferred standard for Section 5 prevents "diluting" an incumbent's majority black district from, say, 75 percent to 55 percent, "even if the adjoining district went from 25 percent to 45 percent [black, thus] converting a probable Republican district to a Democratic seat."[126] In essence, Scott favors the creation of more districts with only the minimum percentage of minority voters necessary to elect the candidate of a majority group's choice.

The barely majority-minority districts at issue in *Shaw v. Reno* and *Miller v. Johnson* and endorsed by Scott bear out his position (see fig. 2 in chapter 5). Yet it cannot be assumed that the presence of a substantial or influential minority voter bloc in an electoral district means that the representative elected from that district will be responsive to his or her minority constituents.[127] In some cases, the opposite can occur. For example, despite the fact that black voters supported the Democratic candidate by over 90 percent in three of the influence districts at issue in *Georgia v. Ashcroft*, Republicans won in those districts. In two other influence districts, African Americans elected Democrats. However, shortly after the election, those two Democratic representatives switched to the Republican Party, and three other Democrats running unopposed end elected by minority influence districts did the same. By the beginning of the legislative session following the election, seven of the seventeen state senators elected from minority influence districts were Republican; the partisan converts were central to the shift in power in Georgia's Senate from Democratic to Republican.[128] It is thus difficult to fathom that such outcomes comport with Justice O'Connor's expectation in *Ashcroft* that minority influence districting would foster "representat[ion] sympathetic to the interests of minority voters."[129] In fact, representatives elected from these districts have generally not been responsive to the interests of their minority constituents.[130] This is precisely what, according to the state of Georgia, minority influence districts were supposed to prevent. At the very least, it is "premature" to rely on or generalize about influence to districts "without [the Supreme Court] at first clarifying" what such districting entails and how minority influence should be measured.[131]

Ultimately, the VRA was reauthorized as the Fannie Lou Hamer, Rosa Parks, and Coretta Scott King Voting Rights Act Reauthorization and Amendments Act of 2006. The act retained Section 2 as it stood, and extended Section 5 with an "*Ashcroft* fix" for another twenty-five years. Echoing the outcomes transformation of Section 2 in 1982, the *Ashcroft* fix stipulated that the purpose of Section 5 is to protect the ability of minority voters "to elect the preferred candidates of their choice."[132] Unlike in 1982, the Senate approved the bill unanimously and after virtually no debate. However, after the bill was passed, a Senate minority report expressed "significant" reservations about the reauthorizations.[133] President George W. Bush gave an address to the NAACP in which he appealed to the Senate to pass the bill with no amendments, leading some to surmise that Bush's words were a significant factor in the speedy and overwhelming Senate approval.[134] Others have claimed, in turn, that the 2006 reauthorization of the VRA was less a result of bipartisanship than of partisan and racial coercion. For example, Carol Swain wrote shortly thereafter that "fears of being called racist played no small role in defining and constraining the contours of the debate" over the act and that the Senate "undoubtedly felt the pressure exerted by outspoken black members of Congress." She also took issue with Watt's negotiations with Republican leaders, the "unusual" show of bipartisanship in the Senate, and Bush's "special incentive to appease" the NAACP. Where Bobby Scott lauded the president's appeal to the Senate, Swain characterized it, along with the

Senate's speedy and unanimous approval of the reauthorization, as black coercion of the legislative and the executive branches. She was particularly concerned that the Senate's hand was forced before it had time to complete its final report on the bill.[135]

Republican Sensenbrenner's and Feeney's observations about the reauthorization of the VRA at least partially refute Swain's partisan conclusions. It is very doubtful that either congressman could be coerced by the CBC to support the caucus's intent for Section 5. Like members of the caucus and others who have opposed the *Ashcroft* and *Bossier Parish* decisions for their hazy standards and potential for minority vote retrogression, Feeney held the Court majority accountable for veering away from its pre-1990s voting rights decisions and replacing them with unclear and unwieldy precedents. And Sensenbrenner has long held that most objections to Section 5 are either misguided or willfully ignorant of persisting electoral discrimination. With respect to the Senate's quick approval of the bill, he recalled, somewhat proudly, hand-delivering to the Senate, with Conyers, the more than fourteen thousand pages of evidence amassed by the House as a means of emphasizing that the thoroughness of the record obviated the need for the Senate to compile further information. In Sensenbrenner's view, the Senate's minority report was simply "not on message."[136]

The Ramifications of the CBC's Lobbying Efforts: Success Breeds Retrenchment

That the CBC has been so instrumental in persuading Congress to retain and strengthen the pre-clearance provisions of the act three times, especially in the face of fierce partisan, regional, and ideological opposition, is remarkable. The CBC's role in transforming the VRA since 1982 from equalizing voting opportunities for racial minorities to equalizing their opportunities to actually elect the candidates of their choice exceeded most expectations for the caucus. The fortified VRA, combined with a more precise 1990 census count, compelled many southern states to create majority-black districts where few or none had previously existed. This development was due in part to a relatively race-conscious DOJ that called for at least one majority-minority congressional district in states with large black populations that had failed to elect black representatives since the Reconstruction era.

In turn, the creation of more majority-black districts encouraged more African Americans to run for Congress.[137] The presidential elections of

1992, in which Democratic candidate Bill Clinton openly courted the black vote, also contributed to relatively high African American voter turnout. As a result, a record forty black candidates were elected to Congress in that year. Several of these candidates were elected from states that had not sent African American representatives to Congress since the turn of the twentieth century. Despite Senator Dole's rider preventing Section 2 of the VRA from guaranteeing proportional representation, by 1992, the number of African Americans in the House reached near proportionality.

The 1982 amendments to the VRA also reaped results that, ostensibly, the CBC never intended. The growth in the CBC's size and potential legislative influence after the 1992 elections was stymied almost immediately by Congress and the Supreme Court. In effect, the caucus's VRA victories engendered two types of opposition to them: (1) partisan resistance from House Republicans, and (2) constitutional retrenchment by the Supreme Court's conservative majority.

Internal Checks on the CBC: Republican Resistance

The gains in the CBC's membership after the 1990 reapportionments and the ensuing congressional elections greatly increased the caucus's presence in Congress and, potentially, its power to pursue its civil rights agenda. Between 1992 and 1994, the CBC played a pivotal role in twenty-one pieces of legislation.[138] As CBC members gained more seniority, they gained more powerful positions in Congress and in the Democratic Party. Accordingly, the CBC's descriptive presence in Congress translated into significant substantive representation. However, the 1994 midterm congressional elections resulted in major losses for the Democratic Party, with a corresponding loss of support of the CBC's goals. The CBC's enlarged ranks presented a formidable and unprecedented challenge to the incoming Republican majority; by 1995 the GOP defunded it along with several other caucuses. Although the CBC had long received the bulk of its funding from the CBCF, such support cannot replace the political legitimization conferred by the House, which is in many ways far more valuable than external funding.[139]

External Checks on the CBC: Judicial Opposition to
Race-Based Districting

Shortly before the partisan retrenchment of the mid-1990s, the judicial branch had begun to check the caucus's (and by extension Congress's) power with respect to the VRA. Starting in 1993, the Supreme Court took a more restrictive approach to Sections 2 and 5. Given the CBC's role in expanding the scope and intent of these provisions, the Court was unquestionably retrenching against the CBC as well. At issue in a series of districting cases (*Shaw v. Reno, Miller v. Johnson,* and *Shaw v. Hunt*) was the constitutionality of race-based districts. Of particular concern were irregularly shaped majority-black districts drawn to (1) enable black voters living in regions with a long history of electoral discrimination to elect candidates of their choice and (2) enhance the opportunities for black candidates. By 1997, the Court had firmly established a color-blind voting rights jurisprudence that limited states' power to draw such districts in order to comply with the VRA. In 2003, the Court held in *Georgia v. Ashcroft* that congressional districts with a lower-than-threshold black voting age population were not necessarily retrogressive and thus did not violate Section 5. Here the Court reinterpreted Section 5 by measuring the "effectiveness" of the minority vote based on a district's potential to yield substantive rather than descriptive representation of minority voters.[140] Although the CBC has often demonstrated otherwise in Congress, the Court's rationale in *Ashcroft* reinforced the view that descriptive and substantive representation are mutually exclusive modes of representation and that the former is an illegitimate mode.

The Rehnquist Court is notable for its commitment to federalism and to restoring state autonomy. As subsequent chapters will detail, it opposed expansive interpretations of the VRA and race-conscious interpretations of the Fourteenth Amendment's Equal Protection Clause as it applied to minority voting rights. For example, the Court was adamant in *Shaw v. Reno* that the Fourteenth Amendment does not allow race to be the primary factor in districting. In other words, race-based districting violates the constitutional rights of all voters to an equal electoral process, regardless of whether a state has a history of racial discrimination at the polls. Echoing the intent of the Dole amendment, the Rehnquist Court insisted that Congress never meant for the VRA to guarantee equal electoral outcomes for racial minorities. Holding that the department had incorrectly interpreted the VRA, the Court also checked the DOJ's power to require states to draw minority-majority districts. Finally, echoing Republican opposition to Section 5's pre-clearance requirements, the Rehnquist Court has held that the DOJ violates the principles of federalism and states' rights when it compels covered states to create additional majority black congressional districts where possible and where none had previously existed.

Conclusion: The Price of the CBC's Legislative Accomplishments

In light of the Court's minority voting rights decisions since 1993, the CBC's success with the VRA has come at a substantial cost to its power and influence and, by extension, to that of the African American electorate. The CBC's involvement in the 1982 amendments to the VRA unquestionably bore remarkable fruit. Yet ten years later, the caucus was hobbled by the return of control of the House to the Republican Party. During this period, the CBC's intent for the VRA was checked by the Court's restrictive jurisprudence of race, districting, and representation. While the power of incumbency has helped mitigate the worst effects of this retrenchment, it is nonetheless more difficult for black Democratic candidates to challenge white candidates or to capture open seats, especially in the South.

In keeping with its mission, the CBC has no choice but to advocate for a stronger VRA, including the use of race-based measures to accomplish the act's goals, even though the CBC's success appears to have instigated, at least in part, partisan and judicial retrenchment. In effect, the CBC has been hoisted by both the Republican Party and the Supreme Court onto its own minority voting rights petard. Ironically, the Court's retrenchment is felt most intensely in the most problematic regions of the South. At times, the Court has been more hostile to benign gerrymandering on behalf of blacks in the formerly Confederate South than it has to similar gerrymanders in California and Illinois that have primarily benefited Latino voters.[141] These developments may be evidence of the CBC's "complete forfeiture" of power.[142] Or, perhaps they are the inevitable ramifications of its race-conscious mission as the conscience of Congress. Either way, if the enhancement of the historically compromised black vote is viewed as an enhancement of pluralist democracy, the partisan and judicial retrenchments against the VRA do not simply penalize the CBC or check Congress's intent for the act. They also betray the spirit of the Equal Protection Clause, and the American dreams of equality and democracy for all. Chapter 4 explores the CBC's efforts as amicus curiae to convince the Supreme Court of this view.

4 | The Congressional Black Caucus: Pushing Constitutional Boundaries

"The Court is a good mirror, an excellent mirror . . . of the struggles of dominant forces outside of the Court."

—Felix Frankfurter

The CBC Engaging the Supreme Court as Amicus Curiae in Minority Voting Rights Litigation

Chapter 3 recounted the efforts of the Congressional Black Caucus (CBC) to strengthen the Voting Rights Act (VRA) against new and continuing electoral problems. In so doing, the CBC has also sought to buttress the act against what it perceives as the Supreme Court majority's retrogressive minority voting rights jurisprudence since the early 1990s. Whereas that chapter looked at the caucus in its legislative capacity, here I examine a little-discussed aspect of the CBC's substantive representation of its constituents: its extralegislative efforts as amicus curiae in key voting rights cases. This examination analyzes the amicus briefs the caucus submitted to the Court in *Rodgers v. Lodge, Miller v. Johnson, U.S. v. Hays, Shaw v. Hunt,* and *Northwest Austin Municipal Utility District Number 1 v. Holder.*[1] In submitting such briefs, the caucus acts akin to a civil rights interest group. Congressional caucuses are not usually considered interest groups. However, in filing amicus briefs on behalf of voters whose political power is affected by Supreme Court decisions, the CBC satisfies much of the criteria for interest groups while simultaneously performing an important representative function.[2] The analysis of these briefs focuses on the changing substance and tone of the caucus's arguments. In particular, it considers how the Court and the caucus have influenced each other. It is easy to assume that the influence would flow only from the Court to the caucus, especially since the Court so rarely mentions amicus briefs in its opinions.

However, the CBC may influence the Court, albeit indirectly, by insisting that a race-conscious approach to redistricting cases and minority voting rights falls squarely within Congress's intent for both the Fourteenth Amendment and the VRA.

The efforts of the CBC and its fellow legislators to strengthen the VRA in 1982 in a way that fostered the creation of safe black districts also fostered a paradox of race and representation. On the one hand, the increase in majority-minority districts drawn after the 1990 reapportionments led to a significant increase in the number of blacks and other minorities elected to the House, thus enhancing the diversity of the legislative branch to a degree unprecedented since the Reconstruction era. On the other hand, white voters have repeatedly challenged the districting that enhanced black political power, and the Supreme Court has repeatedly minimized states' use of race to enhance such power. Thus the CBC's role in amending the VRA appears to have provoked popular and judicial resistance to the law and the ideology behind it. In a very real sense, the CBC's efforts to defend such districting constitute an effort to protect black political power—and itself—from the potentially retrogressive effects of a color-blind voting rights jurisprudence. In sum, the CBC's endorsement of race-based districting in its amicus briefs may have goaded the Court into checking congressional power by interpreting the law in a way that undermines Congress's intent.

There is no shortage of current studies on the use of amicus curiae briefs on judicial decision-making. Most, however, overlook the CBC in this role. Most also agree that groups seeking change through litigation assume that such briefs can influence the Court, or at least can help shape the debate on an issue. Conclusions about *how* amicus briefs influence the Court have been inconsistent.[3] Paul Collins's investigation of the relationship of such briefs to judicial decision making finds a correlation between nonunanimous Court decisions and an increase in the number of briefs filed by interest groups. He concludes that such briefs are "staples of group interest activity" that help "light the fires of dissensus" on the Court and motivate dissenting justices "to express their displeasure with the majority's interpretation of the law."[4] Because dissents or concurrences may later be transformed into majority opinions, Collins's finding is no small point. The most well-known example of such a transformation is Justice John Marshall Harlan's lone dissent in *Plessy v. Ferguson* becoming the unanimous opinion in *Brown v. Board of Education*. In the area of minority voting rights, Justice Clarence Thomas's concurrence in *Holder v. Hall* provided the bulk of the majority opinion ten years later in *Georgia v. Ashcroft*.

Generally speaking, external parties with a direct stake in a case before the Court submit amicus curiae briefs to present facts or positions that the litigants may not have raised or of which the Court may not be aware, including an issue's broader legal and political implications.[5] To the extent that Court decisions shape public policies, interest groups may also attempt to shape policies by filing amicus briefs.[6] The CBC's amicus arguments that race-conscious districting is in keeping with Congress's intent for the VRA exemplify such an effort. In highly controversial cases, it is not unusual for a multitude of organizations to submit amicus briefs. For example, two 2003 affirmative action cases, *Gratz v. Bollinger* and *Grutter v. Bollinger,* elicited sixty-nine briefs on behalf of the appellees and nineteen on behalf of the appellants. The involvement of so many organizations in Supreme Court litigation by means of amicus curiae briefs can give litigation "the distinct flavor of group combat."[7] Interest groups often deploy amicus briefs to challenge the idealistic but mistaken view of judges as cloistered and quasi-omniscient decision makers. According to Collins, amicus briefs contribute democratic input into the judicial arena, and may thus improve the quality of judicial decision making.[8] The Court's acceptance of a steady flow of amicus curiae briefs suggests that it is at least receptive to the arguments contained in them. For example, in one of the 2003 affirmative action decisions, the Court majority explicitly referred to several amicis' endorsements of the use of race in graduate school admissions to buttress its holding that a diverse graduate student body was a compelling reason to take race into account in such admissions.[9]

Very little has been written about the CBC's efforts to lobby the Court as amicus curiae. For the caucus to take on this role illustrates its efforts to challenge and think beyond the dominant position in a case. Acting as an amicus curiae, the CBC also continues the practice of small or politically marginalized groups turning to the courts for protection from majoritarian dominance. The CBC's role as amicus comports with an early examination by Clement Vose of the deployment of amicus briefs by the National Association for the Advancement of Colored People (NAACP) in its battle against racially restrictive housing covenants and school segregation. Vose found that the organization's lawyers tailored the briefs to speak to the individual personalities on the bench. He also found that the NAACP's amicus briefs provided useful links between formal organizations with broader general interests and litigants in Supreme Court cases. In his view, because "judicial review . . . constitutes an invitation for groups" to challenge legislation, the NAACP's involvement in civil rights cases as amicus curiae was to be expected.[10] In light of the fact that the NAACP has been a leadership model for the caucus, its efforts to "exploit ... judicial review" by lobbying the Court on behalf of African American voters are also to be expected.[11] In addressing the Court, the CBC also signals to its constituents and the civil rights community more broadly its advocacy of their interests.

Table 1 lists all of the amicus curiae briefs that the caucus has submitted

TABLE 1.   Amicus Curiae Briefs Submitted by the Congressional Black Caucus

Year	Case Name	CBC's Position Affirmed	Legal Issue
1981	*Rodgers v. Lodge*	Yes	At-large districting and vote dilution
1984	*Jean v. Nelson*	No	Detention of undocumented Haitian emigrés
1989	*Astroline v. Sherburg*	Yes	Minority set-asides for broadcasting firms
1989	*Metro Broadcasting v. F.C.C.*	Yes	Minority set-asides for broadcasting firms
1990	*Ayers v. Mabus*	Yes	Desegregation of public universities
1990	*U.S. v. Fordice*	Yes	Desegregation of public universities
1992	*McNary (I.N.S.) v. Haitian Centers*	No	Executive orders of interdiction for detained Haitian emigrés
1994	*Adarand v. Peña*	No	Minority set-asides and contracting
1994	*U.S. v. Hays*	No	Majority-minority gerrymanders and equal protection
1995	**Miller v. Johnson**	No	Majority-minority gerrymanders and equal protection
1995	**Shaw v. Hunt**	No	Majority-minority gerrymanders and equal protection (revisitation of *Shaw v. Reno*)
2003	**Branch v. Smith**	No	Race-based districting and scope of VRA's Section 5 "pre-clearance" requirement
2003	*Gratz v. Bollinger*	No	Race and university admissions, undergraduate
2003	*Grutter v. Bollinger*	Yes	Race and university admissions, graduate
2009	**Northwest Austin Municipal District Number 1 v. Holder**	Yes	Section 5 pre-clearance

Note: This table was compiled by the author. Cases indicated in boldface are those considered in chapters 4 and 5 of this book.

in various federal and Supreme Court cases; the voting rights cases explored in this and the next chapter appear in boldface. A cursory glance reveals a mixed record of success for the CBC and thus for minority political interests. The frequency with which the Court's position conflicts with the CBC's puts the findings by Vose and Collins at odds with Girardeau Spann's contention that the constitutional safeguards to offset external and majoritarian influences fail and thus consign the Court to be an "agent of the majority" at the expense of minority interests.[12] It is difficult if not impossible to determine who is more correct on this question, especially with such a small case study as the one in this volume.[13] One may even question why the caucus bothers to submit such briefs at all. In the long run, these questions may not matter. What matters most has less to do with who wins in a particular minority voting rights debate and more with the CBC's role in provoking deeper and more nuanced considerations of the role of race in constitutional and statutory laws in such debates.

The chief issues in the CBC's briefs for *Rodgers v. Lodge, U.S. v. Hays, Miller v. Johnson, Shaw v. Hunt,* and *Northwest Austin v. Holder* are minority vote dilution, the use of race in redistricting, and the constitutionality of Section 5 of the VRA. These five briefs are important because they address cases that test the scope and intent of the VRA in the context of the Equal Protection Clause of the Fourteenth Amendment. Implicitly, they also test the Court majority's tolerance of the CBC's contributions to amending the VRA. Table 2 puts these cases into a fuller historical background. It includes laws and cases that do not specifically concern minority voting rights but are nevertheless germane. Because earlier civil and voting rights statutes were weak, unenforced, or invalidated by the Court, one might conclude that the federal government never intended for them to be very effective. However, the number of constitutional and statutory provisions passed to protect blacks' civil rights is a striking reminder of the tenacity of racial discrimination in American politics and society and is at the least an indication of Congress's efforts to grapple with the problem.

As table 1 illustrates, by 1993 the Court began to retrench against the VRA by interpreting it and the Equal Protection Clause more narrowly. This was not the first such retrenchment. In 1980's *Mobile v. Bolden,* the Court held that plaintiffs claiming vote dilution—in this case from an at-large electoral scheme—must prove intent to discriminate. Two years later, in *Rodgers v. Lodge,* the Court retreated from this criterion. Acknowledging the increasing difficulty of finding smoking guns of discriminatory intent, it held that proof of harm based on a preponderance of circumstantial evidence was sufficient to make a claim of minority vote

TABLE 2. Key Developments in African Americans' Voting Rights

Year	Law or Case	Intent or Issue
1865	Thirteenth Amendment	Abolition of chattel slavery
1866	Civil Rights Act	Provision of full citizenship for blacks; invalidation of "Black Codes"
1868	Fourteenth Amendment	Provision of full citizenship for blacks
1870	Fifteenth Amendment	Prevention of denial of suffrage based on race
1870	Force Bill (1st)	Enforcement of the Fourteenth Amendment
1871	Force Bill (2nd)	Enforcement of the Fifteenth Amendment
1871	Force Bill (3rd), also known as Ku Klux Klan Act	Prevention of racial intimidation and violence by private citizens' groups
1873	*Slaughter-House Cases*	E.P. clause of Fourteenth Amendment intended to protect blacks' civil rights at national but not state level
1875	Civil Rights Act	Prohibition of racial segregation of public accommodations
1880	*Strauder v. West Virginia*	Extended *Slaughter-House* rationale by applying E.P. clause to state laws excluding blacks from juries
1883	*Civil Rights Acts*	Struck down Civil Rights Act of 1875. E.P. clause of Fourteenth Amendment not intended to foster racial integration.
1897	*Plessy v. Ferguson*	Separate-but-equal policies for public accommodations do not violate the Thirteenth or Fourteenth Amendment
1915	*Guinn v. U.S.*	"Grandfather clauses" that trigger literacy tests violate the E.P. clause
1944	*Smith v. Allwright*	Invalidates use of white-only primary elections
1954	*Brown v. Board of Ed.*	Separate-but-equal segregation of public schools violates the E.P. clause
1957	Civil Rights Act	Enforcement of the Fifteenth Amendment
1960	Civil Rights Act	Enforcement of the Fifteenth Amendment
1960	*Gomillion v. Lightfoot*	Racial gerrymanders that effectively disenfranchise blacks violate the Fifteenth Amendment
1964	*Reynolds v. Sims*	Reapportionment must be balanced; introduces principle of "one person one vote" that guides contemporary redistricting
1964	Twenty-fourth Amendment	Prohibits state imposition of poll taxes for federal elections
1964	Civil Rights Act	Enforcement of the Fourteenth Amendment
1965	Voting Rights Act	Enforcement of the Fifteenth Amendment
1966	*South Carolina v. Katzenbach*	VRA's pre-clearance provision is constitutional

(continues)

TABLE 2.—*Continued*

Year	Law or Case	Intent or Issue
1973	*White v. Regester*	Proof of discriminatory effect is sufficient to prove discriminatory intent in the absence of explicit evidence of the latter.
1975	VRA of 1965 amended	Extended protections to language minorities; extended pre-clearance requirements until 1982
1976	*Beer v. U.S.*	Districting plans with discriminatory intent do not violate VRA as long as they do not result in minority vote retrogression.
1977	*U.J.O. v. Carey*	Majority-minority districting to rectify previous discrimination is constitutional.
1980	*Mobile v. Bolden*	Evidence of discriminatory intent is required to make an equal protection claim or a claim of vote dilution.
1982	VRA of 1965 amended	Section 2 given an effects orientation to check the Court's decision in *Bolden;* Section 5 pre-clearance provision extended until 2007
1982	*Rodgers v. Lodge*	Proof of discriminatory effect suffices as proof of intent to dilute minority vote.
1986	*Thornburg v. Gingles*	Establishes three-pronged "*Gingles* test" for minority vote dilution based on (a) cohesion of the minority electorate, (b) compactness/ contiguity of district lines, and (c) evidence of racial polarization.
1993	*Shaw v. Reno*	Establishes the right to a color-blind districting process; bizarrely shaped majority-minority districts may provide basis for claim of E.P. violation
1995	*Miller v. Johnson*	Bizarrely shaped majority-minority districts may be unconstitutional; burden of proof is on state to justify such a use of race.
1995	*U.S. v. Hays*	Vacated and remanded due to plaintiffs' lack of standing
1996	*Shaw v. Hunt*	States must show that bizarrely shaped majority-minority districts are sufficiently narrowly tailored to satisfy a compelling state interest.
1997	*Bossier Parish I*	Discriminatory intent does not violate the VRA if there is no discriminatory effect.
2000	*Bossier Parish II*	Section 5 of VRA does not prohibit pre-clearance of an electoral plan that has a discriminatory intent but a nonretrogressive purpose; separates Section 2's non-

TABLE 2.—*Continued*

Year	Law or Case	Intent or Issue
		dilution purpose from Section 5's non-retrogression purpose.
2003	*Georgia v. Ashcroft*	Violations of Section 5 of VRA do not trigger Section 2 protections
2003	*Branch v. Smith*	Delayed electoral plans due to Justice Department pre-clearance delays do not violate VRA.
2006	VRA of 1965 amended	Extends Section 5 pre-clearance provision for an additional 25 years; strengthens language-based protections
2009	*NAMUDNO v. Holder*	Section 5 of VRA is constitutional.

Note: This table was compiled by the author.

dilution.[14] This pause in the Court's retrenchment was only momentary. As noted in chapter 3, it also coincided with Congress's 1982 amendment of the VRA, which was motivated in part to check the *Mobile* decision. *Shaw* and subsequent decisions signaled a renewed and energetic judicial retrenchment against state and federal efforts to protect minority voting rights via race-conscious measures. These decisions in turn triggered energetic responses from the CBC that stand in stark contrast to its initial brief in *Rodgers v. Lodge*. Over time, the CBC intensified its race-conscious content and tone as the Court extended its color-blind voting rights jurisprudence.

A Diplomatic Exchange: Rodgers v. Lodge *(1982)*

As amicus curiae briefs go, the CBC's brief for *Rodgers* was fairly straightforward.[15] It followed a conventional format, urging the Court to affirm the decisions of the lower courts that had upheld the claims of the black litigants. The brief's relatively formulaic structure makes for an instructive backdrop against which to contrast the more animated tone of the CBC's subsequent briefs. At issue in *Rodgers* was an at-large districting plan for a five-member board of commissioners of Burke County, Georgia. Plaintiffs charged that the plan diluted the voting strength of the county's majority-black electorate, rendering it impossible for black voters to elect a representative of their choice. Burke County's long history of disfranchising its black residents prevented the election of black board members even after the VRA's passage. The district court found that this history of racial discrimination, in concert with at-large districting, abridged the voting rights of the county's black residents. The district court ordered the county to implement a multimember system, and the appellate court upheld that ruling.[16] In its brief, the CBC first urged the Supreme Court to affirm the judgments of the lower courts, noting that the order to utilize at-large districting was a suitable remedy for earlier violations of the Fourteenth and Fifteenth Amendments as well as Section 2 of the VRA. On that point, the caucus emphasized that Burke County's at-large arrangement was precisely the type of discrimination that Congress intended for Section 2 to prohibit.[17]

The caucus next turned to the process of voting in Burke County, focusing on the issue of burden of proof:

> The only issues before [the] Court are whether the quality and nature of the evidence . . . of dilution and purposeful discrimination were sufficient to satisfy appellees' burden of producing evidence, and whether the District Court's finding . . . that appellees had met their burden . . . was clearly erroneous.[18]

On this point, the caucus endorsed the criteria in *Zimmer v. McKeithen*, a case in which the Fifth Circuit Court determined that a showing of a "totality of the circumstances" was sufficient for proving intentional discrimination in the absence of explicit evidence.[19] The CBC saw *Zimmer* as significant not just because of the lower court's recognition of the value of circumstantial evidence at a time when explicit proof of discrimination was rare, but also because it acknowledged the gravity of racially polarized bloc voting.[20] The CBC's brief for *Rodgers* made only minimal references to the history of racist suppression of black political power in Burke County; it simply noted that the county had an "extreme" level of racial discrimination and called attention to "ongoing efforts by a white minority to exercise dominion over a black majority" by denying or abridging blacks' political power.[21] The brief's boldest moment was its declaration that the intent criterion in *Mobile v. Bolden* was not appropriate for vote dilution claims because such

> claims require proof that the challenged action was based on a racially discriminating purpose. The correctness of this assumption, however, need not be determined [in this case] for it clearly appears from the record that evidence presented at trial was more

than sufficient to prove that defendants had the requisite discriminatory purpose.[22]

Overall, the CBC's brief for *Rodgers* was largely procedural and almost conversational. In both content and tone, it was as close to color-blind as possible in light of the CBC's constituency and race-conscious mission. On their own, neither of these points is particularly noteworthy. Amicus curiae briefs are typically written in dispassionate or deferential language.[23] However, by emphasizing precedents and lower court decisions over racial factors, the CBC muted its race-conscious voice. This approach served the caucus well enough for this case, especially given the close timing between the *Rodgers* decision and Congress's revision of the VRA. A decade later, however, the CBC changed its approach to advocating for majority-minority voting rights.

Strained Relations: Miller v. Johnson *(1995)* *and* U.S. v. Hays *(1995)*

The CBC did not submit an amicus brief for *Shaw v. Reno*. Several factors explain why. First, at the time the litigation commenced, the caucus was occupied by high-profile issues such as affirmative action and the Haitian refugee crisis.[24] Second, because the challenged districting was drawn in compliance with the VRA and because the Court had rendered several favorable voting rights decisions in the past, the caucus did not feel compelled to submit a brief for *Shaw*. Caucus members quickly learned from that decision, however, that white voters would find it as easy to challenge remedial post-VRA racial gerrymanders as blacks had found it to challenge racist gerrymanders of the late Jim Crow era. Prior to *Shaw*, the shape of a majority-minority district drawn to protect minority electoral strength did not generate the kind of attention that the *Shaw* districting did. Put otherwise, the *Shaw* decision caught the CBC off guard. Third, because congressional Republicans had just defunded the caucus, it had far fewer resources to solicit an amicus curiae brief. Finally, not every CBC member believed that such briefs were worth the expense.[25]

By the mid-1990s, the caucus found itself grappling with a new reality. To be sure, the advantage of incumbency helped the caucus maintain its newly expanded presence in Congress. Yet the CBC had to engage in a new battle to hold its ground against deepening judicial, ideological, and partisan retrenchments against the kind of districting that helped expand that presence. Consequently, its briefs for *Miller v. Johnson* and *U.S. v. Hays* were defensive and prescriptive rather than simply advisory and were more historically and socially contextualized. Compared to the *Rodgers* brief, the CBC's tone in *Miller* and *Hays* is less congenial and decidedly more race-conscious.

At first glance, *Miller* and *Hays* look redundant in that they involve similar challenges to oddly shaped majority-black congressional districts. However, a closer look reveals several key distinctions between the two cases. For *Hays*, many of Louisiana's districts were redrawn after a challenge was initiated but before that case made it to the Supreme Court. By the time the case reached the Court's docket, only one of the original plaintiffs still resided in the challenged districts, causing the Court to vacate the case on the grounds that the original plaintiffs no longer had standing.[26] In addition, the size of Louisiana's congressional delegation had dropped from eight to seven as a result of the 1990 census. Conversely, in *Miller*, Georgia gained a seat after the 1990 census, affording the state more opportunity to increase the number of majority-black districts. Despite these distinctions, both states shared the goal of protecting the black vote: Where Louisiana attempted to maintain the level of black representation in the face of loss, Georgia attempted to strengthen that level given an enhanced opportunity to do so. These similarities may explain why the CBC made virtually identical arguments in its amicus briefs for these cases.[27]

The issues in *Rodgers* differed substantially from those in *Miller/Hays*. In *Rodgers*, black plaintiffs claimed that at-large electoral schemes diluted the electoral strength of African American voters in violation of Section 2 of the VRA. In *Miller* and *Hays*, white plaintiffs claimed that oddly shaped majority-minority districts drawn to mitigate historical racial discrimination at the polls violated the Equal Protection Clause. Moreover, in *Rodgers*, the lower courts had upheld the African American plaintiffs' claims. Thus the main function of the CBC's brief in that case was to endorse those decisions. In *Miller* and *Hays*, the lower courts' decisions were reversed by the *Shaw* precedent. The likelihood that the justices would follow that precedent thus put the CBC in a more of a defensive position than was the case in *Rodgers*.

In its *Miller* and *Hays* briefs, the CBC sought primarily to convince the Court that *Shaw* was a poor precedent for challenges to majority-minority districts. To support this claim, the caucus provided detailed accounts of the various electoral practices and procedures that had long harmed blacks in Louisiana and Georgia. With each example, the caucus emphasized the states' racially exclusive histories and how they shaped the surrounding political and racial contexts in ways that distorted both electoral processes and outcomes. In so doing, the caucus pulled history to the forefront of considerations of black political power. For example, both briefs open by declaring, "In the context of American history and contemporary reality, minority-majority districts are often the only way of fully achieving the pluralist aspirations of American politics and remedying the longstanding exclusion of African Americans from full participation in government."[28] Here, the CBC did more than emphasize the history and persistence of racism; it also immediately positioned itself as an advocate of race-based remedies to race-based discrimination.

The caucus then reviewed the historical effects of electoral discrimination on black political power, emphasizing the long-standing dearth of African American representation in Congress as a whole:

> For far too long, this nation was unresponsive and often hostile to the needs of its African American citizens. [By] 1957 southern congressmen almost uniformly joined the "Southern Manifesto," rejecting the doctrine of *Brown. v. Board of Education*. . . . [T]oward the ideal of a representative democracy, one that encourages the inclusion of *all* Americans in political discourse, . . . [p]rogress has been slow in coming. Indeed, only after the 1992 congressional elections did the number of African American members of the Congress rise from 26 to 40.[29]

Having expanded its focus from regional to national effects of electoral discrimination, the caucus emphasized the utility of majority-minority districting as a remedy to such discrimination:

> Even today, white attitudes hardened by state-sponsored *de jure* segregation often result in racially polarized voting and contribute to a variety of other [discriminatory] circumstances. . . . [T]he brutal truth of contemporary American politics is that, absent minority-majority districts, African American representation would virtually disappear from Congress. . . . Only two [African Americans in 1992] were elected from majority-white districts. Not a single African American representative from the Deep South states covered by Section 5 of the Voting Rights Act was elected from a majority-white district.[30]

The CBC might be perceived as unnecessarily miring its arguments in the history of American racism. However, its emphasis on this history served several important purposes. First, it called attention to the *Shaw* majority's selective discussion of the history of racism in America. More important, it underscored the fact that the challenged districts in *Shaw* had helped remedy that history by enabling North Carolinians to elect African Americans to Congress for the first time since 1901. Finally, the caucus's emphasis on this history helped it lay the groundwork for its endorsement of race-based districting as a constitutionally permissible remedy for continuing racial discrimination.

Turning to the question of the electoral cohesiveness of black voters in the challenged districts, the caucus rejected the *Shaw* majority's contention that racial commonality alone is an insufficient determination of common political interests. It also challenged the Court's implication that racial commonality among the members of black community is itself egregious, asserting that racially driven political behavior is part and parcel of pluralist America:

> Even beyond their generally cohesive support for certain explicitly race-conscious legislative measures, African Americans often form discrete communities of interest. Recognition of this thread of shared interests does not involve the type of pernicious stereotyping referred to by this Court in *Shaw v. Reno.* . . . Similar to other ethnic [and] religious . . . groups, African Americans, who share a common cultural heritage, often share a common cultural perspective on many issues the government faces.[31]

The CBC further defended its race-conscious advocacy of black interests by noting that like those of other groups, the CBC's efforts to advance the particular concerns of African Americans "is appropriate and critical."[32] It next emphasized the need for race-conscious districting in Louisiana and Georgia by reviewing the history of racist electoral practices in those states and the persistence of racially polarized voting there and elsewhere. According to the CBC, such polarization is exacerbated by single-member, winner-take-all electoral systems that tend to dilute minority political power. In this view, such processes necessitate race-based districting to prevent further dilution of that power:

> As *Shaw* recognized, all districting is race-conscious. . . . We also know, as practical politicians aware of the voting behavior of citi-

zens inside and outside our districts, that minority-majority districts are the only way of providing African American voters with an opportunity to elect the representatives of their choice. Thus, if the American political system is to achieve real integration . . . while continuing to use single-member districts . . . race-conscious minority-majority districts are essential.[33]

The caucus recalled how in *Thornburg v. Gingles,* the Court rejected a double standard of racial identity that allowed whites to assert "traditional" ethnic interests but prohibited similar assertions by blacks. Comparing that precedent to *Shaw,* the brief asserted boldly that the Court majority's protection of the interests of all voters by barring only majority-black gerrymanders "turns the Fourteenth Amendment completely on its head."[34] The caucus further contended that by *Shaw's* logic

the original intended beneficiaries of the Fourteenth Amendment—African American slaves and their descendants—would be punished by that very Amendment. This is not the law and the Court must unequivocally reject [such] infirm logic.[35]

From the CBC's perspective, the challenged districts in North Carolina, Georgia, and Louisiana were not unconstitutional. Rather, the *Shaw* decision was unconstitutional because it interpreted the Fourteenth Amendment in a way that deprived *only* blacks of districting intended to protect their political power in those states.

The CBC reinforced this point by refuting the *Shaw* majority's equation of the challenged districts with racial segregation and balkanization. The caucus first noted that other racial and ethnic groups have long been allowed to determine their political identities and interests and that political identification by racial, ethnic, or religious background is a core aspect of political behavior in America. It then declared that African Americans have the same right as other groups to assert their racial interests in the political arena without being condemned as segregationists. Finally, the CBC emphasized that a collective black racial consciousness does not prevent black members of Congress from representing their white constituents: "Members of the caucus represent all the residents of their districts, whatever their race. Our doors are always open to all constituents. We perform the traditional service functions with the same vigor for white constituents as we do for African American constituents."[36] With this point, the caucus did not simply challenge the *Shaw* majority's presumptive skepticism of black legislators' ability to represent their non-black constituents.[37] The caucus also suggested that the majority's equation of remedially race-based districts with racist gerrymanders belied the latter's racial bias. In turn, this bias compromised the Court's color-blind commitment to minority voting rights in much the same way that Justice Harlan's *Plessy* color-blind dissent affirmed racial hierarchy. Rejecting the implication that African Americans or other minorities cannot represent the interests of white constituents as "indefensible," the caucus noted the long history of white legislators who acted against the interests of their black constituents; in so doing, the CBC called attention to the Court majority's elision of this history.[38]

Finally, the CBC asserted that the majority wrongly conflated oddly shaped remedial safe black districts with racial segregation. Declaring that this aspect of the *Shaw* rationale was based more on conjecture than fact, the caucus noted that neither Louisiana's nor Georgia's districting plans gave "rise to the potential harms hypothesized by the Court." It then pointed out that majority-minority districts drawn in compliance with the VRA do not exacerbate residential patterns because "Louisiana [and Georgia], like many other states, [are] *already* separated and segregated, and [their] voting patterns are *already* divided along racial lines."[39] In other words, the Court skirted the root causes of contemporary racial separation, including the correlation between racially discriminatory housing patterns and racial discrimination at the polls.

The CBC then brought another factor to the Court's attention: The majority-black districts in these cases were far more racially balanced than the majority-white and oddly shaped surrounding districts:

> The . . . challenged minority-majority districts . . . are among the *least* segregated districts in the Nation [and are] characterized by a significant degree of racial integration. Only slightly more than half of [these districts'] voters—55% [and 60%]—are African American. When these districts are compared to their white-majority counterparts, such as North Carolina's Fifth, which is *85% white* . . . or Georgia's Ninth, which is *94.9% white,* the integrated nature of these [challenged] districts . . . is clear.[40]

In closing the briefs, the CBC challenged the Court to "unequivocally . . . reject the theory that a 60% [and 55%] African American constituency . . . is segregated while an 95% [or 80%] white district . . . is not," especially when many other districts were oddly shaped.[41] In exposing the *Shaw* majority's biased conception of what makes for an invidious racial gerrymander, the caucus concluded that the majority's openness to challenges of majority black districts by white voters exposed two similar but distinct double standards: (1) an oddly shaped slightly majority black district is segregated and balkanized, while an oddly shaped and overwhelmingly white district is not; and (2) an oddly shaped majority-minority district is tantamount to apartheid if it joins geographically dispersed members of that group, while a similarly situated white district is not.

The CBC clearly traded the procedural, race-neutral approach in its *Rodgers* brief for a more vigorous, race-conscious advocacy of majority-minority districting to mitigate past and continuing racial discrimination against African Americans. It perceived the decision in *Shaw v. Reno* as an attack not just on the Court's earlier precedents that were more favorable to blacks' electoral interests but also on the intent of the 1982 revisions of the VRA. Hence, the caucus took a more confrontational stance in its subsequent briefs, in which it did not merely talk to the Court but talked back to the Court: "We submit that the *Shaw* decision was wrongly decided and should be revised."[42] The CBC was reacting to a serious dilemma: The *Shaw* decision trapped the caucus between the Scylla of the Court's color-blind jurisprudence, which threatens the political gains made by blacks since the VRA was amended in 1982, and the Charybdis of the CBC's reliance on precisely the type of districting that *Shaw* deemed unconstitutional. The caucus in turn found itself in the unenviable position of having to defend itself in the process of defending such districting. Accordingly, the tone of its amicus briefs went from congenial to provocative and eventually to confrontational.

Casting Down the Gauntlet: Shaw v. Hunt *(1996)*

The caucus intensified its race consciousness in its brief for *Shaw v. Hunt*, as indicated by several of the brief's section headings: "The History of Discrimination in North Carolina Justified the Creation of Two Majority-Minority Districts"; "North Carolina Had a Compelling Interest in Engaging in Race-Conscious Districting to Remedy the Legacy of Racial Discrimination in the North Carolina Political System"; "Majority-Minority Districts Are Necessary Tools to Offset the Effects of Racially-Polarized Voting and Past Discrimination."[43] Building on its arguments in the *Miller* and *Hays* briefs, the caucus emphasized that North Carolina's history of racial discrimination has continuing effects on that state's political and racial landscape. In this instance, the CBC provided more detailed examples of white supremacists' disfranchising tactics that included defying or circumventing Reconstruction-era laws, purging the Republican Party, and restoring a racial caste system. In reciting this litany, the CBC contended that the lingering effects of North Carolina's "long, ugly history" of racism provided sufficiently compelling reasons for the state to use race as a primary factor in districting.[44]

In its briefs for *Hays* and *Miller*, the CBC challenged the *Shaw* majority's claim that African Americans could not or would not satisfactorily represent constituents who were not black. In its brief for *Shaw v. Hunt*, the CBC refuted that claim much more sharply. It first provided more documentation that the two black representatives of North Carolina's challenged districts represented all of their constituents regardless of race and partisanship. It also reiterated the history of white nonresponsiveness to North Carolina's black constituents. This time, the CBC connected these points to the principle of innocence until guilt is proven:

> Because the appellants did not—and could not—submit proof that Representatives [Eva] Clayton and [Mel] Watt have failed to represent their interests, the Court should presume that [they] have fully represented appellants and the rest of their constituents. . . . As a practical matter, the racial makeup of the challenged districts renders it improbable that [Clayton and Watt] would ignore their white constituents. . . . By contrast, for centuries many white legislators . . . acted against the interests of their African American constituents.[45]

In buttressing its account of the efforts made by Eva Clayton and Mel Watt (the two black representatives elected by the challenged districts), the CBC noted that

> Congresswoman Clayton . . . has installed a toll-free phone line to enhance the ability of her . . . constituents to communicate with her. In addition, she visits all counties within her district during weekends and congressional recesses, and employs field representatives and case workers who maintain regular, publicized hours. . . . Congressman Watt . . . mailed every resident in his district a Guide to Constituent Services . . . instituted a policy that his phone calls not be screened . . . employs a mobile caseworker [and] regularly mails information to mayors and city managers in his district. . . . [Clayton and Watt] have conducted several town meetings where black and white constituents alike express their concerns and opinions.[46]

Once again, the CBC questioned the validity of *Shaw v. Reno* as the controlling precedent in this and similar cases. This tactic represents a sharp departure from the standard protocol for amicus briefs, which are generally more advisory than judgmental. In its *Miller* and *Hays* briefs, the CBC suggested that it would be unwise to continue the precedent it set in *Shaw v. Reno*. For *Shaw v. Hunt*, the caucus took that argument a significant step further, declaring that "*Shaw* and *Miller* were wrongly decided" and challenging the Court majority to reconsider its color-blind approach to these cases:

> In the event this Court finds itself obligated by the standards set forth in *Shaw* and *Miller* to hold that the challenged districts violate the Equal Protection Clause, we submit that the Court should take this opportunity to repudiate the holdings of those two cases.[47]

For the CBC, the potential political cost to African Americans of building on the *Shaw v. Reno* rationale gave the Court a "special justification" to depart from that rationale in *Shaw v. Hunt*.[48] The CBC did not propose completely abandoning the principle of stare decisis but instead endorsed a case-by-case approach. This approach reflects the caucus's view that precedents should be considered within the full historical context of a given case, particularly in highly divisive matters such as the districting cases—all of which were decided by a five-to-four majority.

Throwing down a final gauntlet, the CBC likened *Shaw* to *Plessy v. Ferguson*—fighting words given the typically dispassionate tone of amicus briefs. Invoking the Court's preceding observation in *Adarand v. Peña*, the caucus asserted that remaining true to an "intrinsically sounder" doctrine in prior cases would better serve the principle of stare decisis than would allegiance to a new precedent that is inconsistent with that doctrine. Put more starkly, the Court "should be no less reluctant to depart from the holdings of *Shaw* and its progeny, because, like *Plessy v. Ferguson*, *Shaw* was wrong the day it was decided."[49] The CBC closed its brief by exhorting the Court majority to examine the issue of remedial racial gerrymanders from the perspective of historically suppressed minority voters:

> Although all parties long for the day when one's race has little or no effect on the quality of one's life . . . the Caucus realize[s] that because that day has not arrived, majority-minority districts are necessary. Americans . . . see the world through prisms colored by their

. . . pasts. For this reason, a district that to some resembles a "bug splattered on a windshield," may to others look more like a winding path leading to political inclusion. . . . The reality of life in the United States prevents African Americans from enjoying the luxury of pretending America is color blind. As this Court makes [this] decision . . . it must accept what most African Americans and many Americans of all races know to be true: race still matters.[50]

Holding Ground: Northwest Austin v. Holder *(2009)*

This case was the first to test Section 5 after its most recent reauthorization. The plaintiffs (the Northwest Austin Municipal Utility District Number 1) sought to "bail out" of Section 5's pre-clearance provision. In particular, they claimed that any interpretation of the VRA that prevented small political subdivisions from bailing out would render Section 5 unconstitutional. Essentially, this case invited the Court to strike down Section 5. Given the centrality of this provision to the CBC's mission, the caucus submitted an amicus brief. It was joined this time by the Congressional Hispanic Caucus and the Asian Pacific American Caucus.[51] Emphasizing the diversity of this coalition as well as its members' common political challenges, substantial portions of the brief focused on the historical disenfranchisement and political suppression of minority voters writ large.[52]

The *Northwest Austin* brief reads as a fusion between the CBC's *Rodgers* and post-*Shaw* briefs. Although its arguments are race-conscious and are framed in a distinctly historical context, its tone is not combative. Along with presenting the CBC and its cosigners as a racially united front, the brief stands out for three emphases: (1) the connection between the VRA and a more diverse political system; (2) the fragility of that diversity; and (3) the forward-looking nature of Section 5.

The amici opened by emphasizing the significance of their existence as congressional caucuses. They asserted their shared purpose of "provid[ing] representation and constituency service for millions of American voters" whose political power had long been suppressed by electoral discrimination. They noted that their constituents' ability to elect their "preferred candidates is an important barometer of [minority voters'] incorporation" into the American polity. That "Congress [is] more racially diverse and inclusive" is thus a direct result of the "successful enforcement" of Section 5. Crediting their presence in Congress as the "clearest evidence" of a changed legislative environment, the caucuses "strongly contend[ed] that the preclearance requirement . . . remains a permissible and effective statutory tool for eliminating and deterring voting discrimination in the political process."[53]

The brief then turned to the persistence of retrogression and minority vote dilution, holding that the VRA's successes in combating these problems should not be taken lightly. Here, the amici directly refuted the appellants' and others' claims that Section 5 is no longer warranted because America has finally entered an era in which electoral discrimination no longer poses a serious threat to minority political power. Pronouncing such claims as inconsistent with reality, "particularly when it comes to extending the franchise to non-white citizens," the amici offered evidence of "election ceilings" that until as recently as 2000 prevented Latino and Native American candidates from winning in majority-white districts. They also noted that such ceilings continue to limit the success of black congressional candidates running in majority-white districts.[54] Here, the brief emphasized that the diversification of the electoral arena is

> of a relatively recent vintage . . . when compared to the extended period in which the denial and abridgment of the franchise was the norm. . . . While the advancements for minority voters are rightly lauded, the lesson of America's difficult history of race and politics teaches that these gains are often fragile. . . . Although the successes of the Voting Rights Act have been substantial, they have not been fast and they have not been furious.[55]

The brief next emphasized that the record offered during the 2006 reauthorization of the act "was replete with evidence showing . . . widespread, intransigent and recent" problems, including the "naked refusal" of some jurisdictions to comply with Section 5. Reminding the Court that the expansion of democracy in America has been characterized by periods of retrenchment and retraction, the amici contended that Section 5's success compelled Congress to extend it rather than strike it down.[56] Here, the brief cited Mel Watts's and John Conyers's observations during the 2006 reauthorization hearings that

> Though there is much to celebrate, efforts to suppress or dilute minority votes . . . are still all too common. . . . [A]lthough the successes of the VRA have been substantial, ... [n]ow is not the time to jettison the . . . provisions that have been instrumental to the success we applaud today.[57]

The emphases on increasing representational diversity, and the fragility of that diversity, along with a forward-looking endorsement of Section 5, are perhaps the most important aspects of this brief. These emphases demonstrate the ongoing dispute between the CBC and the Court regarding the role of race in civil and voting rights. According to the CBC and its fellow amici, Section 5 does not simply benefit historically disfranchised minorities but promotes the "larger institutional goal . . . of pluralist democracy" by ensuring that "all citizens in the United States enjoy the benefit of a more accessible and equal political system."[58] Consequently, pluralism, descriptive representation, and remedially race-conscious districting are mutually beneficial:

> Pluralist democracy recognizes the value of diversity within the political process [and] helps establish a level playing field for individuals with cross-cutting interests and ideas to engage in the pushing, hauling and trading that is commonly associated with politics. . . . [R]ace may be one of the factors that inform perspectives and highlight otherwise overlooked effects of a policy proposal.[59]

The brief concludes that the VRA "helps government move closer to achieving the goals of a more pluralist democracy" and lauds the "genius" of the constitutional system for its openness to innovative methods like Section 5 as among "the best examples" of America's commitment to achieve those goals.[60]

In *Northwest Austin,* the Court upheld Section 5, albeit cautiously. In this moment of congruence with the CBC, the Court's rationale has deep historical resonance. In characterizing Section 5 as the proverbial rising tide that lifts all boats, the CBC and its fellow amici in *Northwest Austin* reflect earlier black leaders' approaches to racial equality. As discussed in earlier chapters, Martin Luther King Jr. consistently argued that America as a whole, not just African Americans, stood to benefit from dismantling institutionalized racism. A key aspect of W. E. B. Du Bois's theory of dualism was the implicit assumption that desegregation would redeem the souls of white folk as it reconciled those of black folk. Booker T. Washington also condemned the mutually damaging effects of racial segregation and hierarchy on blacks and whites. This position also exemplifies the more contemporary theory of blacks' "universal quest for freedom" that is characterized by blacks attempting to push the boundaries of equality, liberty, and democracy not just for themselves but for all citizens.[61] Abolitionists such as David Walker and Frederick Douglass fought to end slavery not just to liberate blacks but to redeem America. From a different angle, the brief's closing point exemplifies Derrick Bell's interest-convergence theory—that those in power will concede to the demands of a minority group only if the former also gain from the concession (for elaborations on these points, see chapters 1 and 2).

This aspect of the *Northwest Austin* brief correlates with the Court's opinion in the affirmative action case of *Grutter v. Bollinger*. A key aspect of the Court's decision in the latter case is its shift from allowing racial classifications to rectify past and existing inequality to allowing racial classifications to promote equality via diversity. Justice Sandra Day O'Connor made explicit references to several of the amici's endorsements of affirmative action as indispensable to fostering diverse leadership. In the *Northwest Austin* brief, the amici noted O'Connor's commendation of Justice Thurgood Marshall's ability to offer different perspectives on an issue by recounting his own life experiences to his colleagues.[62] This perspective reflects Supreme Court justice Sonya Sotomayor's conviction that a justice's core identities can enrich his or her jurisprudence.[63] In sum, the amici in *Northwest Austin, Miller,* and *Shaw v. Hunt* argue that descriptive representation is neither merely symbolic nor illegitimate, racially exclusive, or inimical to substantive representation. Rather, it is part and parcel of substantive and universal modes of representation.

Conclusion: Legislative Success Triggers Judicial Retrenchment

Thus far, the Court majority has rejected the CBC's appeals to expand its interpretation of the Equal Protection Clause to allow for a remedially race-conscious approach to redistricting. Yet it has implicitly reflected the caucus's expansive approach to that clause in recent years, in areas not involving minority voting rights. In *Grutter v. Bollinger*, the justices upheld the University of Michigan's use of race in its law school admissions policy (ironically, those challenging affirmative action endorsed *Shaw v. Reno* as the most applicable precedent). In *Lawrence v. Texas*, the Court majority made a particularly expansive interpretation of the Equal Protection Clause to overrule *Bowers v. Hardwick*. In that case, the majority took the bold step of declaring that *Bowers* was not only wrong in 2003 but was wrong when it was decided in 1986.

Although the positions of the CBC and the Court majority converged somewhat in *Northwest Austin*, it is unlikely that this convergence will last very long. The caucus's limited overall success as an amicus curiae in convincing the Court of the centrality of race to districting, elections, and pluralism contradicts others' conclusions about the general effectiveness of amicus briefs.[64] The Court majority has restricted the use of race to enhance the political power of groups that have been historically suppressed on the basis of race. In other words, the Court has responded negatively to most of the caucus's arguments. For its part, the caucus has sought in the legislative arena to strengthen the VRA against judicial constrictions of it.

As of this writing, the 2010 redistricting has incited legal challenges from several camps (including the Justice Department) to the shape of and racial, ethnic, and partisan composition of districts in California, Illinois, Louisiana, and Texas. At the request of Texas's attorney general, the Supreme Court agreed to expedite its hearing of interim redistricting plans created by a three-judge panel. Alabama and Georgia sought to circumvent the Justice Department's pre-clearance scrutiny by taking their plans directly to the federal court in the District of Columbia; Shelby County, Georgia, in particular has challenged Sections 4 and 5 of the VRA. Recent legislation passed in Florida seriously restricts the process of voter registration. Over a dozen states have instituted voter identification laws in recent years.[65] The CBC has a direct stake in all of these issues, while the ideological balance on the Supreme Court remains unchanged. The cross fire between the caucus and the Court is thus unlikely to abate any time soon.

The CBC's rhetoric in *Miller* and *Hays* and *Shaw v. Hunt* was much more race-conscious and historical than its rhetoric in *Rodgers*. The *Northwest Austin* brief was less race-conscious. But to the extent that the arguments in the latter brief were historically framed, they were racially contextualized as well. Given African Americans' persisting vulnerability to electoral discrimination in the early 1980s, the *Rodgers* brief is notable for its minimal references to the historical and racial contexts that surround the case and for its failure to mention any sort of race-conscious solution to blacks' struggle to gain and retain political power, particularly in the South. That the *Rodgers* brief followed this traditional format may merely indicate astute and experienced maneuvering on the part of the CBC, especially since the VRA was under reconsideration at that time. Yet skirting the issue of race was antithetical to its mission as the conscience of Congress.

The racial intensification of the CBC's arguments was triggered by the *Shaw* holding that any race has standing to make a claim that race-conscious districting "that is so extremely irregular on its face that it rationally can be viewed only as an effort to segregate the races for the purposes of voting" is a violation of the Fourteenth Amendment guarantee of a color-blind districting process.[66] From the Court majority's color-blind perspective, this rationale is an egalitarian one, yet from the race-conscious perspective of the CBC, it is not fair. These divergences demonstrate that the CBC remains concerned with electoral outcomes while the Court majority is concerned with electoral processes. From the former perspective, *Shaw* and its progeny are particularly troubling because they invite the electoral retrogression of black political power while enhancing the advantage of white voters (who never claimed harm from the districting they challenged).[67] The substantive and rhetorical changes in the CBC's post-*Shaw* briefs confirm Girardeau Spann's thesis that racial minorities cannot rely on the Court to protect their interests. From this viewpoint, the 1990s redistricting decisions have left the CBC with little choice but to approach the Court as an adversary whose commitment to combating electoral inequality with racially neutral processes threatened to undermine blacks' political interests.

According to an early study on amicus curiae briefs submitted by civil rights organizations, an effective brief must meet three basic criteria. It must be novel, presenting new points that are not mentioned in the litigants' briefs. It must be provocative, either by creating a healthy doubt about the arguments of the main brief or by advocating its position on moral grounds. Finally, it must be redemptive, presenting arguments that attempt either to salve justices' consciences or mitigate justices' hesitation to lean toward those on whose behalf an amicus brief is submitted.[68] While the CBC's voting rights briefs satisfy these criteria, they largely failed the main goal of convincing the Court majority to reconsider its skepticism of race consciousness. Unless the ideological balance on the Court shifts to the left, the antagonism between the CBC and the Court majority over the relationship of race to representation will continue. For the caucus, the Court majority's color-blind voting rights jurisprudence—specifically, its reliance on the concept solely as a process rather than as an outcome as well—is dangerously shortsighted and almost literally blind. Hence, although American politics are becoming more egalitarian than ever, they remain fettered by knots of persisting racism and by judicial inability to loosen those knots. The next chapter will explore how the Court majority's voting rights jurisprudence potentially undermines black political power, restricts federal and state authority to protect that power, and compromises the expansive concepts of equality and democracy as expressed by the CBC and black leadership since the 1800s.

5 | The Supreme Court: Pushing Back

"The Supreme Court's majority opinion in Shaw v. Reno, applying
the Equal Protection Clause to preclude African Americans from
attaining significant political power in this nation, turns the intent
. . . of the Fourteenth Amendment on its head."
—A. Leon Higginbotham Jr., 1994

Contesting Boundaries: Judicial Reshaping of the VRA

Chapters 3 and 4 assess the position of the Congressional Black Caucus
(CBC) on the relationship of race, representation, and law through its legislative role in reauthorizing the Voting Rights Act (VRA) and as amicus
curiae in key voting rights cases. This chapter reviews the Supreme Court's
decisions in those cases, thereby demonstrating one of the central claims
of this book: The CBC's role in strengthening the VRA in a way that allows
for remedial uses of race when redistricting and later in endorsing such an
approach to the Court effectively triggered color-blind judicial restrictions on such uses of race. Starting with *Shaw v. Reno* in 1993, the Court
majority has protected white plaintiffs' (and ostensibly all voters') rights
to a color-blind districting process. In so doing, the justices have pinned
black political power between narrow interpretations of the laws intended
to protect that power. In effectively hoisting the CBC onto its own race-
conscious petard, the Court majority has imperiled black political power
as well.

This chapter examines the Court's opinions in *Shaw v. Reno, Miller v.
Johnson, Shaw v. Hunt,* and *Northwest Austin Municipal Utility District
Number 1 v. Holder.*[1] The *Shaw* decision alone has generated a wealth of
scholarship. Consisting largely of law review articles, most of this literature is critical of the minority voting rights trajectory established in that

precedent. This examination makes no attempt to duplicate or extend that work. Instead, it examines these decisions as the Court majority's implicit responses to the CBC's endorsements of a race-conscious minority voting rights jurisprudence. Like most of the existing analyses of *Shaw* and its progeny, the analysis here is critical of the Court majority's reasoning. However, it makes this critique from the CBC's perspective and in the context of African American political thought. Although the Court never directly mentions the CBC's amicus briefs, the opinions respond indirectly to the caucus's position. For example, in rejecting the states' arguments in these cases—many of which the CBC amplified in its briefs—the Court rejected the caucus arguments as well. The same can be said for the Court's rejection of the oversight exercised by the Department of Justice (DOJ) covered by Section 5 and of its reinterpretation of Congress's intent for Sections 2 and 5 of the VRA.

This chapter focuses on the Court majority in these cases because it has been such a unified and consistent one.[2] The central argument here is that with respect to minority voting rights, the majority has exerted a particularly authoritative role in interpreting the Fourteenth Amendment and the VRA in a way that checks congressional and executive power to make and enforce those laws—and that completely rejects the CBC's perspective.

Given the Court majority's and the CBC's divergent approaches to the role of race in districting and representation, it is not surprising that the former would reject the latter's arguments. However, these disagreements have important implications for those whose political power depends on aggressive enforcement of the VRA, including remedially race-conscious interpretations of the act. For example, the members of the American polity might come to better understand and work with each other via race-conscious districting that diversifies political representation and thus leadership.[3] Regrettably, the complexities of this view are all too easily obscured by the volley of ideological and political debates regarding the role of race in law and society. The majority's rationale in *Shaw v. Reno* exemplifies this problem by making three false parallels between remedial and egregious uses of race.

False Parallels: Shaw v. Reno

The central question in *Shaw* was whether the use of race in creating oddly shaped majority-minority districts gave rise to the claim that such a use violates the Equal Protection Clause of the Fourteenth Amendment. Following the 1990 census, North Carolina gained one congressional seat.

Its initial districting plan had one majority-black district. Because parts of North Carolina are covered by Section 5, it submitted that plan to the Justice Department for pre-clearance. The DOJ rejected the initial plan, directing North Carolina to draw a second majority-black district. The DOJ later cleared the revised plan, which featured two districts, each of which was slightly over 50 percent black. These districts were also very irregularly shaped. White voters challenged the revised plan, alleging that the use of race in creating the two black districts (Districts 1 and 12) violated established redistricting principles, along with the Fourteenth Amendment's Equal Protection Clause. They initially challenged the constitutionality of the VRA as well. In effect, this case tested "the propriety of race-based state legislation designed to benefit members of historically disadvantaged racial minority groups."[4] It is important to note that the appellants never made a claim of racial harm.

The opinion in Shaw seemed driven almost entirely by the appearance of the challenged districts. Writing for the majority, Justice Sandra Day O'Connor paid considerable attention to and seemed largely animated by outside observers' dramatic descriptions of the districts, which included such vivid phrases as "snakelike," a "Rorschach ink-blot test," a "bug-splat on a windshield," and even as potentially deadly (driving down the interstate running through District 12 with both car doors open would kill most of its voters).[5] In evaluating the constitutionality of these districts, O'Connor drew the following parallels by equating (1) irregularly shaped districts that were slightly over 50 percent black to irregularly shaped districts that were more than 90 percent white; (2) North Carolina's remedial race-based districting to South Africa's system of racial apartheid; and (3) post-VRA remedial uses of districting to Jim Crow–era segregation. All of these parallels are false.

Equating the Challenged Districts to
Gomillion v. Lightfoot

Early in its opinion, the Shaw majority equated North Carolina's districting plan to the gerrymander in a 1960 case, Gomillion v. Lightfoot. In Gomillion, an Alabama statute allowed Tuskegee's legislature to change its existing municipal boundaries from a square to an "uncouth . . . strangely irregular twenty-eight sided figure" that excluded all but four of its approximately four hundred registered black voters.[6] Under the original boundaries, African Americans comprised approximately 80 percent of Tuskegee's 6,700 residents, while the new boundaries reduced the munic-

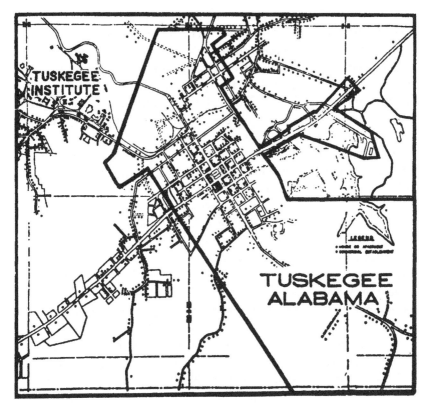

Fig. 1.   Map of redistricting at issue in *Gomillion v. Lightfoot.* (Image printed from HeinOnline, http://heinonline.org.)

ipality's black population to 1,750. In effect, the statute converted an over-whelmingly black municipality into a smaller but even more overwhelm-ingly white political enclave.[7] Figure 1 illustrates the *Gomillion* districting plan. (The heavily lined square is the original shape of the districting plan, and the heavily lined shape within the square is the redrawn plan chal-lenged by black voters.)

The *Gomillion* Court determined that the new boundary lines "deprived the [black] petitioners of the municipal franchise" and "de-spoil[ed] . . . only colored citizens of their . . . voting rights." Holding that state actions "generally lawful may become unlawful when done to ac-complish an unlawful end," the justices granted standing for Tuskegee's black voters to make a claim that the statute denied their rights under the Fifteenth Amendment.[8] In a short but noteworthy concurrence, Justice

Charles Evans Whittaker asserted that the black plaintiffs' rights were indeed violated, but under the Fourteenth rather than the Fifteenth Amendment. In his view, Tuskegee's qualified black voters were not denied the right to vote per se; while they were excluded from Tuskegee's boundaries and thus from its municipal elections, they could vote in other elections. Consequently, no violation of the Fifteenth Amendment had occurred. But because the districting plan treated black voters differently, it violated the Equal Protection Clause of the Fourteenth Amendment.[9] Since that decision, and as the VRA has vastly improved blacks' access to the ballot, most contemporary minority voting rights litigation raises Fourteenth rather than Fifteenth Amendment claims.

Justice O'Connor's rationale in *Shaw* extends Whittaker's concurrence in *Gomillion*. Against the backdrop of that case, she emphasized that "reapportionment is one area in which appearances do matter." In her view, it was "unsettling how the challenged districts resemble[d] the most egregious racial gerrymanders of [America's] past," such as *Gomillion*.[10] Relying on Whittaker's concurrence in that case, she noted that with respect to redistricting, all racial classifications trigger strict scrutiny:

> A racial classification, regardless of purported motivation, is presumably invalid and can be upheld only upon an extraordinary justification. . . . *Gomillion*'s holding is compelled by the Equal Protection Clause. [It] thus supports the [*Shaw*] appellants' contention that district lines obviously drawn for the purpose of separating voters by race require careful scrutiny under the Equal Protection Clause regardless of the motivations underlying their adoption.[11]

In citing Whittaker's concurrence as the appropriate precedent for *Shaw*, however, O'Connor elided the fact that Tuskegee's redistricting plan sought to suppress the black vote, whereas North Carolina's redistricting plan intended in part to counteract the legacy of such suppression. Instead, the shape of the districts seemed to blind the *Shaw* majority to the state's intent behind them, along with the framers' intent for the Equal Protection Clause.

At first glance, North Carolina's Districts 1 and especially 12 raise suspicions. Yet while appearances can be important, they do not always tell the whole story. When examined in their full context, the bizarre shapes of the districts do not indicate an effort to "segregate . . . voters on the basis of race [or] citizens into separate voting districts on the basis of race."[12] According to North Carolina, the shapes indicate compliance with the Jus-

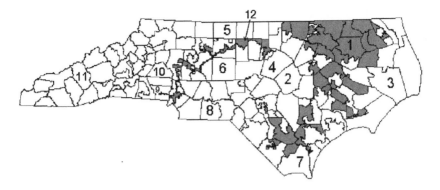

Fig. 2.   Map of redistricting at issue in *Shaw v. Reno*. (Original image from http://www.ncga.state.nc.us/representation/Content/Plans/PlanPage_DB_1991. asp?Plan=1992_Congressional_Base_Plan_10&Body=Congress.).

tice Department's oversight by creating districts that would help offset decades of racial discrimination at the polls. In this respect, the districts accord with Congress's—and the CBC's—intent behind the 1982 revision of Section 2 of the VRA. The district shapes also indicate state legislators' efforts to balance several driving and competing factors in the redistricting process. The chief factor was the partisan imperative to draw districts to preserve incumbency. Second was the challenge of geographically contiguous but noncompact African American residential patterns, where such patterns reflect decades of segregation both by law and custom. Third was North Carolina's mountainous topography, which is conducive to uneven population patterns. Fourth was natural and "traditional" boundary lines such as existing jurisdiction borders, rivers, mountains, and highways, which all tend to be irregularly shaped. District 12, for example, followed a major interstate, around which the population, particularly African American, is densely concentrated. Fifth was computer mapping technology that enabled legislators to carve out districts with greater demographic precision, tending in turn to generate oddly shaped boundary lines.[13] Taken together, these factors made the task of drawing contiguous, compact, equally populated districts extremely challenging and were conducive to districting maps that resembled strange figures. Figure 2 shows the districting map at issue in *Shaw v. Reno*.[14] (The challenged districts, 1 and 12, are shaded in gray.)

Under the *Shaw* rationale, states attempting to draw majority-minority congressional districts in compliance with Section 5 do so at increased risk of violating the Equal Protection Clause. This in turn puts Section 5's antiretrogression principle in tension with Section 2's antidilution principle. Under *Shaw*, legislators in states covered by Section 5 must draw fewer but more compact majority-black districts by packing those voters into a district beyond the number needed for them to elect a candidate of their choice. Or, they may crack voters into minority "influence" districts, in which blacks are not the majority but are sufficient in number to affect the outcome of an election. The problem is that both options risk diluting the minority vote—precisely the problem that Congress sought to prevent when it revised Section 2 in 1982.

The difference between cracking the minority vote and creating minority influence districts has long bedeviled Congress and the Court. In 2003, the Court endorsed such districting in *Georgia v. Ashcroft*. That decision motivated Congress and especially the CBC to assert that the VRA must not be interpreted in a way that equates minority influence districts with majority-minority safe districts. Again, one exception on the CBC is Congressman Bobby Scott, who sees the the choice as theoretically involving more black influence districts at the expense of safe black districts. In practice, however, the choice is "almost always" between more influence districts at the expense of "supersafe" (overly packed) districts and reducing safe districts to a bare but effective electoral majority—as is the case with the two districts at issue in *Shaw v. Reno*. Moreover, as Scott has noted, distinguishing what is packed or cracked from the ideal percentage of black voters in a district depends largely on the racial climate of a given locality, hence his caution against adopting minority influence districting on a wholesale basis.[15]

Those who espouse an exclusively color-blind approach to such cases would likely dismiss the above points. For one, they hinge on benign intent, which the Court majority has often stated is beside the point.[16] The above points are also premised on electoral outcomes, whereas a color-blind approach to the Fourteenth Amendment is premised on equal processes. Yet simply because an argument is repeatedly rejected by a majority of the Court does not negate its value to the discourse regarding minority voting rights and representation. Moreover, the *Shaw* decision demonstrates that the Court's putatively restrained majority was in fact activist when it departed from precedents that allowed for remedial interpretations of the VRA and the Equal Protection Clause.[17] Terms such as *conservatism, liberalism, activism,* and *restraint* tend to oversimplify the complex dynamics of race, representation, and law. No matter how one labels the *Shaw* decision, it is almost an impossible stretch to equate districting that excluded all but four black voters for the purpose of diminishing their political power to districting that included a bare majority of black voters for the purpose of protecting their power. The appellants in *Shaw* were neither excluded from nor harmed by a districting process that equalized the electoral playing field. That they did not make a claim of harm does not make the fact that they were not harmed any less significant.[18]

To equate the *Gomillion* and *Shaw* districts, the Court majority had to cut them from their historical moorings. This may explain the majority's failure to acknowledge that the districts at issue in *Shaw* elected the first blacks from North Carolina to Congress since 1901. In addition, as the CBC pointed out in its amicus brief for *Miller,* for the Court majority to be more disturbed by oddly shaped districts that were barely over 50 percent black than by adjoining oddly shaped districts that were almost 100 percent white is disturbing.[19] It is similarly troubling for the majority to assume that race-conscious districting by a southern state legislature for the benefit of historically oppressed racial minorities was invidious simply because race-conscious districting by such legislatures so often had been invidious in the past. In equating remedial race-consciousness with racism, the majority brands proponents of the former and victims of the latter as racists.

Equating Challenged Districts to
Political Apartheid

Justice O'Connor asserted that the Districts 1 and 12 "bore an uncomfortable resemblance to political apartheid."[20] Although she coined the term "political apartheid," she neither defined it nor offered proof of its existence. Absent any clarification, one was left to equate one state's intent to help remedy the harms of white ascendancy with a national system designed to ensure such ascendancy.[21] The majority also held that North Carolina's (and the DOJ's) intent to remedy electoral discrimination against blacks was an insufficient justification for creating a second irregularly shaped majority-black district. In the justices' view, such districting instead "reinforces stereotypes and threatens to undermine our system of representative democracy" and ultimately is racially "balkanizing":

> Racial gerrymandering, even for remedial purposes, may balkanize us into competing racial factions: it threatens to carry us further from the goal of a political system in which race no longer matters. [Thus,] a reapportionment scheme so irrational on its face that it can be un-

derstood only as an effort to segregate voters into separate voting districts because of their race . . . lacks sufficient justification.[22]

Here, O'Connor reinforced a common misperception among opponents of race-conscious districting, which is that race-based districting causes racial fragmentation and stereotyping. This assumption is problematic in two ways. First, it asserts that racial stereotyping leads to balkanization without acknowledging that the reverse is more often true.[23] Second, putting the proverbial cart before the horse deflects attention from the root causes of balkanization in America, such as centuries of racial hierarchy and its continuing effects. In taking this perspective, the *Shaw* majority failed to interrogate the significance of bizarrely shaped white-majority districts that adjoined and were thus interlocked with their majority black counterparts, as figure 2 shows. This perspective also apparently prevented the majority from recognizing that the challenged districts were the most racially mixed ones in the state—and thus the least balkanized. Table 3 illustrates this point, along with stark demographic differences between Districts 1 and 12 and the other ten districts. Ironically, the majority invalidated precisely the districts that had the most potential to begin reversing the political effects of generations of political and racial apartheid. It is possible that the majority's trepidations about racist districting of the past fueled skepticism about a remedially race-conscious districting of the present. If so, by declining to give as much weight to the context of the districts as it did to their appearances and by presuming without proof that race-based concepts of representation exacerbate racial problems in America, the *Shaw* majority appeared to be guided more by fears than by facts.[24]

Equating the Challenged Districts
to Segregation

In making false parallels among North Carolina's districting plan, the *Gomillion* gerrymander, and apartheid, Justice O'Connor laid the foundations for a broader equation of race consciousness with racist segregation. She first noted that "the very reason the Equal Protection Clause demands strict scrutiny of all racial classifications is because without it, a court cannot determine whether or not the discrimination truly is benign." This statement means that North Carolina's interest in balancing the electoral playing field for its black voters was not a sufficient justification to draw irregularly shaped majority-black districts, even though many of the state's other districts had extremely irregular boundaries. To be sure, the Court has for several decades routinely applied its strictest scrutiny to racial classifications. However, to presume that any racial classification, regardless of motivation, "is presumptively invalid" and to subject all such classifications to strictest scrutiny whether a policy "burden[s] or benefit[s] the races equally" renders the doctrine of strict scrutiny almost impossible to overcome.[25] This idea also contradicts the Court's earlier position that because considerations of race are inevitable when remedying the effects of past racial discrimination, not every race-based policy should be subjected to a scrutiny that is strict in theory but impossible to justify.[26]

TABLE 3. DB: North Carolina District Summary, Voting Age Populations; Plan: 1992 Cong plan #10—Copy 1; Plan Type: Congressional Base Plan

District Name	Total Voting Age	Voting Age				
		White	Black	Am. Ind.	Asian/PI	Other
District 1	399,969	181,933	213,602	2,428	844	1,110
	100.00%	45.49%	53.40%	0.61%	0.21%	0.28%
District 2	420,087	328,676	84,311	2,173	3,074	1,963
	100.00%	78.24%	20.07%	0.52%	0.73%	0.47%
District 3	413,263	324,808	81,170	1,755	2,922	2,608
	100.00%	78.60%	19.64%	0.42%	0.71%	0.63%
District 4	428,984	336,850	81,210	1,239	7,782	1,903
	100.00%	78.52%	18.93%	0.29%	1.81%	0.44%
District 5	428,782	364,886	60,204	822	1,650	1,221
	100.00%	85.10%	14.04%	0.19%	0.38%	0.28%
District 6	428,096	393,271	30,188	1,433	2,407	798
	100.00%	91.87%	7.05%	0.33%	0.56%	0.19%
District 7	414,413	306,754	71,071	26,489	4,201	5,898
	100.00%	74.02%	17.15%	6.39%	1.01%	1.42%
District 8	403,678	305,366	84,386	8,699	2,956	2,271
	100.00%	75.65%	20.90%	2.15%	0.73%	0.56%
District 9	421,615	380,364	33,849	1,275	5,059	1,069
	100.00%	90.22%	8.03%	0.30%	1.20%	0.25%
District 10	421,456	397,476	20,837	700	1,409	1,036
	100.00%	94.31%	4.94%	0.17%	0.33%	0.25%
District 11	430,457	396,064	27,438	5,126	1,237	592
	100.00%	92.01%	6.37%	1.19%	0.29%	0.14%
District 12	411,687	186,115	219,610	1,529	3,283	1,150
	100.00%	45.21%	53.34%	0.37%	0.80%	0.28%
Total	5,022,487	3,902,563	1,007,876	53,668	36,824	21,619
	100.00%	77.70%	20.07%	1.07%	0.73%	0.43%

Note: Compiled from North Carolina General Assembly data available at http://www.ncga.state.nc.us/representation/Content/Plans/PlanPage_DB_1991.asp?Plan1992_Congressional_Base_Plan_10&Body=Congress (accessed April 4, 2012).

O'Connor condemned the challenged districts because they combined "individuals who belong to the same race, but who are otherwise widely separated by geographical and political boundaries, and who may have little in common with one another but the color of their skin."[27] By departing from earlier precedents, the majority opinion in *Shaw* bound the hands not only of legislators in states covered by Section 5 but also of minority voters, whose interests are generally cohesive even if their residential patterns are not contiguous or compact. In the process, the majority overlooked two important realities. First, most African Americans possess not simply a racial consciousness but a racial group consciousness. Second, race and group consciousness can and often do transcend geographical boundaries.[28]

The opinion acknowledged that a state legislature is "always aware of race when it draws district lines" and that "race consciousness does not inevitably lead to impermissible race discrimination."[29] The majority's aversion to Districts 1 and 12 thus appears less driven by irregular shapes per se than by irregular shapes drawn around black voters. Indeed, O'Connor suggests that black candidates elected from majority-black districts would be unable or unwilling to represent their non-black constituents:

> When a district obviously is created solely to effectuate the perceived common interests of one racial group, elected officials are more likely to believe that their primary obligation is to represent only the members of that group, rather than their constituency as a whole.[30]

As with her apartheid parallel, O'Connor offered no proof of this claim, even as North Carolina was compelled to prove that blacks' political cohesion transcended geographical boundaries. Her opinion does not consider that African American representatives of Districts 1 and 12 would attempt to represent their entire constituency.[31] She was surely aware of the long history of white nonresponsiveness to black constituents, which likely fueled her and others' skepticism of descriptive representation. Yet she and others on the Court majority were apparently unaware of the early example of the racially inclusive and egalitarian agenda of black Reconstruction legislators, a history that clearly refutes her claim. She also made no mention of the fact that North Carolina's legislators, most of whom were white, were attempting in part to remedy the racially discriminatory legacy of the state's past. Instead, by making this claim, O'Connor and the majority engaged in precisely the racial stereotyping they claimed to refute.

O'Connor next stipulated "that racial bloc voting and minority group political cohesion never can be assumed, but specifically must be proven in each case."[32] This stipulation reveals another inconsistency on the part of the majority: While it requires proof of political cohesion among minority *voters*, it simply presumes racially biased representation by minority *representatives*. O'Connor also emphasized that racial classifications "reinforce the belief, held by too many for too much of our history, that individuals should be judged by the color of their skin."[33] Here, she invoked one of Martin Luther King Jr.'s most widely known—and arguably most widely misunderstood—aspirations. Like so many who rely on this particular goal, O'Connor took it out of context. A complete reading of the "I Have a Dream" speech reveals a clear emphasis on reparations. Taken as a whole, the speech condemns racial inequality far more than it calls for color blindness. In particular, those who rely on the "content of our character" phrase in the speech tend to overlook King's explicit call in other writings for "Negro bloc" voting as an essential political tactic "to make [the black] voice known" and to achieve racial equality.[34] To strip the challenged districts of their historical and political contexts to condemn them, and to buttress that condemnation with decontextualized misinterpretations of King, is at the very least disturbing.

The Court ultimately held in *Shaw v. Reno* that all voters have a constitutional right to a color-blind electoral process.[35] This holding reveals dual tracks of protection in regions covered by Section 5. These dual tracks, in turn, create a tension between the VRA and the Constitution in which (1) whites are guaranteed a constitutional right to a color-blind electoral process by the Equal Protection Clause of the Fourteenth Amendment while (2) blacks are better off claiming statutory protection from discrimination by relying on the VRA. In one view, by applying a "racial double standard" with which to determine the constitutionality of two oddly shaped majority-black districts among ten other oddly shaped majority-white districts, the Court gives "undue solicitude" to white voters.[36] In another, the *Shaw* rationale undermines the concept of color-blind egalitarianism to which it is committed.[37] The result, as discussed earlier, is an Equal Protection Clause that is turned on its head.

Judicial Revision of the VRA: Miller v. Johnson

In key respects, *Miller v. Johnson* simply builds on the *Shaw v. Reno* precedent by holding that Georgia's irregularly shaped minority-black District 1 was tantamount to racial segregation. In *Miller,* the Court also fortified its equation of oddly shaped majority-black districts to *Gomillion*-type racist gerrymanders.[38] In *Shaw*, the Court held that plaintiffs had standing to challenge oddly shaped majority-minority districts under the Equal Protection Clause. Writing for the majority in *Miller*, Justice Anthony Kennedy laid out the following criteria:

> Parties alleging that [Georgia] has assigned voters on the basis of race are neither confined in their proof to evidence regarding the district's geometry and makeup nor required to make a threshold showing of bizarreness. . . . The plaintiff's burden is to show, either through circumstantial evidence of a district's shape and demographics or more direct evidence going to legislative purpose, that race was the predominant factor motivating the legislature's decision to place a significant number of voters within or without a particular district. To make this showing, a plaintiff must prove that the legislature subordinated traditional race-neutral districting principles . . . to racial considerations.[39]

Miller is distinguished from *Shaw* by its attention to federalism, where the Court framed a significant portion of its review of Georgia's districting plan in the context of what it saw as the proper balance of power between states and the federal government. By emphasizing the differences between the Court's and the Justice Department's interpretation of the VRA, the decision also brought the system of checks and balances to the foreground.

Acknowledging that redistricting is a "most difficult subject for state legislators," the opinion noted that states must have the autonomy to decide the best way to balance competing interests, including the "complex interplay of forces" involved in reapportionment. Repeating Justice O'Connor's observation in *Shaw* that legislators are always aware of race during the process of reapportionment, Kennedy conceded that the "distinction between being aware of racial considerations and being motivated by them may be difficult to make." Compared to other districts, Kennedy also conceded that "the geometric shape of the Eleventh District may not seem bizarre on its face"; however, in light of the district's minority population density, the Court asserted that "the story of racial gerrymandering . . . becomes much clearer." Based on that story, the Court majority rejected Georgia's claim that it had drawn District 11 "to offset the loss of [that] population caused by the shift of predominantly black portions" to another district (itself a response to Justice Department oversight). It also rejected Georgia's explanation that the precision of redistricting software is conducive to drawing more fine-tuned and thus more irregular district boundaries.[40]

Federalism, Checks and Balances, and
Compelling State Interests

More than the *Shaw* precedent, *Miller v. Johnson* illustrates the Supreme Court majority's willingness to reinterpret federal law. By raising the bar on what constitutes a compelling state interest, the Court imposed its vision of the VRA onto states covered by Section 5. In the process, it imposed its interpretation of the act onto the legislative and executive branches as well. For example, Justice Kennedy emphasized the majority's agreement with the lower court's finding that the DOJ would accept nothing less than Georgia's "abject surrender" to the department's agenda to maximize the black vote.[41] He then phrased the Court's rejection of the DOJ's race-conscious enforcement of Section 5 in the rhetoric of surrender:

> Where a State relies on the [DOJ's] determination that race-based districting is necessary to comply with the [VRA], the judiciary retains an independent obligation in adjudicating consequent equal protection challenges to ensure that the State's actions are narrowly tailored to achieve a compelling interest. . . . Were we to accept the [DOJ's] objection itself as a compelling interest adequate to insulate racial districting from constitutional review, we would be surrendering to the Executive Branch our role in enforcing the constitutional limits on race-based official action. We may not do so.[42]

Kennedy went on to declare that "judicial power cannot be shared with the Executive Branch"; because the "Supreme Court is the ultimate interpreter of the Constitution . . . we think it inappropriate for a court engaged in constitutional scrutiny to accord deference to the Justice Department's interpretation" of the VRA.[43] In this view, enforcement of Section 5 by compelling covered states to create majority-minority districts wherever possible takes the enforcement power of the executive branch far beyond what Congress intended. Thus, in rejecting compliance with the VRA as a compelling reason to create an additional, irregularly shaped majority-minority district, the Court majority essentially reinterpreted the legislative intent for the VRA.

With respect to federalism, Kennedy repeated that federal courts must recognize "the intrusive potential of judicial intervention into the legislative realm" of states when evaluating redistricting plans and must be "sensitive to the complex interplay of forces that enter a legislature's redistricting calculus."[44] Yet it appears that the majority was so concerned about what it deemed Georgia's abdication of autonomy to the DOJ that the justices effectively compelled the DOJ to surrender its power of administrative interpretation of the VRA to the judiciary:

> There is little doubt that the State's true interest in designing the Eleventh District was creating a third majority-black district to satisfy the Justice Department's pre-clearance demands. . . . Whether or not in some case compliance with the [VRA], standing alone, can provide a compelling interest independent of any interest in remedying past discrimination, it cannot do so here. . . . The congressional plan challenged here was not required by the [VRA] under a *correct* reading of the statute.[45]

This aspect of the majority opinion limited state and federal power to remedy the persisting underrepresentation of black citizens in a race-conscious manner. The problem for the majority may not have been the surrender of Georgia's autonomy to the DOJ but Georgia's surrender to the department's race-conscious administration of the VRA. In any event, by rejecting the DOJ's pursuit of race-based districting as a mistaken interpretation of the VRA, the *Miller* Court rejected Congress's and the CBC's intent for Section 5 of the act.

Overall, the Court majority appeared considerably more troubled by the DOJ's race-conscious administration of the VRA in *Miller* than it was in *Shaw*. For example, in describing the department's oversight of legislative reapportionment, Justice Kennedy employed terms such as "demands" for "abject surrender" compared to more common and less dramatic terms like "requirements" and "compliance." The majority also overlooked the congruence of objectives between the DOJ and states: to protect the voting rights of a group whose power had for decades been subordinated by states and localities. In holding that the Justice Department had an incorrect reading of the VRA, the majority failed to stipulate what the correct reading was. The only correct reading thus appears to be the Court majority's reading. If this is true, the Court majority compromised both federalism and the system of checks and balances.

In closing his opinion in *Miller*, Kennedy emphasized the Court majority's commitment to color-blind voting rights jurisprudence, declaring that it "takes a shortsighted and unauthorized" view of the VRA "to demand the very racial stereotyping the Fourteenth Amendment forbids."[46] This conclusion illustrates once more that the majority equates race consciousness with racism, segregation, and apartheid. Consequently, its reading of the VRA contrasts sharply with the CBC's and Congress's intent for Sections 2 and 5 of the act. In using the term "unauthorized," the Court challenged not only the Justice Department's power but also Congress's authority to amend the VRA in a race-conscious manner. Here, the majority exposed its own shortsightedness by disconnecting Congress's intent for the VRA from the history and legacy of electoral racial discrimination in states covered by Section 5, despite the fact that the CBC supplied the *Miller* Court with a thorough account of that history in its amicus brief.

The *Miller* decision signals further retrenchment against congressional and executive authority over the VRA. If the *Shaw* decision turned the framers' intent for the Fourteenth Amendment upside down, the *Miller* decision inverted the VRA. Those who now stand to lose the most by the Court's decisions are precisely the people whose best interests it has at other times claimed to have at heart: minority voters in the South. These are the people who can least afford to lose the political gains that are afforded by the strengthened VRA, gains that have come from a few oddly shaped minority safe districts interspersed among many more oddly shaped majority-white districts.

Judicial Restriction of the VRA: Shaw v. Hunt

The decision in *Shaw v. Reno* laid the groundwork for challenges to majority-minority districting by equating inclusive, race-conscious districts with odd shapes to exclusive, racist districts with odd shapes. In *Shaw v. Hunt,* essentially a remand of *Shaw v. Reno,* the Court considered whether North Carolina's districting plan was sufficiently narrowly tailored to satisfy its interests without violating the Equal Protection Clause. The majority subsequently held that because the Fourteenth Amendment's chief purpose is to eliminate state-sponsored racial discrimination, racial classifications such as those used in North Carolina's districting plan "are antithetical to the Fourteenth Amendment."[47] At the same time, it held that under "certain circumstances," racial distinctions may be permissible. According to Chief Justice William Rehnquist, who wrote the majority opinion for this case, discrimination must be identified . . . with some specificity before [a state] may use race-conscious relief. . . . A generalized assertion of past discrimination in a particular industry or region is not adequate because it provides no guidance for a legislative body to determine the precise scope of the injury it seeks to remedy. Second, the institution that makes the racial distinction must have had a strong basis in evidence to conclude that remedial action was necessary before it embarks on an affirmative action program.[48]

While this opinion leaves the door open for remedial race-based districting, the conditions for doing so are problematic in several ways. They burden states covered by Section 5 with providing a specific evidence of discriminatory intent when clear or irrefutable evidence of such intent is almost nonexistent. Rehnquist did note that the Court has not always provided "precise guidance" in the matter of race-based districting because it has "always expected that the legislative action would substantially address, if not achieve, its avowed purpose." Rather than specify the criteria at this point, however, Rehnquist simply reasserted the majority's interpretation of the VRA. As in *Miller,* the Court majority found that North Carolina's creation of two majority-black districts was not required under a "correct" reading of Section 5 and that as drawn, the districts were "not a remedy narrowly tailored to the State's professed interest in avoiding Section 2 liability."[49] This holding conflicts with Congress's express intent to amend the VRA to guard against the effects of racial discrimination at the polls. It also threatens to undermine minority political power in regions where it was just becoming established under the auspices of Section 5.

Rehnquist next noted that to justify race-based districting, a state must prove that a minority group is both sufficiently large and sufficiently compact to comprise a majority in a single-member district. Emphasizing the criterion of geographical compactness, the Court determined that the districting plan was not narrowly tailored to satisfy the state's compelling interest in avoiding Section 2 liability. Rejecting the DOJ's "expansive interpretation[s] of Section 5," the majority held that "failure to maximize [minority electoral power] cannot be the measure of Section 2." It thus found "singularly unpersuasive" North Carolina's argument that it was compelled by the DOJ to draw as many majority-minority districts as possible to avoid violating the VRA. According to the Court majority, the state's argument "derives from a misconception of the vote-dilution claim."[50]

Although the Court majority's attention to district shape in *Miller* and *Shaw v. Hunt* was brief compared to *Shaw v. Reno,* shape was the driving force behind all three decisions. Appearances were, after all, what triggered this litigation. According to Justice O'Connor, in *Shaw v. Reno*, the irregular shape of such districts, combined with the fact that they were predominantly black, convinced the majority to grant white plaintiffs standing to claim that such districts violated the Equal Protection Clause. In *Miller*, shape was "relevant not because bizarreness is a necessary element of . . . constitutional wrong . . . but because it may be persuasive circumstantial evidence that race for its own sake . . . was the legislature's dominant and controlling rationale in drawing its district lines."[51] In *Shaw v. Hunt*, the majority emphasized again that "no one looking at District 12 could reasonably suggest that the district contains a geographically compact population of any race."[52]

These decisions laid the groundwork for the majority to interpret Sections 2 and 5 completely independent of each other a few years later in *Reno v. Bossier Parish School Board I* and *II*. Building on that pair of precedents in *Georgia v. Ashcroft*, the majority "specifically held that a violation of Section 2 is not an independent reason to deny pre-clearance under Section 5 . . . and . . . refuse[d] to equate a Section 2 vote dilution inquiry with the Section 5 retrogression standard."[53] As discussed in chapter 3, for the Court to interpret these provisions in this manner conflicts with Congress's intent for them to reinforce each other. This intent is manifested not only by legislative deliberations regarding the act but by Congress's infusion of the results-oriented language of Section 2 into Section 5.[54] These decisions shift the balance of institutional power toward the Court and thus toward the federal government. Such a result is an ironic exception to Rehnquist's more typical commitment to the concept of dual federalism and state autonomy. In checking Congress's expansive interpretation of Sections 2 and 5 along with the Justice Department's administration of the latter, the Court may simply have sought to restore that autonomy. In effect, however, the Court freed the states of executive oversight only to tether them to judicial oversight. The ramifications of these decisions go beyond checks and balances and federalism. They risk harming the political power of minority voters caught in the institutional cross fire over the meaning and scope of democracy in America.

Holding Ground: Northwest Austin Municipal Utility District Number 1 v. Holder

Northwest Austin is the first adjudication of Section 5 after Congress extended it in 2006. The case involves a tiny municipal district raising large questions and presented major implications for the VRA, federalism, checks and balances, and minority political power. The first question raised in this case was whether Section 5's bailout provision must be applied to a subdivision that, like *Northwest Austin,* does not register voters. Here, appellants sought not to strike down Section 5 altogether but to allow subdivisions within a covered region to be exempted from coverage. The second question was the perennial one of whether Section 5 is a valid exercise of Congress's enforcement power under the Fifteenth Amendment.

The timing of *Northwest Austin* is significant because it is one of the first major voting rights issues brought to the Court under Chief Justice John Roberts's leadership, arriving, as one observer put it, "at the intersection of . . . Roberts' past and the Supreme Court's future."[55] (At the time the case was argued, Roberts's position on the VRA was unclear. When questioned by Senator Ted Kennedy about his position on the act, Roberts responded that it was "an important legislative tool" to ensure the right to vote and that he had "no issue" with the fact that the "act's constitutionality ha[d] been upheld." He then noted that extending the VRA was "a separate question" on which, because the question was likely to come before the Court, he could not speak. He also echoed his support of the Reagan administration's preference for Section 2 to have an intent rather than an effects standard.)[56] The decision in this case is significant for the Court's deference to Congress regarding Section 5 and for the limitations of that deference. It is significant for its eight-to-one majority, which stands in stark contrast to the five-to-four majority in the cases discussed previously.[57] Finally, the case is significant in that both sides can claim some victory.

Appellants and opponents of Section 5 can claim victory because the Court held that the North Austin Metro district—and all political subdivisions beyond those enumerated in the VRA—are eligible for bailout from the provision. Writing for the majority, Roberts concluded that "specific precedent, the structure of the VRA," and underlying (albeit unspecified) constitutional concerns "compel a broader reading of the bailout provision." Under this reading, once a state has been designated for Section 5 coverage, the "definition of political subdivision has no operative significance in determining the reach" of that provision. Here, the Court based its rationale on what it understood as Congress's 1982 "embrace of piecemeal bailout" rather than a more comprehensive concept of it. Consequently, the Court rejected the U.S. attorney general's position as appellee—a position that echoed Congress's 2006 approach—as an "untenable" interpretation of the bailout provision that rendered it "all but a nullity." With respect to federalism, the opinion affirmed the appellant's position that "current" burdens that the VRA imposes on states must be justified by "current" needs, based on the recognition that "the evil that Section 5 is meant to address may no longer be concentrated in the jurisdictions singled out for preclearance." Finally, Roberts noted that the VRA's effect on federalism has generated "serious misgivings" on the Court. In particular, Section 5's scrutiny of "*all* changes to state election law—however innocuous" goes beyond the ambit of the Fifteenth Amendment's enforcement mechanism.[58]

Proponents of Section 5, especially the CBC, can claim victory because the Court declined the plaintiffs' invitation to strike down the provision altogether. After recounting the genesis and development of the VRA, Roberts emphasized the "undeniable" success of the act. He then confirmed that Congress established a sufficient record to justify extending Section 5, in keeping with the *Boerne* precedent that called for such a record. "Keenly mindful" of its power of judicial review, the Court declined to decide on Section 5's constitutionality as long as other political "ground[s] on which to dispose of the case" existed. On this point, Roberts pointedly rejected Justice Clarence Thomas's claim that "the principle of constitutional avoidance" did not prevent the Court from striking down Section 5.[59] At the same time, the opinion repeated that the preclearance requirement raises serious constitutional questions and that the provision only barely satisfies the Court's imperative that the VRA's remedies must be proportional to the ills they treat.[60]

As with the *Grutter v. Bollinger* affirmative action decision, the *Northwest Austin* majority cast the purpose of VRA in a preventive, forward-looking rather than remedial light. In so doing, Chief Justice Roberts glossed over the CBC's concerns regarding and evidence of the tenuous nature of Section 5's success. With its call for a "broader" and more "current" reading of the VRA in this case, the decision essentially fortified the *Miller* and *Shaw v. Hunt* holdings that Congress's intent for the act was "incorrect." Thus, the *Northwest Austin* majority's affirmation of the constitutionality of Section 5 is negated somewhat by the justices' hesitant support of the provision. Several other aspects of the opinion signal an aversion to Section 5. For example, Roberts pointed out that pre-clearance is determined by federal authorities in Washington, D.C., as opposed to local authorities. He also emphasized the "stringent" nature of the act's purpose of rooting out not just electoral discrimination but "flagrant" discrimination." He did not, however, acknowledge Texas's long history of discrimination against Latino and black voters, the states' rights concept of federalism that frustrates local enforcement of Section 5, or the fact that flagrant discrimination has been replaced by subtle but no less harmful forms.[61] Thus what initially appears as congruence between the Court and the CBC on Section 5 masks the same disagreement that has existed between them since the 1990s districting cases. Likewise, what initially sounds like judicial deference to legislative intent portends future restriction of "extraordinary legislation otherwise unfamiliar to our federal system."[62]

Conclusion

Since the 1990s, the Court majority has applied the Fourteenth Amendment to cases involving race and redistricting in a manner that invites conflicts among the three branches of the federal government.[63] Although the Court does not explicitly refer to the CBC or any of its amicus arguments in its opinions, the Court's decisions clearly reject the CBC's position in these cases, along with the CBC's and Congress's intent for the VRA. The Court majority has also rejected the Justice Department's interpretation of Section 5 of the act. The 2009 decision in *Northwest Austin* suggests that the Roberts Court may embark on a similar trajectory regarding the most recent extension of Section 5. For example, in 2009, the same Court majority restricted the scope of Section 2 by holding in *Bartlett v. Strickland* that the provision does not compel states to consider race when districting for state legislatures, county boards, city councils, and school districts in regions where blacks do not make up a voting majority of the population. The majority also held that Section 2 does not compel states to draw "crossover" districts in such instances (districts that depend on white crossover voters to elect the minority's candidate of choice). Because the *Bartlett* ruling does not apply to congressional districting, its implications may be limited; however, it suggests that the Court, at least as currently constituted, will continue to constrain states' race-conscious efforts to comply with the VRA.

The debates between the CBC and the Court majority illuminate inherent tensions in the balance of powers as well as federalism. With its exclusively color-blind interpretations of the Fourteenth Amendment and the VRA, the Court majority has checked congressional power to protect racial and ethnic minorities against racially and ethnically discriminatory electoral processes. In so doing, it has violated the framers' intent for both laws. A corollary tension exists between the Court and the executive branch—specifically, the Justice Department's race-conscious and results-oriented administration of the VRA. Again, in these respects, the Court majority's invalidation of Congress's and the DOJ's interpretations of the VRA has shifted the balance of power in favor of the Court. Similarly, federalism tensions are exacerbated by the Court's restriction of state power to draw benign racial gerrymanders to remedy existing and prevent further electoral discrimination. With respect to protecting minority political power, these decisions skew the system of federalism as they undermine the VRA.

In condemning the districting at issue in *Shaw v. Reno,* Justice O'Connor quoted a rather sarcastic quip in a study by an eminent voting rights expert of North Carolina's districting plan, "Ask not for whom the line is drawn; it is drawn to avoid thee."[64] This perspective, however, allows the majority to blind itself to an equally important point of view, that of a black voter in North Carolina, who might respond, "Ask not for whom the line is drawn; it is drawn to include me."[65] The majority's invocation of this quip is also misleading in that it suggests that the author of the article disapproved of the North Carolina districting plan in particular and race-based districting in general. In fact the author, Bernard Grofman, has expressed mixed views about this issue. On the one hand, he has argued that racially driven problems call for race-conscious remedies. He has also argued that district shapes should be allowed to accommodate irregular topographical features (such as those found in North Carolina) that make it difficult to draw compact, contiguous district boundaries. On the other hand, he considers what amounts to surgical carving of highly irregularly shaped districts to pick up as many minority voters as possible to be constitutionally suspect. To reconcile the problem of a scattered minority population with the Court's requirement for geographical compactness, Grofman has proposed creating a "cognizability standard," or "the ability to characterize the district boundaries in a manner that can be readily communicated to ordinary citizens of the district in commonsense terms based on geographical referents."[66] However, this standard would do little for minority voters who have common political interests but are geographically dispersed, such as those in North Carolina.

If the Court majority considered more perspectives and factors—all of which the CBC articulated in its amicus briefs—it might have had more difficulty presuming that all race-conscious districting is invidious. It might also open the Court as a whole to a more heterodox approach to race, law, and democracy. Although this point might be perceived as wide-eyed optimism, potential exists for it on the Court majority. In his memoir, Justice Thomas repeatedly extols the virtues of heterodox over orthodox thinking, although he tends to take this approach more to his general thinking about race than to his interpretation of the Equal Protection Clause.[67] For the interests of racial minorities, a constitutionally hetero-dox approach that includes race consciousness is preferable to the major-ity's ostensibly neutral perspective that reflects only one point of view and that is more blind to the reality of persisting racial discrimination than to race itself. This in turn raises the question of whether neutrality itself is overrated as the ideal approach to solving the problem of racial inequality. To borrow from Martin Luther King Jr., a Court that is "so objectively an-alytical that it is not subjectively committed" to eradicating or remedying racial discrimination may actually hinder America's ability to stride to-ward racial equality.[68]

In some very important respects, the Court and the CBC occupy two sides of the same coin of debate over race, law, and representation. Both contingents are disturbed by the political inequities that exist between blacks and whites. Both would like to level the electoral playing field for historically disadvantaged minorities. At the risk of oversimplification, these issues boil down to whether to adopt a long- or short-term ap-proach. The Court majority promotes color-blind electoral processes that may gradually yield more egalitarian political outcomes and a society where race no longer matters.[69] The CBC champions a speedier process toward political and other aspects of equality, which in its view requires more aggressive race-conscious methods. In *Shaw v. Reno*, the Court noted North Carolina's (and the CBC's subsequent) claim that the delib-erate creation of majority-minority districts is the most effective if not the only way to overcome long-term and persistent effects of racially polar-ized voting.[70] However, the majority declined to settle the question in that case and subsequently retreated from that observation in *Shaw v. Hunt* and *Georgia v. Ashcroft*. Congress attempted to settle this question when it revised the VRA in 2006, motivated in part to check the Court's decision in *Georgia v. Ashcroft*. Soon thereafter, however, the Court returned fire in *Bartlett v. Strickland* regarding Section 2, positioning itself to do the same after *Northwest Austin v. Holder* with respect to Section 5.

The Court closed *Miller* by dismissing as "short-sighted" the DOJ's and the CBC's race-conscious intent for the VRA.[71] Not surprisingly, the cau-cus has in turn condemned the Court's color-blind approach to racial dis-crimination as short-sighted. These competing perspectives are illustrated by the Court's faith in the ideal of color blindness versus the caucus's grounding in the reality of race consciousness. This includes the reality that racially polarized voting results in part from fear and mistrust of black candidates.[72] The majority's closing comments in *Miller* indicate its tendency toward idealism: "Only if our political system and our society cleanse themselves of . . . discrimination will all members of the polity share an equal opportunity to gain public office regardless of race."[73] Based on the arguments put forth by the CBC in its amicus briefs, it would likely reverse the phrasing of the Court's appeal: Only if all members of the polity acquire a realistic, equal opportunity to gain public office will our political system and society achieve the ideal of cleansing itself of discrimination against racial minority candidates. In other words, color blindness is but one means toward egalitarianism, not the end in and of itself.

Prior to the passage of the VRA, racial discrimination against blacks, especially in the South, was rampant. With the exception of the truly redemptive but brief Reconstruction era, few southern blacks were able to vote, and fewer still were elected to public office until after 1965. Thanks to the VRA and to an activist Supreme Court that supported the act and subsequent amendments of it, the number of African American elected officials has increased significantly. However, fractious racial bloc voting between both blacks and whites remains more the norm than the exception in many regions. The uncomfortable reality is that racial identification, both affirmative and invidious, is still strong in the American polity. The Court has obviously come a very long way from its thinking in *Plessy v. Ferguson*. Yet the majority's unyielding commitment to color blindness may be too much of a good thing if, like the *Shaw* precedent, such commitment fosters stereotypical and potentially retrogressive decision making or if it undermines the original intent of the Fourteenth Amendment and the VRA. The following and final chapter will compare contemporary minority voting rights jurisprudence to the Court's initial interpretations of that amendment. It will emphasize the salience of those interpretations, along with early black political thought, to contemporary legal debates over race, voting rights, and representation.

6 | Reconciling the Present with the Past

"This so-called democracy has failed the Negro. . . . [T]he entire civil
rights struggle needs a . . . broader interpretation. We need to look at
this civil rights thing from another angle—from the inside as well as
the outside . . . a new interpretation to the civil rights struggle that
will enable us to come into it, take part in it."

—Malcolm X

Revisiting the Supreme Court's First Interpretations of
the Fourteenth Amendment

This book has explored the cross fire between the Congressional Black
Caucus (CBC) and the Supreme Court majority over the role of race in redistricting, representation, and law. This cross fire is triggered by institutional debates over color blindness and race consciousness. What is the best
method to eradicate racial discrimination and promote racial equality?
Does color blindness guarantee equality? Under what circumstances is race
consciousness constitutional? This book has emphasized the Court majority's overreliance on color blindness in key redistricting cases. It has also attempted to illustrate the general confusion over both concepts. Even a cursory examination of the rhetoric of black leaders from the antebellum era
to the CBC indicates that color blindness has never been their sole or ultimate goal. The goal has been, and continues to be, racial equality, with
color blindness but one means toward that end. Accordingly, black leaders
have consistently endorsed race-based approaches to racial equality, as exemplified by the caucus's position with Congress and the Court regarding
redistricting and the Voting Rights Act (VRA). For its part, the Court majority endorses color blindness as the ultimate goal based on the presump-
tion that color blindness will automatically lead to racial equality. In the

process, the justices tend to equate race-conscious districting with racist districting. These distinctions between means and ends and between race consciousness and racism tend to be lost on the Court majority.

Since the landmark *Brown v. Board of Education* decision, the Court has superimposed its concept of color blindness onto the Fourteenth Amendment with respect to redistricting and increasingly treats race consciousness as antithetical to that amendment. This chapter explores the Court's earliest interpretations of that amendment and compares them to the Court's current applications of the Equal Protection Clause to cases involving race and redistricting. In the spirit of Malcolm X's aspiration, I argue that early black political thought—considered with the Court's initial approach to the Fourteenth Amendment—offers a "broader interpretation" and a suitable fulcrum on which to balance contemporary tensions over race, law, and minority political power.

The Fourteenth Amendment stipulates that certain rights may not be abridged by the state on the basis of color. As written, it applies to individuals and classes of individuals. Similarly, the Fifteenth Amendment classifies by race, color, and previous condition of servitude. These first two classifications include people of African descent, while the third applies exclusively to them. The congressional record of the framing of the Fifteenth Amendment indicates that it "was to be as capable of growth as the capacity of Americans to mature."[1] Under the principle of color blindness, the Court's decisions in *Shaw v. Reno, Miller v. Johnson,* and *Shaw v. Hunt* have hollowed out the Fourteenth and Fifteenth Amendments.[2] As asserted by the CBC during legislative deliberations and in its amicus curiae briefs, a color-blind approach to racial equality risks perpetuating existing inequities. The caucus does not hold that color blindness is invalid or that it should be abandoned. It has contended instead that minority voting rights cases call for the Court to look squarely at rather than beyond race. In the CBC's view, to simply will away race-based measures— as demonstrated by Chief Justice John Roberts's facile conclusion that "the way to stop discrimination on the basis of race is to stop discriminating on the basis of race"—is not merely wishful thinking but also potentially harmful thinking.[3]

The Court rightly recognizes that the institutions of slavery and segregation were premised on and designed to promote white supremacy and acknowledges the judicial branch's complicity in decisions such as *Dred Scott v. Sandford,* the *Civil Rights Cases,* and *Plessy v. Ferguson.* Since rejecting these decisions, however, it has tended to overcompensate by presuming that all racial classifications are suspect, regardless of their intent. In the process, it overlooks its earlier, egalitarian race-conscious precedents. For example, shortly before the *Brown* decision, the Court struck down white-only primaries and political parties as well as segregated colleges with relatively race-conscious rationales.[4] Several decades earlier, in the *Slaughter-House Cases* and *Strauder v. West Virginia,* the Court held that Congress intended for the Fourteenth Amendment to protect the civil rights of freed blacks both as individuals and as a class. Since then the Court has expanded the scope of the amendment to encompass other racial, ethnic, gender, sexuality, and wealth classifications. The Court's initial race-conscious precedents remain instructive for contemporary litigation involving the use of race in redistricting, especially when color-blind measures alone are not enough to remedy or prevent minority vote dilution.

The Slaughter-House Cases *(1873)*

The *Slaughter-House Cases* were the first to invoke the Fourteenth Amendment. This combined litigation was adjudicated during the rise of the Industrial Revolution, arguably paving the way for the Court's development of doctrine of economic due process that insulated private enterprise from state and federal interference.[5] The chief emphasis on this case is usually given to the Court's nearly fatal constriction of the Fourteenth Amendment's Privileges or Immunities Clause. As a result, the significance of its race-conscious rationale tends to be overlooked. Yet that aspect of the decision is a vital reminder that the Fourteenth Amendment was primarily intended to protect "the slave race." At issue in this litigation was a Louisiana statute, passed in response to a cholera epidemic, to consolidate all of New Orleans's slaughterhouses into a single private facility. Individual butchers were required to use this facility, including payment of a fee for use. The resulting monopoly effectively dispossessed the city's individual butchers. In challenging the statute, the butchers argued that it violated the Due Process, Equal Protection, and Privileges or Immunities Clauses of the Fourteenth Amendment. They also contended that it violated the involuntary servitude clause of the Thirteenth Amendment.

In adjudicating these amendments for the first time, the Court quickly dispensed with the butchers' Thirteenth Amendment claim. It did so based on a decidedly race-conscious reading of that amendment that also reflected the history behind and framers' intent for it:

> To withdraw the mind from the contemplation of this grand yet simple *declaration of the personal freedom . . . of four millions of*

slaves—and with a microscopic search endeavor to find in it a reference to servitudes which may have been attached to property in certain localities requires an effort, to say the least ... [T]he *obvious* purpose [of the Thirteenth Amendment] was to forbid all shades and conditions of African slavery.[6]

With this rationale, the Court distinguished between the founding fathers' concept of slavery and chattel slavery; where the former constrained one's freedom to *do*, the latter constrained one's freedom to *be*.

The Court then turned to what the Fourteenth Amendment meant for the system of federalism, particularly the degree to which it protected citizens from state as opposed to federal infringement on civil liberties. First, it distinguished between "citizenship of the United States, and a citizenship of a State, which are distinct from each other, and which depend upon different characteristics or circumstances in the individual."[7] In response to the appellants' claim that Louisiana's statute violated their privileges and immunities under the Fourteenth Amendment, the Court held that the scope of that clause was limited by the system of federalism:

Of the privileges and immunities of the citizen of the United States, and of [those of] the citizen of the State ... it is only the former which are placed by this clause under the protection of the Federal Constitution, and ... the latter, whatever they may be, are not intended to have any additional protection by [it].[8]

In response to the butchers' equal protection claim, the Court declared,

Under no construction of that provision that we have ever seen, or any that we deem admissible, can the restraint imposed by the State of Louisiana upon the exercise of their trade by the butchers of New Orleans be held to be a deprivation of property within the meaning of that provision.[9]

Noting repeatedly that the primary (although not the sole) intended beneficiaries of the Fourteenth Amendment were former slaves and their descendants, both as individuals and as a class, the Court rejected the butchers' claim of a right to equal protection and due process under the amendment.

The most cursory glance at these [Reconstruction] articles discloses a unity of purpose ... the freedom of the slave race. ....

[O]n the most casual examination of the language of these amendments, no one can fail to be impressed with the one pervading purpose found in them all, lying at the foundation of each, and without which none of them would have been even suggested; we mean the freedom of the slave race . . . and the protection of the newly-made freeman and citizen from the oppressions of those who had formerly exercised unlimited dominion over him. It is true that only the Fifteenth Amendment, in terms, mentions the negro by speaking of his color and his slavery. But it is just as true that each of the other articles was addressed to the grievances of that race.[10]

In upholding Louisiana's statute, the Court did far more than limit the scope of the Fourteenth Amendment. It signaled its disinclination to shift the system of federalism further than the amendment already had. The Court also emphasized the framers' intent for the Fourteenth Amendment to protect newly emancipated blacks from state "laws which imposed upon the colored race onerous disabilities and burdens, and curtailed their rights in the pursuit of life, liberty, and property to such an extent that their freedom was of little value."[11] Paradoxically, in limiting the scope of the amendment in this manner, the Court propped open a door through which states could infringe on blacks' civil rights. Yet its initial affirmation of the race-conscious intent for the amendment remains relevant to contemporary voting rights decisions and is instrumental to keeping the door open to affirmative uses of race to remedy or offset persisting racial discrimination in the electoral realm.

Strauder v. West Virginia (1879)

This case was decided shortly after the pivotal Hayes Compromise of 1877. Unlike the *Slaughter-House Cases*, which involved a statute that had nothing to do with race, *Strauder* was about a West Virginia statute stipulating that "all white male persons who are twenty-one years of age and who are citizens of this State shall be liable to serve as jurors, except as herein provided. The persons excepted are State officials."[12] Strauder, a black man convicted of murder by an all-white jury, claimed that the statute denied him the same benefit of West Virginia's laws as white citizens enjoyed, thereby violating the Equal Protection Clause. The chief legal question for the Court was whether the Fourteenth Amendment was violated when "in the composition or selection of jurors . . . all persons of [the defendant's] race or color may be excluded by law, solely because of their race or color, so that by no possibility can any colored man sit upon the jury."[13]

In addressing this question, the Court first acknowledged the potential negative ramifications of this law for black defendants:

> It is hard to see why the statute . . . should not be regarded as discriminating against a colored man. . . . It is not easy to comprehend how it can be said that while every white man is entitled to a trial by a jury selected from persons of his own race . . . and a negro is not, the latter is equally protected by the law with the former.[14]

Invoking *The Slaughter-House* precedent, the Court asserted that

> the true spirit and meaning of the [Reconstruction] amendments . . . cannot be understood without keeping in view the history of the times when they were adopted, and the general objects they plainly sought to accomplish. [The Fourteenth Amendment] was designed to assure to the colored race the enjoyment of all the civil rights that under the law are enjoyed by white persons [and] denied to any State the power to withhold from them the equal protection of the laws.[15]

Here, the Court did more than simply extend the precedent of the *Slaughter-House Cases*. It bolstered its race-conscious interpretation of the Fourteenth Amendment in that decision by reminding litigants of the unique historical and political contexts surrounding its ratification. It also affirmed the notion of equality inherent in that amendment by explicitly equating the civil rights of blacks to those of whites. Finally, it emphasized the remedial aspects of the amendment:

> The framers of the constitutional amendment must have known full well the existence of [racial] prejudice and its likelihood to continue against the manumitted slaves and their race, and that knowledge was doubtless a motive that led to the amendment. . . . Without the apprehended existence of prejudice [the Equal Protection Clause] would have been unnecessary, and it might have been left to the States to extend equality of protection.[16]

With this affirmation, the Court closed the door that the *Slaughter-House* decision had opened for states to discriminate against their citizens. In exchange, however, the justices left ajar several other doors through which states could do so. For example, the Court interpreted the Constitution to allow states to

> confine the selection to males, to freeholders, to citizens, to persons within certain ages, or to persons having educational qualifications. We do not believe the Fourteenth Amendment was ever intended to prohibit this.[17]

History is of course replete with evidence of how states availed themselves of the opportunity to restrict blacks' and others' civil rights. The *Civil Rights Cases* and *Plessy v. Ferguson* exemplify the growing tolerance, on the Court and more broadly, of facially neutral laws that effectively discriminated against blacks. Disfranchising tactics such as literacy and interpretation tests, poll taxes, registration requirements, and character assessments became ubiquitous throughout the South. The Court's initially narrow and race-conscious reading of the Fourteenth Amendment also contrasts sharply with the broad penumbra of rights and classifications it has subsequently come to protect. Again, I am not calling for an abandonment of the concept of color blindness or of color-blind interpretations of the Constitution. I am, however, calling for strict color-blind constitutionalists and adherents of originalism to acknowledge that the Fourteenth Amendment was not originally intended by all of its framers to preclude race-conscious remedies to racial discrimination, and that the Court did not always interpret the amendment in such a manner. As chapter 4 demonstrates, the CBC went through great lengths in its amicus briefs for *Miller v. Johnson* and *Shaw v. Hunt* to point out that the amendment's "design was to protect an emancipated race."[18] In her dissent in *Miller*, Justice Ruth Bader Ginsburg also contrasted *Strauder's* race- and group-based rationale to subsequent precedents that have taken a more individualist approach to the Fourteenth Amendment.[19] Despite these reminders, today's Court majority declines to acknowledge these precedents.

As discussed in chapter 1, the concept of color blindness has evolved from a lone, unpopular position on the Supreme Court into one of America's most vaunted ideals. The *Plessy* decision was a national validation of a regional racial caste system. Coming on the heels of crushed opportunity for a more fully inclusive democracy, Justice John Marshall Harlan challenged the Court to commit itself to both the principle and practice of equality.

The Court majority ignored Harlan's challenge for nearly two decades before beginning to alter its approach to the equal protection of blacks, starting with its invalidation of the use of grandfather clauses to trigger literacy tests in *Guinn v. U.S.* Today, not only does the Court majority hold the Constitution to be color-blind, but its rulings in the 1990s districting cases, especially *Shaw v. Reno,* suggest that society has reached that point as well. Indeed, America has become more egalitarian over the past century and has the Court to thank for much of this progress. Efforts by all levels and branches of government to equalize the political landscape have been instrumental in paving the way to more diverse legislatures, judiciaries, and bureaucracies and finally to the election of an African American president. Despite these important accomplishments, however, American society is not color-blind—or, to use a more current term, postracial. Racial and other forms of discrimination remain deeply entrenched in our society, as do profound inequities with respect to political power, wealth, educational attainment, health, crime, and incarceration rates. These realities call for a rethinking of the concepts of both race and equality, including reinvigorating the *Slaughter-House Cases* and *Strauder* and contemporary precedents that are more open to race-conscious interpretations of the law.

From Ideals to Realities

In its minority voting right decisions, the Court majority has held fast to color blindness, in part because the concept is seen to comport with the core American value of individualism. For example, in *Shaw v. Reno,* the majority emphasized that "the individual is important, not his race, his creed or his color."[20] In *Miller v. Johnson,* the Court held that "the Government must treat citizens as individuals, not as simply components of a racial . . . class."[21] Justice Ginsburg dissented from such conclusions, noting that

> In adopting districting plans, . . . States do not treat people as individuals. Apportionment schemes, by their very nature, assemble people in groups. . . . If Chinese-Americans and Russian-Americans may seek and secure group recognition in the delineation of voting districts, then African-Americans should not be dissimilarly treated. Otherwise, in the name of equal protection, we would shut out the very minority group whose history in the United States gave birth to the Equal Protection Clause.[22]

In *Shaw v. Hunt*, the Court repeated that racial classifications are antithetical to the Fourteenth Amendment.[23] With this line of reasoning, the majority did not simply pave over its early race- and group-conscious interpretations of the Fourteenth Amendment in the *Slaughter-House Cases* and *Strauder*. It evaded the reality that collective wrongs at times require collective remedies. It also overlooked the fundamental pluralist precept that, as Ginsburg dissented, political interests are most often expressed on a group basis. The gist of the *Shaw* legacy is that the Court majority treated blacks differently from whites: While whites can claim that their right to equal protection is violated when race is a factor in creating oddly shaped majority-black districts, blacks remain vulnerable to the same harm when they are the minority in an oddly shaped majority-white district. Not only does this outcome protect white dominance, it "undermines the promise of political equality contained in the Fourteenth Amendment and Fifteenth Amendments . . . and the VRA."[24]

The concept of color blindness is noble. Yet while America should be proud of its progress toward equality, it must recognize that this goal is far from accomplished. In this respect, the Court's presumptive skepticism of nearly all uses of race is premature. As early black leaders and the CBC have pointed out, the difference between ideal and reality is key. For the Court to almost blithely apply the ideal of color blindness to a society in which racism is still a reality is problematic. So, conversely, is the majority's hostility to benign uses of race to remedy invidious uses. To the extent that color blindness can lead to blindness to invidious uses of race, the approach potentially harms precisely the people it is supposed to protect.

The Court acknowledged these paradoxes when it confirmed in 2003 that diversity remains a compelling reason to take race into account when admitting students to graduate programs. Still, its anticipation that such uses would be obsolete in twenty-five years reveals its unwillingness to grapple fully with the fact that race remains salient in American society. The February 2009 remarks of attorney general Eric Holder and the ensuing controversy over them illustrate this point: "To get to the heart of this country one must examine its racial soul. . . . [I]n things racial we have always been and continue to be, in too many ways, essentially a nation of cowards. . . . [W]e, average Americans, simply do not talk enough with each other about race."[25] Rather than clarify the complexities of race and representation, the Court majority's exclusively color-blind voting rights jurisprudence exacerbates them by papering egalitarian ideals over starkly unequal realities.[26] The conclusion that "racial gerrymander[s] may exacerbate the very patterns of racial bloc voting that majority-minority districting is sometimes said to counteract" illustrates how easy it is to conflate the causes of racial divisiveness with the effects of it.[27] Moreover, the justices have not come to terms with the fact that black leaders, legislators, and scholars have long pointed out: African Americans still share beliefs and a sense of racial commonality that override class divisions and geographic dispersion.[28] By revisiting its initial interpretations of the Fourteenth Amendment in the *Slaughter-House Cases* and *Strauder,* the majority might resolve these tensions in a way that comports with an originalist interpretation of the Constitution.

From Conflicting to Complementary Approaches to Race and Representation

Some observers have lamented that the Court has advanced minority interests at the expense of those of the majority. According to this view, the founding fathers never intended the judiciary to be a "continuing constitutional convention" that subverts the will of the people. A related contention is that the conflicting concepts of equality among the Fourteenth Amendment's framers prove that they did not intend for the Equal Protection Clause to be interpreted as broadly as the Warren and subsequent Courts have done. This position raises questions about whether the *Brown* Court could legitimately outlaw segregation by wielding its power to correct an evil that the majority of the people were not ready to cure. Should such "government by judiciary" become necessary, it can only be legitimately granted by the people, ostensibly through popular demands or sustained social movement activism.[29]

Others hold that the Court is expected to insulate minority rights from the majority's curtailment of them. Rather than condemn the Court for betraying the will of the people, this view condemns its advancement of a "veiled majoritarian" agenda at the expense of minority interests. From this perspective, *Brown* and the Court's civil rights activism of the 1960s–70s are exceptions to its otherwise majoritarian decision making. These exceptions, moreover, have appropriately contributed to the Court's jurisprudence of minority rights and to the public policies that emerge from these decisions. Hence, the problem does not rest solely with a majoritarian Supreme Court. It also rests with "the people"—specifically, racial and ethnic minorities. In other words, minorities (along with liberal law and policy makers) overly rely on the Court's protective capacity without sufficiently acknowledging its majoritarian tendencies. Taking this point further, *Brown* effectively lulled protected classes into dependence on a periodically sympathetic judiciary at the expense of the pursuit of direct political power and influence. Evidence of the Court's majoritarian tendencies in its minority voting rights jurisprudence is seen in its key precedent, *Shaw v. Reno*, which is largely premised on demeaning and counterproductive stereotypes about racial minorities. Not only are such opinions at odds with the spirit of the Equal Protection Clause, but they also prevent such protection from existing. The remedies for this problem are threefold: (1) minorities must "relinquish their vulnerability" to a Court that cannot not sufficiently protect their interests, (2) minorities must more effectively press their perspective to the Court when litigation is the only option, (3) minorities must step up their political participation.[30]

Through a selectively originalist interpretation of the Fourteenth Amendment in the 1990s districting cases and the assumption that "even in the pursuit of remedial objectives, an explicit policy of assignment by race may serve to stimulate our society's latent race consciousness," the Court majority has contributed to a nearly wholesale condemnation of race-based remedies to racial discrimination.[31] As many members of Congress noted during the 2006 reauthorization of the VRA, the result is a series of fractured and increasingly complex decisions that are also difficult precedents to follow. These problems are exacerbated by two others. First, by failing to acknowledge the fundamental differences between race consciousness and racism, the Court appears motivated to avoid the specter of "reverse racism." This concept is in several ways a red herring. For example, to characterize a state's remedial use of race as reverse racism implies that because "traditional" racism has been the norm, it is somehow less objectionable than "reverse" instances of it. It is a stretch to equate racial classifications intended to remedy the effects of oppressive laws and practices with racism when such classifications are not motivated by racial animus or supremacy. Rarely are condemnations of reverse racism accompanied by condemnations of traditional racism, much less with the same vigor. Accusations of reverse racism also seem to presume that at least since the civil rights movement, the effects of white racism have been nearly eradicated, thus obviating the need for remedial uses of race. At their worst, such accusations lead to "bankrupt" color-blind voting rights jurisprudence that shows "undue solicitude for white voters' prerogatives," creates a racial double standard, and ultimately treats minority voters unequally.[32] If one subscribes to the definition of racism as a deviation from a universal norm of fairness and equality, one must then acknowledge that racism can be practiced by anyone with the power to disadvantage or impose his will onto others.[33] By this definition, the oppression of whites by nonwhites would simply be racism, not "reverse" racism.

Second, by relying on just a few dozen of Martin Luther King Jr.'s words, often taken out of context, color-blind constitutionalists engage in a semantic sleight of hand. Michael Eric Dyson expounded on this problem several years ago in his observation that those who invoke King's "I Have a Dream" speech to oppose affirmative action ignore King's race-conscious analyses of America's racial dilemma in that speech and in his other speeches and writings. Such selective references to the speech also miss what is effectively a call for reparations in the opening paragraphs of it. In his characteristically provocative manner, Dyson has proposed a ten-year moratorium on invocations of the speech, to be replaced with other selections from King. However, such a moratorium might defeat Dyson's purpose. Americans would benefit far more by reading the entire speech. This fuller reading of the piece along with King's other seminal writings and addresses would clearly reveal that he endorsed race-based approaches along with color-blind efforts to achieve his dream of racial equality.[34]

The Transformative Potential of Early Black Political Thought: From Ideological Outlier to Ideological Fulcrum

The fundamental tensions between the CBC and the Supreme Court over race consciousness and color blindness are not new. Black leaders have long engaged in similar debates over race, identity, and equality. These early debates remain relevant to contemporary American political and legal thought. Frederick Douglass, for example, tended to avoid race-conscious terms, at least until his split with women suffragists over the Fifteenth Amendment. He also tended to speak in individualist terms. For example, comparing himself to his race-conscious peer Martin Delany, Douglass declared, "I thank God for making me a man simply . . . but Delany always thanks Him for making him a black man."[35] Although Douglass did not eschew his blackness, he tended to be more individualist- than group-oriented, and racial group consciousness was secondary to his efforts to attain justice for all individuals, regardless of their identification. Yet Douglass's individualism conflicted not only with the realities of the chattel slavery but also with Jim Crow's collective degradation of blacks. His individualism also conflicted with the race consciousness of many of his peers as well as those who rose to leadership after his death, including W. E. B. Du Bois.

It may seem odd to contrast Du Bois to Douglass in light of their shared commitment to integration. While Du Bois was indeed a staunch integrationist, he was a lifelong student of race. His efforts to deconstruct prevailing notions of racial hierarchy were inevitably race- and group-conscious, from his seminal theory of dualism—the existence in the blacks' psyche of a "two-ness . . . an American, a Negro . . . two unreconciled strivings, two warring ideals in one dark body"—to his advocacy of pan-Africanism in the latter decades of his long life.[36] Du Bois's theories are thus central to the evolution of a positive, *collective* black consciousness. He advocated integration not for its own sake but as a gauge to measure racial equality, and endorsed both race- and group-conscious means toward that end, the latter of which is evidenced by his involvement in both the Niagara Movement and the National Association for the Advancement of Colored People. While he considered integration a fundamental step toward racial equality, he was convinced that one's racial group identity anchored one's individual identity.[37] This perspective on race and racial identity comports with contemporary findings that among African Americans, racial group identity serves as a proxy for individual identity.[38] Du Bois's theories of race also reflect the spirit of the Supreme Court's first interpretations of the Fourteenth Amendment.

In 1920, Du Bois observed that the "discovery of personal whiteness among the world's peoples is a very modern thing." This observation emerged from his 1903 pronouncement that "the problem of the 20th century is the problem of the color line."[39] Often overlooked in Du Bois's writings is the idea that race is not in and of itself the problem. Rather, the drawing of that line—premised on notions of white supremacy—by whites around blacks was the problem. It is the same problem that the Supreme Court determined in the *Slaughter-House Cases* and *Strauder* that the Fourteenth Amendment was intended to prevent. Du Bois argued that an entire race "handicapped" by centuries of oppression "ought not to be asked to race with the world, but rather allowed to give its time and thought to its own social problems."[40] This point was later amplified by the civil rights and Black Power movements. More recently, the CBC reinforced this idea in its amicus briefs, specifically in the context of race-conscious districting. Also overlooked is that while Du Bois's theory of dualism describes a tortured sense of self, the concept of "two warring ideals" can be mutually enriching. For example, he envisioned a time when blacks and whites "may give . . . to each those characteristics both so sadly lack" in a world that was "wide enough for two colors, [and] for many little shinings of the sun."[41] This conceptualization of integration goes far beyond contemporary judicial and legislative discussions of it. Du Bois's concept of race consciousness bridges the gap with color blindness and reflects goals sought by early black leaders, the CBC and ostensibly the Supreme Court majority.

In this light, America might be destined for a third reconstruction, this time focused on the concept of representative democracy. Reconstructing American democracy for the third time would first require *de*constructing prevailing concepts of representation. In many respects, early black leaders such as David Walker, Martin Delany, Henry Highland Garnet, Henry McNeal Turner, and W. E. B. Du Bois attempted to do so. Whites at times denounced these leaders as seditious, even revolutionary. Given that black folk have been an indispensable component of American life since this nation's inception, their demands that the political system be transformed into one that respects and fully incorporates them into the body politic are predictable. What remains revolutionary is a concept of representation in which fair political outcomes are as important as equal political opportunities. After all, "in the end, it is the end that matters."[42] This is not a call for increased black political power at the expense of others. As the members of the CBC, their predecessors, and black scholars over time have repeatedly pointed out, an outcomes orientation is not about racial retribution, nor need it be a zero-sum prospect.

Throughout their participation in American life as both observers and elected officials, blacks have pursued policies that benefit African Americans as well as the larger populace. Examples of inclusive legislation proposed by black Reconstruction leaders include public funding for schools and hospitals, prison reform, and land redistribution. In the latter stages of the civil rights movement, Martin Luther King Jr. proposed a racially inclusive, class-oriented "Bill of Rights for the Disadvantaged." King emphasized that in addition to blacks, "millions of white poor . . . would also benefit from such a bill" and that it was a "simple matter of justice that America, in dealing with the task of raising the Negro from backwardness, should also be rescuing . . . the forgotten white poor."[43] A little over a decade later, in 1978, the CBC helped realize this aspect of King's dream when it cosponsored the Humphrey-Hawkins Act.[44] This act was notable for being "non-race-specific" and for "benefit[ing] whites as well as blacks." Although not a panacea, the act's intent and provisions clearly reflect one of the chief legacies of black Reconstruction legislators: an inclusive approach to black racial uplift.[45] Ten years after the passage of the Humphrey-Hawkins Act (borrowing heavily from black Reconstruction legislators' and later King's playbooks), sociologist William Julius Wilson advised black and other liberal legislators to pursue "the hidden agenda" of "improv[ing] the life chances of truly disadvantaged groups such as the ghetto underclass by emphasizing programs to which the *more advantaged* groups of *all* races . . . can positively relate."[46]

Contrary to perceptions that they would or could not measure up to the task, black legislators have demonstrated all of the representational styles laid out by Hannah Pitkin in her classic study of representation. They are *descriptive* representatives in that they racially and in many cases socially "correspond in composition with the community" of newly enfranchised blacks. They *stand for* the interests of their black constituents in a way that many white legislators have been unable or unwilling to do. They provide important *symbolic* representation in that they succeed in "foster[ing] belief, loyalty, [and] satisfaction with their leaders, [and] among the people" that they represent, including but not limited to blacks. Black legislators perform the function of *trustee* by legislating less as a result of direct constituent influences and more based on what they deem to be in these constituents' best interests. They also act as *agents* by representing the will of their more savvy and more expressive constituents.[47] In sum (and to the chagrin of those who would prefer more progressive or innovative approaches), black representatives have largely acted in a very conventional manner, even under very unconventional circumstances, such as the Reconstruction era. Contrary to the Court majority's trepidations over minority representation of minority constituents in *Shaw v. Reno,* African American legislators have pursued substantively egalitarian and universal goals as part of their race-conscious approach to representation.

The ratification of the Fourteenth and Fifteenth Amendments enabled blacks to demonstrate their capacity to be rational political actors. It took a century, along with a full-blown civil rights movement and several acts of Congress, to enforce those rights. After a little over one generation of greatly increased political opportunities, African American political outcomes remain decidedly unequal, and the overall status of blacks still lags behind that of whites and most other American racial and ethnic groups. There is no disputing the significant gains in political activity and power that have occurred since the civil rights movement. At the same time, there is little disputing the idea that black political influence remains limited largely to urban regions with high concentrations of African Americans. It also continues to depend on its historically complicated relationship with the Democratic Party and on the occasionally precarious racial and ethnic coalitions within the party, which, taken together, make the

CBC's job of representing African Americans' political interests extremely challenging.[48] It is thus clear that equal opportunities alone have not been sufficient to offset the effects of contemporary racism and discrimination, much less the damage done by more than three centuries of slavery and racial oppression.

Because traditional pluralism tends to be premised on all things being equal, it does not hold the same promise for African Americans as it does for other populations. Some observers have contended that the theory better applies to African Americans as they increase their access to the ballot, enter politics, and influence the formation of public policies that address their interests.[49] Such arguments are often grounded in the fact that the black electorate has grown in size and influence since the passage of the VRA. In the context of an opportunity orientation and in an *absolute* sense, this statement is true. The number of black elected officials has also grown sharply since the passage of the act. However, when evaluated from an outcomes-oriented and *relative* perspective, pluralism falls short, especially with respect to the degree of black political power and influence. For example, absolute black gains in political access are remarkable largely because they started so close to zero. When compared to other racial and ethnic minority groups that have made a faster and more complete entry into American society, African Americans have not made comparable gains in political, social, and economic outcomes. At the national level, blacks, particularly in the House and the executive branch, have an unprecedented presence. However, blacks still comprise only about 3 percent of all elected officials, compared to roughly 13 percent of the overall population. In sum, whether the glass of black political outcomes is half empty or half full depends on whether one is measuring absolute or relative changes in blacks' political status.

This point returns us to earlier discussions of the tension between individual and group perspectives when theorizing about representation. Pluralism allows for group identities but assumes that those identities are mutable and cut across racial and ethnic lines. However, while racial interests and identities can be flexible, race as a legal construct is not.[50] Moreover, because race remains central in American society, it is likely that most African Americans will continue to espouse a racialized concept of representation. Like their nineteenth-century counterparts, contemporary African American political leaders likely will gauge equality of representation by political and social outcomes for the race as a whole rather than by improved opportunities for individuals. In an opportunity-oriented individualist world, the glass of political outcomes appears to be half full, if not at times overflowing. But again, from an outcomes-centered collective black perspective, the glass remains half empty at best.

Conclusion

If early black political thought were considered by more legislators and decision makers as a key political context variable, it might help ease the conflicts over how best to achieve racial equality. Black leaders since the early nineteenth century have consistently subscribed to the core American tenets of freedom, equality, and democracy even as they have endorsed them in a race- and group-conscious manner. A central tenet of black political thought is that it is indeed possible to accomplish racial equality and cooperation through remedially race-conscious measures. Black leaders from David Walker to Barack Obama have endorsed a balancing perspective by expressing the centrality of racial inequality to America's common concerns.[51] In the process, the CBC has consciously sought to balance political perspectives and power by revising the VRA and by presenting to the Court the merits of race-based districting. This body of thought thus offers the Supreme Court a useful ideological fulcrum on which to balance color-blind and race-conscious perspectives.

To the extent that black political thought is obviously limited to a "black/white jurisprudential paradigm," it does not speak to America's full diversity.[52] Still, it provides a rich and instructive narrative about American political development, law, and race relations. Indeed, increased familiarity with the voices of early black political thinkers demonstrates that they are not simply voices of the past. These voices do not speak solely about the black experience in America. The racial, political, and legal observations made by black leaders of the past offer thoughtful, nuanced, and cogent alternatives to the simplistic approaches that constrain contemporary debates regarding race, representation, and democracy in America. All Americans can learn and progress from these observations.

This book has illuminated the implicit but very real debates between the CBC (along with Congress more generally) and the Supreme Court majority over the role of race in a representative democracy. Should that majority become less hostile to race-based remedies for race-based ills, perhaps it will begin again to render decisions that will help restore the momentum of the "quiet revolution" that began with the passage of the VRA and that accelerated after the 1982 amendment to it. Ideally, this revolution would extend beyond the South to encompass the entire nation, strengthen the political power of black and other minority voters, endure without threat of retrogression in the span of a single generation, enhance the quality of democracy in America, and cease rather than continue the existing cross fires over race, law, and representation. Ideally, in the words of Langston Hughes, such a revolution would "let America be America again."[53]

Notes

INTRODUCTION

1. This book uses the terms *majority-minority districts* and *safe districts* interchangeably to refer to electoral districts purposely drawn to include a minority voting-age population of above 50 percent.

2. X, *Malcolm X Speaks*, 31.

3. King, *Where Do We Go from Here*, 23–66; King, *Why We Can't Wait*, 137–42.

4. These were common arguments among the nearly seventy amicus curiae briefs submitted on behalf of the University of Michigan and the nearly twenty such briefs submitted on behalf of the appellant, Barbara Grutter.

5. Balkin and Siegel, *Constitution in 2020*, 96.

6. States covered as a whole by Section 5 are Alabama, Alaska, Arizona, Georgia, Louisiana, Mississippi, South Carolina, Texas, and Virginia. States covered in part/by particular counties are California, Florida, New York, North Carolina, and South Dakota. Some townships in Michigan and New Hampshire are also covered by the provision. See http://www.justice.gov/crt/about/vot/sec_5/types.php (accessed April 4, 2012).

7. For such analyses, see Bositis, *Congressional Black Caucus*; Swain, *Black Faces, Black Interests*; Robert C. Smith, *We Have No Leaders*; Singh, *Congressional Black Caucus*; Bositis, *Redistricting and Minority Representation*; Paul Frymer, *Uneasy Alliances*; Fenno, *Going Home*; Tate, *Black Faces*; Bositis, *Voting Rights and Minority Representation*.

8. For such scholarship, see Grofman, Handley, and Niemi, *Minority Representation*; Davidson and Grofman, *Quiet Revolution in the South*; Guinier, *Tyranny of the Majority*; Lublin, *Paradox of Representation*; Grofman, *Race and Redistricting*; Clayton, *African-Americans and the Politics of Congressional Redistricting*; Galderisi, *Redistricting in the New Millennium*; Epstein, *Dividing Lines*.

9. Thorough assessments of the act can be found in Kousser, *Colorblind Injustice*; Epstein et al., *Future of the Voting Rights Act*; Epstein, *Dividing Lines*; Valelly, *Voting Rights Act*.

10. Most such analyses appear in law journals. See Aleinikoff and Issacharoff, "Drawing Constitutional Lines," 583–87; Guinier, "Groups, Representation, and Race-Conscious Districting"; A. Leon Higginbotham Jr., Clarick, and David, "*Shaw v. Reno*"; Karlan, "*Georgia v. Ashcroft*"; Persily, "Promises and Pitfalls"; Kousser, "Strange, Ironic Career."

11. Michael C. Dawson and Cathy Cohen, "Problems in the Study of the Politics of Race," in *Political Science*, ed. Katznelson and Milner, 488–510.

12. Balkin and Siegel, *Constitution in 2020*, 96–97 (original emphasis omitted).

13. Ibid., 96. See also A. Leon Higginbotham Jr., Clarick, and David, "*Shaw v. Reno*."

14. Peller, "Race Consciousness," 791.

15. Ibid., 847.

16. Lowndes, Novkov, and Warren, *Race and American Political Development*, 2, 84.

17. See Swain, *Black Faces, Black Interests*; Robert C. Smith, *We Have No Leaders*; Singh, *Congressional Black Caucus*; Frymer, *Uneasy Alliances*.

18. See Canon, *Race, Representation, and Redistricting*; Tate, *Black Faces*; Hammond, *Congressional Caucuses*.

19. The term *consciousness-raising* was coined during the modern American feminist movement. It refers to a form of political action that allows women to analyze through discourse with each other the conditions of their individual lives and to consider how what had seemed like isolated problems of subordination were in fact common constraints. The practice is very similar to "rap sessions" conducted during the Black Power phase of the civil rights movement. Perhaps not surprisingly, given the CBC's formation in 1971, the concept of consciousness-raising correlates closely with CBC's original mission statement, in which it describes itself as the "conscience of Congress." For more on this aspect of the caucus's mission, see chapter 3.

20. For maps of the challenged districts in *Gomillion* and *Shaw v. Reno*, see figures 1 and 2 (in chapter 5).

21. Davidson and Grofman, *Quiet Revolution in the South*, 22. Vote dilution is part and parcel of the broader phenomenon of racially polarized voting, both of which will be discussed more thoroughly in subsequent chapters.

22. Ibid., 33.

23. Thomas's concurrence in *Georgia v. Ashcroft* consists of a simple statement: "I continue to adhere to the views expressed in my opinion in *Holder* v. *Hall*. . . . I join the Court's opinion because it is fully consistent with our [Section] 5 precedents" (internal citations omitted).

24. Engstrom, "Influence Districts and the Courts," 2.

25. See Canellos, "Elena Kagan"; Reilly, "Kagan"; *Arizona Free Enterprise Club v. Bennett*.

26. *Allen v. State Board of Elections*, 595. See Ball, Krane, and Lauth, *Compromised Compliance*; Rivers, "'Conquered Provinces'?"

27. Davidson and Grofman, *Quiet Revolution in the South*.

28. http://www.thecongressionalblackcaucus.com/ (accessed July 9, 2010).

29. Balkin and Siegel, *Constitution in 2020*, 101.

CHAPTER 1

1. According to the Court in *Marbury v. Madison*, "It is emphatically the province and duty of the judicial department to say what the law is" (177).

2. See Canon, *Race, Representation, and Redistricting*; Tate, *Black Faces*; Andra Gillespie, *Whose Black Politics?*

3. Harmon-Jones and Mills, *Cognitive Dissonance*, 3–4.

4. *Grutter v. Bollinger,* 341.

5. http://www.thecongressionalblackcaucus.com/ (accessed April 18, 2010); Mill, *On Liberty,* 16–18.

6. Justice William J. Brennan Jr. dissenting in *Regents of the University of California v. Bakke,* 327.

7. Michael Brown et al., *Whitewashing Race,* 193–222; Balkin and Siegel, *Constitution in 2020,* 7.

8. King, *Why We Can't Wait,* 140–41.

9. Dahl, *Dilemmas,* 101–2, 166.

10. Michael Brown et al., *Whitewashing Race,* 196 (internal citation omitted).

11. It can be argued that the founding fathers sought not to secure individual rights as much as to create a viable system of federalism and to protect certain fundamental liberties. However, the Constitution has evolved over time to guarantee and protect both liberties and rights, including racial and group rights.

12. Wills, *Negro President,* 3–11.

13. Gillette, *Right to Vote,* 21.

14. Berger, *Government by Judiciary,* 13–16 (internal quotes omitted), 26–27; Gillette, *Right to Vote,* 31–34. See also Brandwein, *Reconstructing Reconstruction,* 27, 38–41.

15. Berger, *Government by Judiciary,* 134–41, 153–54, 206.

16. Ibid., 204; Brandwein, *Reconstructing Reconstruction,* 5; Epps, *Democracy Reborn,* 97–98; Graber, *Dred Scott,* 1.

17. Mathews, *Legislative and Judicial History,* 15; Valelly, *The Two Reconstructions,* 13.

18. See Frymer, *Uneasy Alliances;* Bell, "*Brown v. Board of Education.*"

19. Graber, *Dred Scott,* 87.

20. As Justice Ruth Bader Ginsburg dissented in *Miller v. Johnson,* the Court also overlooked the race-conscious precedents of *Strauder v. West Virginia.* Her points and this case are examined more closely in chapter 6.

21. See Siegel, "Federal Government's Power."

22. *Plessy v. Ferguson,* 559.

23. See A. Leon Higginbotham Jr., *Shades of Freedom.* See also Brandwein, *Reconstructing Reconstruction,* 213; Klarman, *From Jim Crow to Civil Rights,* 9.

24. *Plessy v. Ferguson,* 559.

25. Golub, "Plessy as 'Passing,'" 593.

26. *Plessy v. Ferguson,* 549 (emphases added).

27. Golub, "Plessy as 'Passing,'" 594.

28. *Brown v. Board of Education II,* 301.

29. *Brown v. Board of Education,* 489, 492–93.

30. See Layton, *International Politics.*

31. Brandwein, *Reconstructing Reconstruction,* 4, 13.

32. Berger, *Government by Judiciary,* 26, 212; Siegel, "Federal Government's Power," 486.

33. Robert C. Post and Reva B. Siegel, "Democratic Constitutionalism," in *Constitution in 2020,* ed. Balkin and Siegel, 33.

34. Bositis, *Black Elected Officials,* 5–7.

35. Ibid.

36. http://www.thecongressionalblackcaucus.com/ (accessed April 4, 2012). This

number includes Illinois senator Roland Burris and the nonvoting delegates from Washington, D.C., and the U.S. Virgin Islands.

37. DeNavas-Walt, Proctor and Smith, *Income, Poverty and Health Insurance Coverage*, 5–6, 14–15.

38. *Shaw v. Reno; Miller v. Johnson; Shaw v. Hunt; Bush v. Vera; Gratz v. Bollinger; Grutter v. Bollinger; Parents Involved v. Seattle School District Number 1.*

39. *Regents of the University of California v. Bakke*, 327.

40. See Spann, *Race against the Court;* A. Leon Higginbotham Jr., Clarick, and David, "*Shaw v. Reno*"; Michael Brown et al., *Whitewashing Race.*

41. See Turner, *Respect Black;* Delany, *Condition, Elevation, Emigration and Destiny;* W. E. B. Du Bois, *Oxford W. E. B. Du Bois Reader;* X, *Malcolm X Speaks;* King, *Why We Can't Wait;* King, *Where Do We Go from Here.* These sources are further investigated in chapter 2.

42. Gillespie, *Whose Black Politics?* 9–15.

43. Thernstrom, *Whose Votes Count?* 242–43.

44. Canon, *Race, Representation, and Redistricting;* Tate, *Black Faces.* Chapter 3 elaborates on these points.

45. A. Leon Higginbotham Jr., Clarick, and David, "*Shaw v. Reno*," 1630.

46. *Parents Involved v. Seattle School District Number 1*, 748.

47. Justice Brennan concurring in *Regents of the University of California v. Bakke*, 627.

48. *Originalism* has various definitions and nuances. Some observers also distinguish between "original intent" (that is, the goal of legislation) and "original understanding" (that is, what legal text means or is interpreted to mean). See Brandwein, *Reconstructing Reconstruction*, 17.

49. Siegel, "Federal Government's Power," 481–82.

50. Ibid., 515–22. See also Post and Siegel, "Democratic Constitutionalism," 29–30.

51. Siegel, "Federal Government's Power," 491–512. For a thorough discussion of discriminatory colonial laws, see A. Leon Higginbotham Jr., *In the Matter of Color.* For a colonial example of such provisions, see *Howell v. Netherland*, a 1770 challenge to a Virginia statute extending chattel status across generations that was argued (unsuccessfully) by Thomas Jefferson.

52. Siegel, "Federal Government's Power," 488.

53. Ibid., 555–56.

54. Brandwein, "Judicial Abandonment of Blacks?" 344–55, 371–73; Golub, "Plessy as 'Passing,'" 592–94.

55. Siegel, "Federal Government's Power," 479, 590; Klarman, *From Jim Crow to Civil Rights*, 5, 20–21, 449.

56. Graber, *Dred Scott*, 1–11.

57. Brandwein, *Reconstructing Reconstruction*, 7.

58. Golub, "Plessy as 'Passing,'" 595–96.

59. Jack M. Balkin, "Fidelity to Text and Principle," in *Constitution in 2020*, ed. Balkin and Siegel, 23.

60. Gillespie, *Whose Black Politics?* 1–11.

61. Joseph, *Dark Days, Bright Nights*, 161–229.

62. Piven, Minnite, and Groark, *Keeping Down the Black Vote*, 164–203.

63. Piven and Cloward, *Why Americans Don't Vote*, 16, 97–101, 251–54; Frymer, *Uneasy Alliances*, 4–7, 27–40, 44–48; Michael Steele, lecture at DePaul University, April 20, 2010, as witnessed by the author. See also Pallasch, "GOP Chairman."

64. Spann, *Race against the Court*, 3, 19–26. Such provisions were further compromised for federal judges during the era of desegregation, many of whom lived in the communities that they were being asked to desegregate and thus had to contend with the disapproval of friends and neighbors. See also Klarman, *From Jim Crow to Civil Rights*, 356; Balkin and Siegel, *Constitution in 2020*, 6; Balkin, "Fidelity to Text and Principle," 22.

65. Klarman, *From Jim Crow to Civil Rights*, 446–50.

66. Graber, *Dred Scott*, 86–89, 226–54.

67. Balkin and Siegel, *Constitution in 2020*, 2–3.

68. The Constitution mandates single-member districting for U.S. congressional seats but does not dictate the electoral plans for other types of offices. See Hallett, *Proportional Representation*, 59–69; Merriam and Gosnell, *American Party System*, 2–5; Duverger, *Political Parties*, 215–18; Abrams, "Raising Politics Up"; Piven and Cloward, *Why Americans Don't Vote*, 65–69, 78–95, 107–12. See also Guinier, *Tyranny of the Majority*.

69. Valelly, *The Two Reconstructions*, 19.

70. Burman, *Black Progress Question*, 112; Crenshaw et al., *Critical Race Theory*, xxix.

71. King, *Where Do We Go from Here?*, 1968, 133.

CHAPTER 2

1. Walton, *African American Power and Politics*, 2–3, 12 (internal citations omitted).

2. See Walton and Smith, *American Politics*.

3. Linda F. Williams, *Constraint of Race*, 19.

4. Michael Brown et al., *Whitewashing Race*, 2–3. This point was central to the plaintiff's arguments in *Northwest Austin Municipal Utility District Number 1 v. Holder* and is discussed in more detail in chapters 4 and 5.

5. Stuckey, *Going through the Storm*, 83–137.

6. See W. E. B. Du Bois, *Souls of Black Folk*.

7. Pitkin, *Concept of Representation*, 120.

8. See Moses, *Creative Conflict*.

9. Some, such as minister and emigrationist Edward Wilmot Blyden, saw chattel slavery as a divinely ordained means to "preserve" and "purify" Africans. But even for Blyden, redemption via slavery was not an end in and of itself but the rightful path to black liberty and uplift. See Marable and Mullings, *Let Nobody Turn Us Around*, 146–57.

10. Walker, *David Walker's Appeal*, ed. Hinks. The *Appeal* has been reissued several times. The first was by his protégé, Henry Highland Garnet, who reissued it along with one of his own addresses in 1848. It did not resurface again until the 1960s, with the nascence of black studies. Hinks's edition is the most recent and is valuable for its informative introduction and its documentation of institutional reactions to the *Appeal*. James Turner's analytical introduction to Walker in his 1993 edition of the *Appeal* is extremely illuminating. It is also the only twentieth-century edition that is presented from the perspective of black nationalism, and that places Walker's rhetoric in the context of modern black political thought.

11. Walker, *David Walker's Appeal*, ed. Hinks, xliii–xliv.

12. Stuckey, *Going through the Storm*, 88–93.

13. Walker, *David Walker's Appeal*, ed. Hinks, 5, 32 (emphasis omitted).

14. Ibid., 5, 24, 39 (emphasis omitted).

15. Ibid., xix, xxxiv.

16. Ibid., 7, 28. Walker's evangelical rhetoric is also characteristic of the Protestant revivalism of the Jacksonian era.

17. Ibid., 41–42.

18. Jefferson, *Notes on the State of Virginia*. For an illuminating and thoughtful analysis of Jefferson's ambivalence about slavery, see Wills, *Negro President*, xii, 14, 47–72.

19. Walker, *David Walker's Appeal*, ed. Hinks, 77–79.

20. Ibid., 32–34, 54–58, 67–73 (emphasis omitted).

21. See Burin, *Slavery and the Peculiar Solution*; Yarema, *American Colonization Society*.

22. Walker, *David Walker's Appeal*, ed. Hinks, 12, 17–18, 29, 64, 73 (emphasis omitted).

23. Ibid., 14–15.

24. Ibid., 27–28.

25. Ibid., 24, 27.

26. Because of laws against educating slaves, those who could read usually had to conceal such knowledge. As Frederick Douglass wrote, "As the master studies to keep the slave ignorant, the slave is cunning enough to make the master think he succeeds" (*My Bondage and My Freedom*, 81). Other covert acts of resistance included arson, disabling farm animals and equipment, feigning illness, sabotaging crops, poisoning water, and feigning loyalty to masters. Some work songs and spirituals were coded calls for resistance. For example, "Steal Away," "The Gospel Train's a-Coming," "Wade in the Water" and "Drinking Gourd" (symbolizing the Big Dipper/North Star) could announce escape plans as much as accompany worship or work.

27. Walker, *David Walker's Appeal*, ed. Turner, 14, 17–18; Walker, *David Walker's Appeal*, ed. Hinks, xli, 95–108.

28. Walker, *David Walker's Appeal*, ed. Hinks, xliv; Stuckey, *Going through the Storm*, 91.

29. Ibid., xxxi.

30. Stewart, *Maria W. Stewart*, 61.

31. Sterling Stuckey, "A Last Stern Struggle: Henry Highland Garnet and Liberation Theory," in *Black Leaders*, ed. Litwack and Meier, 130.

32. Ibid., 134–37.

33. Ibid., 129–30.

34. Garnet, *Let Your Motto*, 10–88; Walker, *Walker's Appeal*, 96.

35. Douglass was not without militancy. A year after Garnet published his speech and Walker's *Appeal*, Douglass confessed that he "should welcome the intelligence to-morrow, should it come, that the slaves had risen in the South." See Stuckey, "Last Stern Struggle," 137–38.

36. Walker, *Walker's Appeal*, 92, 94–95 (emphasis omitted).

37. Ibid., 94–95; Stuckey, "Last Stern Struggle," 144–46.

38. Stuckey, "Last Stern Struggle," 142.

39. Marx, *Capital*, vol. 1, chapter 10, section 7.

40. http://cbc.lee.house.gov/history/history-details.shtml (accessed November 6, 2010).

41. King, *Stride toward Freedom*, 93.

42. See Allen, *Black Awakening;* Marable, *How Capitalism Underdeveloped Black America.*

43. Painter, "Martin Delany," 150, 155.

44. Delany, *Origin of Races and Color,* 23, 89.

45. Painter, "Martin Delany," 149–54, 164–71.

46. According to Article IV, Section 3 of the Constitution, "No person held to service or labor in one state, under the laws thereof, escaping into another, shall, in consequence of any law or regulation therein, be discharged from such service or labor, but shall be delivered up on the claim of the party to whom such service or labor may be due."

47. Fugitive Slave Act of 1850, sections 6 and 10.

48. Painter, "Martin Delany," 153, 159.

49. Delany, *Condition, Elevation, Emigration, and Destiny,* pt. 20. Although blacks in some of these regions had more autonomy than those in the United States, their social status was determined not simply by race but by even more subjective factors such as complexion, facial features, and hair texture. Those deemed to have purely African traits were relegated to the bottom of racial hierarchies. Such hierarchies directly opposed Delany's belief in the virtues of blackness.

50. Painter, "Martin Delany," 155, 160.

51. Delany, *Condition, Elevation, Emigration, and Destiny,* pt. 20.

52. Ibid., pt. 6; Painter, "Martin Delany," 165.

53. Painter, "Martin Delany," 164–68.

54. Douglass, *My Bondage and My Freedom,* 80–83, 429.

55. Ibid., 439–40 (emphasis omitted).

56. Ibid., 444–45.

57. Ibid., 438–40 (emphasis omitted), 396.

58. For the thesis that although morally reprehensible, this decision was correct as a matter of constitutional law, see Graber, *Dred Scott.*

59. Stewart, *Maria W. Stewart,* 37.

60. Flexner, *Century of Struggle,* 39, 43–49 (internal quotations deleted).

61. Rosalyn Terborg Penn, "African American Women and the Vote: An Overview," in *African American Women and the Vote,* ed. Gordon and Collier-Thomas, 13.

62. Stewart, *Maria W. Stewart,* xii–5.

63. Ibid., 15–19, 38, 57–68.

64. The concept of plain talk is significant given the stylistic and syntactic differences between the two published versions of Truth's 1851 "Ain't I a Woman?" address. The first appeared the same year in the *Anti-Slavery Bugle,* while the second appeared more than a decade later as reported by suffragist Frances Gage. The *Bugle* version opens with "I want to say a few words about this matter. I am a [*sic*] woman's rights . . ."; Gage's version opens with "Wall, chilern, whar dar is so much racket dar must be somethin' out of kilter . . ." Moreover, Truth's trademark "ain't I a woman?" question that appears several times in Gage's version never appears in the earlier version. These differences lead to the question of whether Gage exaggerated Truth's syntax in an attempt to make it more appealing to whites or whether Gage's perception of Truth in particular and blacks in gen-

eral led her to report the speech in this more stereotypical manner. See Marable and Mullings, *Let Nobody Turn Us Around*, 67–68; Painter, *Sojourner Truth*.

65. Jason H. Silverman, "Mary Ann Shadd and the Search for Equality," in *Black Leaders*, ed. Litwack and Meier, 93, 97; Shadd, "Mary Ann Shadd Cary."

66. Crenshaw, "Demarginalizing the Intersection of Race and Sex"; Kimberlé Crenshaw, "Mapping the Margins: Intersectionality, Identity Politics, and Violence against Women of Color," in *Critical Race Theory*, ed. Crenshaw et al., 357, 360–66. Because the Court gives more scrutiny to racial than gender discrimination claims, the justices are less able to address the full and intersecting dimensions of racism and sexism.

67. Marable and Mullings, *Let Nobody Turn Us Around*, 72–73.

68. Ibid., 78. Delany's semantic distinction correlates with that made by non-free-holding white men in America's early years between "the franchise" as a privilege to be earned from or granted by states, and "suffrage" as a prayer, or plea, for the vote. See Keyssar, *The Right to Vote*, 9.

69. Dray, *Capitol Men*, 267.

70. Foner, *Freedom's Lawmakers*, xiii–xx, 170–71.

71. Howard Rabinowitz, "Three Reconstruction Leaders: Blanche K. Bruce, Robert Brown Elliott, and Holland Thompson," in *Black Leaders*, ed. Litwack and Meier, 192–93; Dray, *Capitol Men*, 75.

72. Dray, *Capitol Men*, 188–93; Turner, *Respect Black*, 24; Middleton, *Black Congressmen*, xviii.

73. See Foner, *Freedom's Lawmakers*; Middleton, *Black Congressmen*. Because of the paucity and inaccuracy of records, determination of these congressmen's status and racial background can be difficult.

74. Middleton, *Black Congressmen*, 327–28; Dray, *Capitol Men*, 75.

75. Rabinowitz, "Three Reconstruction Leaders," 196; Middleton, *Black Congressmen*, 2–3.

76. Dray, *Capitol Men*, 208–80.

77. Rabinowitz, "Three Reconstruction Leaders," 200; Middleton, *Black Congressmen*, 15; Dray, *Capitol Men*, 228.

78. Rabinowitz, "Three Reconstruction Leaders," 202–3; Middleton, *Black Congressmen*, 85–86.

79. Dray, *Capitol Men*, 173–75.

80. Ibid., 177–78; Rabinowitz, "Three Reconstruction Leaders," 205–8; Middleton, *Black Congressmen*, 87.

81. Dittmer, "Education," 257.

82. Turner, *Respect Black*, vii–viii.

83. Dittmer, "Education," 257–58.

84. Turner, *Respect Black*, 14–23.

85. Dittmer, "Education," 258.

86. Turner, *Respect Black*, 18–25, 60–72, 196. For similar contemporary conclusions, see Frymer, *Uneasy Alliances*.

87. Turner, *Respect Black*, 165–66; Dittmer, "Education," 270. Turner remained passionate about the evils of Jim Crow until his death. Responding to episodes of white atrocities in the South, he exhorted "Negroes, [to] get guns . . . when invaded by the bloody lynchers" and "blow the fiendish wretches into a thousand giblets" (Dittmer, "Education," 270).

88. W. E. B. Du Bois, *Souls of Black Folk*, 4; W. E. B. Du Bois, *Dusk of Dawn*, 130–31.

89. King, "Why We Can't Wait," 149–50; King, "Where Do We Go from Here?" 23–67, 146–48.

90. Walton and Smith, *American Politics*, 115.

91. Elsa Barkley Brown, "To Catch the Vision of Freedom," 73.

92. Flexner, *Century of Struggle*, 297–99.

93. Marable and Mullings, *Let Nobody Turn Us Around*, 170 (internal quotations omitted).

94. Elsa Barkley Brown, "To Catch the Vision of Freedom," 81–82.

95. Marable and Mullings, *Let Nobody Turn Us Around*, 126.

96. Ellen Carol Du Bois, *Feminism and Suffrage*, 88.

97. Evelyn B. Higginbotham, "Clubwomen and Electoral Politics in the 1920s," in *African American Women and the Vote,* ed. Gordon and Collier-Thomas, 136; Coleman, "Architects of a Vision," 32.

98. Marable and Mullings, *Let Nobody Turn Us Around*, 168–69.

99. Sharon Harley, "Mary Church Terrell: Genteel Militant," in *Black Leaders*, ed. Litwack and Meier, 316–18.

100. Ford, *Women and Politics*, 44.

101. Evelyn B. Higginbotham, "Clubwomen and Electoral Politics," 146–51.

102. Wells-Barnett, *Crusade for Justice*, 18.

103. McMurry, *To Keep the Waters Troubled*, 102.

104. McMurry, *To Keep the Waters Troubled*, 107–8, 307–11.

105. Lewis, *W. E. B. Du Bois: Biography of a Race*, 86, 114–49, 155.

106. Marable and Mullings, *Let Nobody Turn Us Around*, 182–84. Washington was averse to competition for leadership, especially from the Du Bois camp, and he often wielded his considerable power and influence to undermine competing interests. For example he reputedly undermined the Niagara Movement before it could fully get off the ground.

107. William Hannibal Thomas was one African American who contended that blacks were inferior to whites. Thomas was a Union Army veteran, an active participant in Reconstruction, and initially a staunch advocate of black civil rights. Thomas had been particularly committed to land redistribution to feed blacks, publishing a monograph on the subject in 1890. In 1901, for reasons that have yet to be fully understood, Thomas published a lengthy book, *The American Negro,* in which he denounced blacks as "moral pervert[s]," "the waste product of American civilization," and "an intrinsically inferior type of humanity." Despite his reliance on spurious data, that a black man would make such claims (and that a major press published them) lent unique credence to existing precepts of racial hierarchy. Thomas eventually eschewed his black identity altogether, asserting instead his mulatto identity, and advocated a racial caste system that privileged mixed-race over "pure" blacks. Not surprisingly, black leaders condemned Thomas as at best a "good negro gone bad" and at worst as a "black Judas." They excoriated the *American Negro* and until recently relegated both Thomas and the book to obscurity. Other accounts claim that he misrepresented his professional qualifications, that he was a charlatan and a bigamist, and that the pain of a war injury that never properly healed might have embittered him. See John D. Smith, *Black Judas,* xix–xxvi, 162–91.

108. Marable and Mullings, *Let Nobody Turn Us Around*, 195–98 (emphasis added).

109. Ibid., 182.

110. King, *Stride Toward Freedom*, 130.

CHAPTER 3

1. Walter Fauntroy, testimony, in U.S. Congress, House, Committee on Judiciary, *Hearings before the Subcommittee on Civil and Constitutional Rights*, 97th Cong., p. 1982.

2. See Davidson and Grofman, *Quiet Revolution in the South*.

3. Fenno, *Congressmen in Committees*, 48.

4. Hammond, *Congressional Caucuses*, ix–xi, 11; Singh, *Congressional Black Caucus*, 107.

5. Hammond, *Congressional Caucuses*, 1; *Congressional Quarterly Weekly Report*, September 27, 2003, 2334.

6. Hammond, *Congressional Caucuses*, 11.

7. *Congressional Quarterly Weekly Report*, September 27, 2003, 2334.

8. Hammond, *Congressional Caucuses*, 125–31.

9. Singh, *Congressional Black Caucus*, 104.

10. Andra Gillespie, "Meet the New Class," in *Whose Black Politics?* ed. Gillespie, 9–37.

11. Canon, *Race, Representation, and Redistricting*, 89; Derfner, "New Black Caucus," 16.

12. Canon, *Race, Representation, and Redistricting*, 47–48.

13. Tate, *Black Faces*, 50–69.

14. Robert C. Smith, *We Have No Leaders*, 111; Singh, *Congressional Black Caucus*, 31–32.

15. http://www.cbcfinc.org/cbc.html (accessed November 11, 2010). The CBC's founding members were Representatives Shirley Chisholm of New York, William Clay of Missouri, George Collins of Illinois, John Conyers Jr. of Michigan, Ronald Dellums of California, Charles Diggs of Michigan, Augustus Hawkins of California, Ralph Metcalfe of Illinois, Parren Mitchell of Maryland, Robert Nix of Pennsylvania, Charles Rangel of New York, and Louis Stokes of Ohio and Delegate Walter Fauntroy of the District of Columbia. Diggs served as the CBC's first chair.

16. *Congressional Quarterly Weekly Report*, September 27, 2003, 2334.

17. Singh, *Congressional Black Caucus*, 22.

18. http://www.cbcfinc.org/cbc.html (accessed July 13, 2010); http://www.thecongressionalblackcaucus.com/ (accessed July 9, 2010).

19. http://www.thecongressionalblackcaucus.com/ (accessed July 9, 2010).

20. Hammond, *Congressional Caucuses*, 14.

21. http://www.thecongressionalblackcaucus.com/issues/cbc-taskforces/ (accessed April 4, 2012).

22. Robert C. Smith, *We Have No Leaders*, 34, 56, 113–14 (internal quotations omitted); Singh, *Congressional Black Caucus*, 73.

23. Singh, *Congressional Black Caucus*, 51, quoting Representative Bill Gray (D-PA).

24. http://www.cbcfinc.org/aboutus.html (accessed April 4, 2012); *Congressional Quarterly Weekly Report*, September 27, 2003, 2334.

25. Pitkin, *Concept of Representation*, 60–91, 112–43; Singh, *Congressional Black Caucus*, 12.

26. *Congressional Quarterly Weekly Report*, September 27, 2003, 2334.

27. Derfner, "New Black Caucus," 16.

28. Gary Franks (R-CT), chose to join the CBC even though his conservatism and partisan loyalties usually put him at odds with the rest of his colleagues; conversely, Republican J. C. Watts of Oklahoma chose not to join the caucus because of its race-conscious orientation (Robert C. Smith, *We Have No Leaders,* 113). These two legislators' stances on the CBC reflect the differences between Franks's more traditional, independent-minded New England Republicanism and Watts's neoconservative partisanship. Where the GOP tended to view Franks as an ideological outlier of the party, it promoted Watts as a color-blind advocate within it. Significantly however, in 2005 Watts submitted an affidavit to the House Judiciary Committee heartily endorsing Section 5 of the VRA, as well as its language-based provisions. These dynamics, along with the GOP's emphasis on color blindness, have complicated its efforts to resonate with black voters, even under the leadership of African American Michael Steele.

29. Singh, *Congressional Black Caucus,* 2.

30. Ibid., 5 (internal punctuation omitted); Turner, *Respect Black,* 72 (emphasis omitted).

31. Frymer, *Uneasy Alliances,* 140; Piven, Minnite, and Groarke, *Keeping Down the Black Vote,* 127–203.

32. Tim Scott of South Carolina and Allen West of Florida were elected to Congress in November 2010. The CBC invited them to join the caucus a week later. As of this writing, West has joined the CBC; Scott has not (Pergram, "GOPers West and Scott"); www.thecongressionalblackcaucus.com/members/directory (accessed April 4, 2012).

33. http://www.thecongressionalblackcaucus.com/members/directory (accessed April 4, 2012).

34. See Edsall and Edsall, *Chain Reaction.*

35. *Congressional Quarterly Weekly Report,* September 27, 2003, 2334. The Congressional Women's Caucus (now called the Congressional Caucus on Women's Issues), the Congressional Hispanic Caucus, and the House Democratic Study Group (the first congressional caucus) were also defunded. According to Section 222 of H.R. 6, passed on January 5, 1995, the "continuation of any legislative service organization . . . shall be prohibited in the 104th Congress. The Committee on House Oversight shall take such steps as are necessary to ensure an orderly termination and accounting for funds of any LSO in existence on January 3, 1995."

36. Hammond, *Congressional Caucuses,* 211.

37. Ibid., 33 (internal citations omitted).

38. Full Employment and Balanced Growth Act, U.S.C. 3151 (1978).

39. Singh, *Congressional Black Caucus,* 84–96; Frymer, *Uneasy Alliances,* 155–63; www.thecongressionalblackcaucus.com/issues/jobs-initiative (accessed April 4, 2012).

40. Singh, *Congressional Black Caucus,* 97–102. The Supreme Court struck down the use of statistical sampling as unconstitutional. The biracial category ultimately was included as an optional category in the 2000 census. For an analysis of the movement that led to these changes to the census, see Kim M. Williams, *Mark One or More.*

41. Clayton, *Presidential Campaign of Barack Obama,* 80–81, 89–103.

42. Frymer, *Uneasy Alliances,* 149.

43. Voting Rights Act of 1965, 42 U.S.C. 1971, 1973 et seq. (2).

44. http://www.justice.gov/crt/about/vot/sec_5/types.php (accessed April 4, 2012).

45. Arthur Flemming, testimony, in U.S. Congress, House, Committee on Judiciary, *Hearings before the Subcommittee on Civil and Constitutional Rights,* 94th Cong., 20–29.

46. Ibid., 20–29, 94.

47. The VRA as originally passed contained limited language protections for non-English-speaking Native American voters in regions in California, the Pacific Northwest, and Alaska.

48. Texas is infamous for its whites-only political parties and primary elections. These devices were invalidated in *Nixon v. Herndon, Smith v. Allwright,* and *Terry v. Adams.*

49. U.S. Congress, House, Committee on Judiciary, *Hearings before the Subcommittee on Civil and Constitutional Rights,* 94th Cong., 76.

50. Ibid., 75.

51. "Congress Clears Voting Rights Act Extension," 527. This rhetoric closely resembles opposition to the Fifteenth Amendment during the Reconstruction era.

52. "Voting Rights Act Extension Approved," 925; "House Passes Strong Voting Rights Extension," 1202.

53. "Voting Rights Act: Debate on Extension Begins," 492.

54. Ibid.; "House Passes Strong Voting Rights Extension," 1202.

55. "Voting Rights Act: Debate on Extension Begins"; "Rules Committee Action," 1044.

56. U.S. Congress, House, Committee on Judiciary, *Hearings before the Subcommittee on Civil and Constitutional Rights,* 94th Cong., 64.

57. "House Passes Strong Voting Rights Extension," 1202.

58. U.S. Congress, House, Committee on Judiciary, *Hearings before the Subcommittee on Civil and Constitutional Rights,* 94th Cong., 81.

59. "Voting Rights Act: Debate on Extension Begins," 489, 492; U.S. Congress, House, Committee on Judiciary, *Hearings before the Subcommittee on Civil and Constitutional Rights,* 94th Cong., 76.

60. U.S. Congress, House, Committee on Judiciary, *Hearings before the Subcommittee on Civil and Constitutional Rights,* 94th Cong., 77; "Voting Rights Act: Debate on Extension Begins," 489; "Expansion of Voting Rights Act Urged," 761.

61. "Subcommittee Action," 876.

62. "Congress Clears Voting Rights Act Extension," 527.

63. "Voting Rights Act: Debate on Extension Begins," 492; U.S. Congress, House, Committee on Judiciary, *Hearings before the Subcommittee on Civil and Constitutional Rights,* 94th Cong., 27.

64. U.S. Congress, House, Committee on Judiciary, *Hearings before the Subcommittee on Civil and Constitutional Rights,* 94th Cong., 94.

65. "Congress Clears Voting Rights Act Extension," 521, 532.

66. Ibid., 521–22.

67. Davidson and Grofman, *Quiet Revolution in the South,* 22.

68. U.S. Congress, House, Committee on Judiciary, *Hearings before the Subcommittee on Civil and Constitutional Rights,* 97th Cong., 4.

69. Ibid., 20.

70. Ibid., 61, 86–88.

71. Ibid., 434, 1850, 1983–85.

72. Ibid., 60.

73. Ibid., 61, 2117, 2130–31.

74. *Allen v. State Board of Elections,* 569.

75. Professor Hugh O. Reid, testimony, in U.S. Congress, House, Committee on Judiciary, *Hearings before the Subcommittee on Civil and Constitutional Rights,* 97th Cong., 420.

76. Ibid., 419–20.

77. *South Carolina v. Katzenbach,* 327–28.

78. "'Intent' a Key Issue," 42; "Voting Rights Act Extended, Strengthened," 375. See also Issacharoff, Karlan, and Pildes, *Law of Democracy,* 714–39.

79. U.S. Congress, House, Committee on Judiciary, *Hearings before the Subcommittee on Civil and Constitutional Rights,* 97th Cong., 2–3, 433; "House Opens Hearings on Voting Rights Act," 819.

80. "Opposition Fading to Voting Act Renewal," 1111.

81. "Talks on Voting Rights Act Now in Progress," 1289.

82. James Sensenbrenner, interview by author, February 24, 2010.

83. U.S. Congress, House, Committee on Judiciary, *Hearings before the Subcommittee on Civil and Constitutional Rights,* 97th Cong., 428.

84. The "totality of the circumstances" test was initially derived from factors formulated by the Fifth Circuit Court in *Zimmer v. McKeithen.* In light of the 1982 revisions of the VRA, the Court's 1986 decision in *Thornburg v. Gingles* gave rise to the "Gingles test," thus incorporating the results orientation of Section 2 into its voting rights jurisprudence.

85. U.S. Congress, House, Committee on Judiciary, *Hearings before the Subcommittee on Civil and Constitutional Rights,* 97th Cong., 18, 62, 2128.

86. U.S. Congress, House, Committee on Judiciary, *Hearings before the Subcommittee on Civil and Constitutional Rights,* 97th Cong., 2149. Senator Orrin Hatch, Attorney General William French Smith, and William Bradford Smith of the DOJ's civil rights division also equated a results standard with proportional representation and, implicitly, racial quotas. See "Hatch vs. Civil Rights Groups," 520; "Voting Rights Act Extended, Strengthened," 320.

87. Issacharoff, Karlan, and Pildes, *Law of Democracy,* 716.

88. U.S. Congress, House, Committee on Judiciary, *Hearings before the Subcommittee on Civil and Constitutional Rights,* 97th Cong., 60–63.

89. Ibid., 1983, 2127.

90. Issacharoff, Karlan, and Pildes, *Law of Democracy,* 716.

91. Ibid., 717.

92. "Administration Draws Fire," 170.

93. "Senate Judiciary Approves Voting Rights Bill," 1043. The wording for this rider was drawn from *White v. Regester.*

94. Kousser, *Colorblind Injustice,* 64–65 (emphasis minimized; brackets omitted).

95. "Voting Rights Act Extended, Strengthened," 373.

96. Voting Rights Act of 1965, 42 U.S.C. Section 1973 (2)(a)(b), as amended June 29, 1982.

97. "Voting Rights Act Extended, Strengthened," 373–74.

98. Sensenbrenner, interview.

99. *Georgia v. Ashcroft,* 461.

100. VRA hearing, "To Examine the Impact and Effectiveness of the Voting Rights Act," October 18, 2005, 52.

101. *Boerne v. Flores,* 507.

102. Mel Watt, interview by author, January 26, 2010; Bobby Scott, interview by author, February 23, 2010.

103. Watt, interview; Sensenbrenner, interview. Watt lauds Sensenbrenner as an "unspoken hero" of the 2006 VRA reauthorization process.

104. Watt, interview.

105. VRA hearing, "To Examine the Impact and Effectiveness of the Voting Rights Act," October 18, 2005, 43.

106. Ibid., 39, 42–43, 53; VRA hearing, "Voting Rights Act: An Examination of the Scope and Criteria for Coverage under the Special Provisions of the Act," October 25, 2005, 90. For recent example of such a problem in a state not covered by Section 5, the Ohio Senate passed a bill in June 2011 that would prohibit poll workers from helping voters find their correct precinct for voting if they came to the wrong place to vote. Reginald Fields, "State Sen. Nina Turner Says More than 14,000 Wrong-Precinct Ballots Were Disqualified in 2008: Politifact Ohio," *Plain Dealer,* July 5, 2011, http://www.cleveland .com/open/index.ssf/2011/07/state_sen_nina_turner_says_mor.html (accessed December 13, 2011).

107. VRA hearing, "To Examine the Impact and Effectiveness of the Voting Rights Act," October 18, 2005, 47–48; VRA hearing, "Voting Rights Act: An Examination of the Scope and Criteria for Coverage under the Special Provisions of the Act," October 25, 2005, 99; VRA hearing, "Voting Rights Act: Evidence of Continued Need," March 8, 2006. Shortly after the 2006 reauthorization of the VRA the Supreme Court upheld Indiana's voter identification law in *Crawford v. Marion County* (553 U.S. 181, 2008). Since then, several states have passed voter identification laws. Eight states did so in 2011 alone, which, along with increasing pressure from civil rights organizations, prompted Attorney General Eric Holder to "urge policymakers at every level to re-evaluate our election systems—and to reform them in ways that encourage, not limit participation." Josh Gerstein, "Eric Holder: Voter ID Law Hurts Minorities," *Politico,* December 13, 2011, http://www.politico.com/news/stories/1211/70400.html (accessed December 13, 2011).

108. *Reno v. Bossier Parish School Board I,* 483, 486.

109. *Reno v. Bossier Parish School Board II,* 329–35.

110. VRA hearing, "Voting Rights Act: Section 5—Preclearance Standards," November 1, 2005, 3–4, citing *Kelo v. City of New London;* VRA hearing, "Fannie Lou Hamer, Rosa Parks and Coretta Scott King Voting Rights Act Reauthorization and Amendments Act of 2006 (Part I)," May 4, 2006, 261–62.

111. VRA hearing, "Voting Rights Act: Section 5—Preclearance Standards," November 1, 2005, 5, 64.

112. VRA hearing, "Voting Rights Act: The Judicial Evolution of the Retrogression Standard," November 9, 2005, 3–4.

113. Ibid., 5.

114. Ibid., 2.

115. VRA hearing, "Fannie Lou Hamer, Rosa Parks and Coretta Scott King Voting Rights Act Reauthorization and Amendments Act of 2006 (Part I)," May 4, 2006, 4.

116. Scott, interview.

117. An example of this occurred during one of the final hearings on Section 5. Conyers and Watt sparred with one witness's continued out-of-context invocations of Lewis's comments to oppose Section 5 despite Lewis's clarifications of those comments.

Roger Clegg, president of and general counsel for the Center for Equal Opportunity, insisted that although he knew that Lewis supported Section 5, Lewis's statement about the positive transformation of the South was inconsistent with that support. Apparently unaware of Lewis's clarifications in earlier VRA hearings, Clegg insisted that Lewis "doesn't deny the accuracy of" Clegg's specific references to him. Clegg went on to challenge Watt's grasp of the voluminous oral and written testimony that, as member of the Subcommittee on the Constitution and as Chair of the CBC, Watt had helped compile (VRA hearing, "Fannie Lou Hamer, Rosa Parks and Coretta Scott King Voting Rights Act Reauthorization and Amendments Act of 2006 (Part I)," May 4, 2006, 59–64).

118. VRA hearing, "Voting Rights Act: The Judicial Evolution of the Retrogression Standard," November 9, 2005, 80–81.

119. Ibid., 7–8.

120. VRA hearing, "To Examine the Impact and Effectiveness of the Voting Rights Act," October 18, 2005, 39–40.

121. VRA hearing, "Voting Rights Act: Evidence of Continued Need," March 8, 2006, 84.

122. VRA hearing, "Voting Rights Act: The Judicial Evolution of the Retrogression Standard," November 9, 2005, 62–63.

123. VRA hearing, "Fannie Lou Hamer, Rosa Parks and Coretta Scott King Voting Rights Act Reauthorization and Amendments Act of 2006 (Part I)," May 4, 2006, 258–63.

124. For the Court's distinctions between "coalition" and "crossover" voting, see *Bartlett v. Strickland.*

125. Scott, interview, emphasis added.

126. Ibid. Black state legislators in Georgia seemingly shared Scott's perspective when they overwhelmingly approved this plan.

127. Engstrom, "Influence Districts and the Courts," 6.

128. Ibid., 25.

129. *Georgia v. Ashcroft*, 482–83.

130. Canon, "Renewing the Voting Rights Act:," 3–24, esp. 11–23.

131. Engstrom, "Influence Districts and the Courts," 6, 25–26.

132. Fannie Lou Hamer, Rosa Parks, and Coretta Scott King Voting Rights Act Reauthorization and Amendments Act of 2006, Section 5(3)(d).

133. Senate Minority Report for the Fannie Lou Hamer, Rosa Parks, Coretta Scott King, and César E. Chávez Voting Rights Act Reauthorization and Amendments Act of 2006, 22–36.

134. Scott, interview.

135. Swain, "Reauthorization of the VRA," 29–34. Swain and J. Morgan Kousser lament the tepidness of the renewed VRA, but for contrasting reasons. For the former, the 2006 reauthorization bows too much to black power and does not go far enough in nationalizing Section 5. For the latter, the reauthorizations are effectively "a defeat in victory" because they do not go far enough to protect minority political power. See Kousser, "Strange, Ironic Career," 760–64. For another thorough analysis of the legislative record of the reauthorization of the act, see Persily, "Promises and Pitfalls."

136. Sensenbrenner, interview.

137. Derfner, "New Black Caucus," 17.

138. Frymer, *Uneasy Alliances*, 176–77; Derfner, "New Black Caucus," 16.

139. Singh, *Congressional Black Caucus*, 68.

140. *Georgia v. Ashcroft*, 487–90. The threshold black voting age population was 44.3 percent. Of the fifty-six districts in Georgia, four fell below that threshold, while thirteen had black voting age populations of between 30 and 50 percent.

141. See Lennertz, "In Dixieland We'll Take Our Stand."

142. Frymer, *Uneasy Alliances*, 177.

CHAPTER 4

1. The CBC also submitted an amicus brief in *Branch v. Smith*. However, that case revolved primarily around administrative delays on the part of the U.S. Justice Department rather than the use of race in districting and thus is not discussed here.

2. Collins, *Friends of the Supreme Court*, 19, 56–63.

3. Kearney and Merrill, "Influence of *Amicus Curiae* Briefs," 767–69. Collins, *Friends of the Supreme Court*, 10.

4. Collins, *Friends of the Supreme Court*, 10, 46, 163–64.

5. Vose, "Litigation," 30; Collins, *Friends of the Supreme Court*, 80.

6. Collins, *Friends of the Supreme Court*, 2.

7. Vose, "Litigation," 27; Collins, *Friends of the Supreme Court*, 40.

8. Collins, *Friends of the Supreme Court*, 2–3.

9. Ibid., 166; *Grutter v. Bollinger*, 18.

10. Vose, "NAACP Strategy," n. 96.

11. Ibid., 25; Collins, *Friends of the Supreme Court*, 20–23.

12. Spann, *Race against the Court*, 14–26, 148–49.

13. Collins, *Friends of the Supreme Court*, 80.

14. *Rodgers v. Lodge*, 616, 624–26. The Court's rationale in this case was partially informed by *Zimmer v. McKeithen*.

15. *Rodgers v. Lodge*, brief of amici curiae for the NAACP Legal Defense and Educational Fund, Inc., and the Congressional Black Caucus in Support of the Appellees (counsels Jack Greenberg, James Nabrit III, Lowell Johnston, Napoleon Williams Jr., and Lani Guinier).

16. *Rodgers v. Lodge*, 615. Blacks comprised approximately 54 percent of Burke County's electorate at that time.

17. *Rodgers v. Lodge*, brief of amici curiae, 2–3.

18. Ibid., 3.

19. Ibid., 4–8, 27–31, 38–40; *Zimmer v. McKeithen*, 619–20, 624–26.

20. *Rodgers v. Lodge*, brief of amici curiae, 22, 29–33, 45, 56–59.

21. Ibid., 4–5, 22–25.

22. Ibid., 8.

23. Vose, "Litigation," 27.

24. The CBC submitted amicus briefs in support of the contracting set-aside program at issue in *Adarand Constructors, Inc. v. Peña* and on behalf of detained Haitian immigrants in *Sale (McNary)/I.N.S. v. Haitian Centers*.

25. Scott, interview; Watt, interview.

26. *U.S. v. Hays*, 747.

27. Both briefs were drafted by A. Leon Higginbotham as counsel of record and Gregory Clarick and Marcella David as counsel for the CBC. Pamela Karlan was an additional counsel in the *Hays* brief.

28. *Miller v. Johnson,* brief of amici curiae for the Congressional Black Caucus in support of the appellants (A. Leon Higginbotham Jr. as counsel of record; Gregory Clarick and Marcella David), 1, 3–4, 16–19, esp. nn. 22–25; *U.S. v. Hays,* brief of amici curiae for the Congressional Black Caucus in support of the United States (A. Leon Higginbotham Jr. as counsel of record; Gregory Clarick and Marcella David; Pamela Karlan as additional counsel), 1, 3–4, 16–18, esp. nn. 22, 23.

29. *Miller v. Johnson,* brief, 10–12; *U.S. v. Hays,* brief, 10–12.

30. *Miller v. Johnson,* brief, 16, 28; *U.S. v. Hays,* brief, 16, 28 (internal citations omitted).

31. *Miller v. Johnson,* brief, 18; *U.S. v. Hays,* brief, 18.

32. *Miller v. Johnson,* brief, 20; *U.S. v. Hays,* brief, 20. See also Vose, "Litigation," 31; Vose, *Caucasians Only.*

33. *Miller v. Johnson,* brief, 27, 33; *U.S. v. Hays,* brief, 27, 32–33 (internal citations omitted).

34. *Miller v. Johnson,* brief, 26; *U.S. v. Hays,* brief, 26, both citing *Thornburg v. Gingles,* 45.

35. *Miller v. Johnson,* brief, 26; *U.S. v. Hays,* brief, 26.

36. *Miller v. Johnson,* brief, 39; *U.S. v. Hays,* brief, 39 (internal citations omitted).

37. *Shaw v. Reno,* 648.

38. *Miller v. Johnson,* brief, 38, n. 28; *U.S. v. Hays,* brief, 38, n. 33.

39. *Miller v. Johnson,* brief, 35, 37–38; *U.S. v. Hays,* brief, 34, 36–37 (emphases in original).

40. *Miller v. Johnson,* brief, 36–37; *U.S. v. Hays,* brief, 35–36 (emphases in original).

41. *Miller v. Johnson,* brief, 26, 43; *U.S. v. Hays,* brief, 26, 43.

42. *Miller v. Johnson,* brief, 9; *U.S. v. Hays,* brief, 9 (internal citations omitted). Here, the CBC was referring to the Court's hesitance in *Planned Parenthood of Southeastern Pennsylvania v. Casey* to overturn *Roe v. Wade.* The caucus, along with the Congressional House Democrats, took the same approach in defending the University of Michigan's affirmative action policies in *Grutter v. Bollinger.* See *Grutter v. Bollinger,* brief of John Conyers, et al. as amici curiae in support of respondents (Paul J. Lawrence and Anthony Miles as counsel of record; Daniel H. Royalty, attorney for amici curiae), 9–10. In that case, the CBC's arguments were apparently more persuasive.

43. *Shaw v. Hunt,* brief of amici curiae for the Congressional Black Caucus in support of the appellees (Marcella David of counsel; A. Leon Higginbotham Jr. as counsel of record; Gregory Clarick, Terri James, and Debo Adegbile), 19–20, 31.

44. Ibid., 5–9.

45. Ibid., 36–37 (internal citation omitted).

46. Ibid., 41–42.

47. Ibid., 43, citing *Adarand Constructors, Inc. v. Peña,* 2097.

48. Ibid., citing *Adarand Constructors, Inc. v. Peña,* 2115.

49. *Shaw v. Hunt,* brief, 43.

50. Ibid., 44–45 (footnotes omitted).

51. *Northwest Austin Municipal Utility District Number 1 v. Holder,* brief of Barbara Lee, Nydia Velazquez, and Michael Honda, et al., as amici curiae in support of appellees (Juan Cartagena, counsel of record; Kareem Crayton).

52. Ibid., 12–13, 15–19.

53. Ibid., 1–2, 5–7.

54. Ibid., 10, 18–19.

186 | Notes to Pages 121–29

55. Ibid., 3, 9–10 (internal citations omitted).
56. Ibid., 10, 14, 20
57. Ibid., 8–9 (internal quotation marks omitted).
58. Ibid., 21.
59. Ibid., 21–22.
60. Ibid., 23.
61. See Walton and Smith, *American Politics.*
62. *Northwest Austin Municipal Utility District Number 1 v. Holder,* brief, 22–23.
63. Sotomayor, "Latina Judge's Voice."
64. Collins, *Friends of the Supreme Court,* 114.
65. Somashekhar, "Louisiana Redistricting Case"; Drange, "California Citizens Redistricting Commission Approves Final Draft Maps"; *Times-Picayune,* "Legislative Black Caucus Will Not Challenge New Louisiana Congressional Map"; Pearson, "African-American Groups Seek to Defend Democratic Map in Court"; Sheinin, "State Sues for Approval of New Legislative Maps"; Sanders, "Voter Registration Groups Sue over New Florida Election Law"; All About Redistricting, "Litigation in the 2010 Cycle"; National Conference of State Legislatures, "Voter Identification Requirements."
66. *Shaw v. Reno,* 642.
67. *Shaw v. Reno,* 641, 659, 687; *Shaw v. Hunt,* brief, 16.
68. Vose, *Caucasians Only,* 166, citing Charles Abrams.

CHAPTER 5

1. This list of cases differs somewhat from those discussed in chapter 4. I do not discuss the decision in *Rodgers v. Lodge* because the caucus and the Court were in such close agreement, likely as a consequence of the fact that it was decided with direct congressional cues—that is, as the VRA was being revised in 1982. Here I emphasize the disagreement between them as a result of those revisions. Because the Court vacated *U.S. v. Hays,* there is no substantive opinion to discuss in that case (and the CBC's briefs for *Miller* and *Hays* were identical).
2. For *Shaw v. Reno,* Sandra Day O'Connor delivered the opinion, in which William Rehnquist, Antonin Scalia, Anthony Kennedy, and Clarence Thomas joined and from which Byron White, Harry Blackmun, John Paul Stevens, and David Souter dissented. For *Miller v. Johnson,* Kennedy delivered the opinion, in which Rehnquist, O'Connor, Scalia, and Thomas joined and from which Stevens, Ruth Bader Ginsburg, Stephen Breyer, and Souter dissented. For *Shaw v. Hunt,* Rehnquist delivered the opinion, in which O'Connor, Scalia, Kennedy, and Thomas joined and from which Stevens, Ginsburg, Breyer, and Souter dissented. For *Northwest Austin,* John Roberts delivered the opinion, in which Stevens, Scalia, Kennedy, Souter, Ginsburg, Breyer, and Alito joined and from which Thomas concurred in part and dissented in part.
3. Abrams, "Raising Politics Up," 477.
4. *Shaw v. Reno,* 633. See figure 2 for a map of the challenged redistricting plan.
5. Ibid., 636.
6. *Gomillion v. Lightfoot,* 340–41.
7. Kousser, *Colorblind Injustice,* 332.
8. *Gomillion v. Lightfoot,* 347–48.

9. Ibid., 350.

10. *Shaw v. Reno,* 641, 647.

11. Ibid., 643–45.

12. Ibid., 647, citing *Gomillion v. Lightfoot.*

13. Kousser, "Strange, Ironic Career," 713.

14. For more images, see North Carolina General Assembly, "1992 Congressional Base Plan #10."

15. Scott, interview.

16. See *Wards Cove Packing Co. v. Atonio; Adarand Constructors, Inc. v. Peña; Missouri v. Jenkins; Parents Involved v. Seattle School District Number 1.*

17. Kousser, *Colorblind Injustice,* 384. See also *United Jewish Organizations Inc. v. Carey; Rodgers v. Lodge; Thornburg v. Gingles.*

18. *Miller v. Johnson,* brief, 30–32; Kousser, "Strange, Ironic Career," 729.

19. *Miller v. Johnson,* brief, 20.

20. *Shaw v. Reno,* 641, 647–48.

21. A. Leon Higginbotham Jr., Clarick, and David, "*Shaw v. Reno,*" 1620–21. According to a more acerbic assessment, "Justice O'Connor was playing language games using Humpty-Dumpty's rules"; see Kousser, *Colorblind Injustice,* 385 n. 23, citing Lewis Carroll's Humpty-Dumpty character: "When I use a word . . . it means just what I choose it to mean—neither more nor less" (emphasis deleted).

22. *Shaw v. Reno,* 650, 657–58.

23. Guinier, "More Democracy," 19.

24. Tate, *Black Faces,* 157.

25. *Shaw v. Reno,* 644–45, 651–53 (internal quotes omitted).

26. *Fullilove v. Klutznick,* 519 (internal citations and quotations omitted). The Court repeated this position fifteen years later in *Adarand Constructors, Inc. v. Peña* and most recently in *Grutter v. Bollinger.*

27. *Shaw v. Reno,* 647.

28. See Dawson, *Behind the Mule;* Tate, *Black Faces.* See also A. Leon Higginbotham Jr., Clarick, and David, "*Shaw v. Reno,*" 1625, 1632–33; Walton and Smith, *American Politics.*

29. *Shaw v. Reno,* 660 (emphasis omitted; internal citations omitted).

30. Ibid., 648.

31. O'Connor's failure to acknowledge these efforts likely explains the CBC's detailed documentation of them in its amicus briefs for *Miller v. Johnson* and *Shaw v. Hunt.*

32. *Shaw v. Reno,* 653, citing *Growe v. Emison.*

33. Ibid., 653, 657.

34. King, "I Have a Dream"; King, *Why We Can't Wait,* 140–41.

35. *Shaw v. Reno,* 642–43, 657–58.

36. Michael Brown et al., *Whitewashing Race,* 215–19.

37. Kousser, *Colorblind Injustice,* 377, 450.

38. *Miller v. Johnson,* 904–5, 911–16.

39. Ibid., 915–17.

40. Ibid., 915–19.

41. Ibid., 917.

42. Ibid., 922 (internal citations omitted).

43. Ibid., 922–25 (internal punctuation and citations omitted).

44. Ibid., 915–17 (internal citations omitted).

45. Ibid., 921 (emphasis added).

46. Ibid., 927–28.

47. *Shaw v. Hunt,* 907 (internal citations omitted).

48. Ibid., 909–10 (internal citations omitted).

49. Ibid., 911, 915.

50. Ibid., 913–17 (internal citations and parentheses omitted).

51. *Miller v. Johnson,* 913.

52. *Shaw v. Hunt,* 916 (internal quotations omitted).

53. *Georgia v. Ashcroft,* 478. See also Kousser, "Strange, Ironic Career," 732–37.

54. Section 2(a) of the VRA guarantees that "no voting qualification or prerequisite to voting, or standard, practice, or procedure shall be imposed or applied by any State or political subdivision to deny or abridge the right of any citizen of the United States to vote on account of race or color." Section 5 ensures in part that covered states or subdivisions do not "have the purpose and will not have the effect of denying or abridging the right to vote on account of race or color."

55. Greenhouse, "Chief Justice on the Spot."

56. "Confirmation Hearing on the Nomination of John G. Roberts, Jr.," 169–73.

57. Justice Thomas dissented from the majority in *Northwest Austin.*

58. *Northwest Austin Municipal Utility District Number 1 v. Holder,* 2511–16.

59. Ibid., 2513. Thomas was particularly averse to this principle, condemning it no fewer than seven times in the first few pages of his minority opinion (2517–18).

60. Ibid., 2511–13 (invoking *Boerne v. Flores*).

61. For earlier evidence of such problems in Texas, see *League of United Latin American Citizens et al. v. Perry,* a 2006 decision on a districting plan that had spawned the concept of "perrymandering" (referring to the efforts by Texas governor Rick Perry to orchestrate a second round of redistricting that advantaged the Republican Party). See also Eggen, "Justice Staff"; Eggen, "Gonzales Defends Approval"; Rosenbaum and Lichtblau, "New Twist." For federal complicity on the part of Republican partisans in Texas's redistricting efforts, see "Section 5 Recommendation Memorandum."

62. *Northwest Austin Municipal Utility District Number 1 v. Holder,* 2509, 2516 (internal citations omitted).

63. Kousser, "Strange, Ironic Career," 692.

64. *Shaw v. Reno,* 636, citing Grofman, "Would Vince Lombardi Have Been Right," 1261 n. 96.

65. Justice Stevens made a similar point in *Miller v. Johnson,* noting the false parallel between the exclusion of black citizens from public facilities and so forth and "the inclusion of too many black voters in [an electoral] district" (931).

66. Grofman, "Would Vince Lombardi Have Been Right," 1259–62.

67. Thomas, *My Grandfather's Son,* 54–57, 61–63, 80, 123, 149.

68. King, *Stride Toward Freedom,* 200.

69. *Georgia v. Ashcroft,* 27.

70. *Shaw v. Reno,* 657.

71. *Miller v. Johnson,* 927.

72. Michael Brown et al., *Whitewashing Race,* 209. See also Gillespie, *Whose Black Politics?*

73. *Miller v. Johnson,* 927.

CHAPTER 6

1. Gillette, *Right to Vote*, 164.
2. Michael Brown et al., *Whitewashing Race*, 193.
3. *Parents Involved v. Seattle School District Number 1*, 748.
4. *Nixon v. Herndon; Smith v. Allwright; McLaurin v. Oklahoma; Sweatt v. Painter*.
5. Lustig, *Corporate Liberalism*, 90–95.
6. *Slaughter-House Cases*, 69 (emphasis added; internal punctuation omitted).
7. Ibid., 74. During this time, the Court was also sharpening the distinction between state and federal citizenship with regard to women's civil liberties and rights. See *Bradwell v. Illinois*, 139, in which the Court held that based on "the opinion just delivered in the *Slaughter-House Cases*," a woman's "right to practice laws in the courts of a state . . . are not controlled by citizenship of the United States." See also *Minor v. Happersett*, 171, 178, in which the Court held that the Fourteenth Amendment "prohibited the state, of which [the woman] is a citizen, from abridging any of her privileges and immunities as a citizen of the United States" and that since "all the citizens of states were not invested with the right of suffrage" and since "women were excluded from suffrage in nearly all of the states," state constitutions that "commit that important trust to men alone are not necessarily void."
8. *Slaughter-House Cases*, 74.
9. Ibid., 81.
10. Ibid., 67–72.
11. Ibid., 70.
12. *Strauder v. West Virginia*, 304.
13. Ibid., 305 (internal citations omitted).
14. Ibid., 309.
15. Ibid., 306.
16. Ibid., 309.
17. Ibid., 310.
18. Ibid.
19. *Miller v. Johnson*, 946.
20. *Shaw v. Reno*, 648, citing Justice William O. Douglas in *Wright v. Rockefeller*.
21. *Miller v. Johnson*, 911 (internal citations omitted).
22. Ibid., 947, citing *Davis v. Bandemer* and Justice John Paul Stevens's dissent in *Shaw v. Reno*.
23. *Shaw v. Hunt*, 908, citing *McLaughlin v. Florida* and *Richmond v. J. A. Croson*.
24. Michael Brown et al., *Whitewashing Race*, 222.
25. Holder, remarks.
26. By no means does the Court's voting rights majority have exclusive ownership of this problem. See Peller's illuminating discussion of liberal hegemony over the concept of race consciousness, which contends that many liberal integrationist whites have recast race consciousness as racism, thereby allowing them to dismiss the concept of race consciousness altogether and to avoid confronting the extent to which they have been advantaged by various manifestations of white supremacy. Peller concludes that the end result is a "discomfort with whiteness [that] has led to a kind of self-negation" and with it a negation of any black race consciousness ("Race Consciousness," 778–90, 839–43). See also Michael Brown et al., *Whitewashing Race*; Bonilla-Silva, *Racism without Racists*.

27. *Shaw v. Reno*, 648.

28. Michael Brown et al., *Whitewashing Race*, 206.

29. Berger, *Government by Judiciary*, 3–4, 141, 458 (internal citations omitted).

30. Spann, *Race against the Court*, 2–3, 19–26, 85, 103–18, 170–71.

31. *Shaw v. Reno*, 641 (internal citations omitted).

32. Michael Brown et al., *Whitewashing Race*, 212–19.

33. Peller, "Race Consciousness," 773.

34. Dyson, *I May Not Get There With You*, 6–7, 15, 24–29.

35. Rollin, *Life and Public Services*, 19; see also http://archive.org/stream/lifepublic servic00inroll#page/n5/mode/2up (accessed April 4, 2012).

36. W. E. B. Du Bois, *Souls of Black Folk*, 5; W. E. B. Du Bois, *Oxford W. E. B. Du Bois Reader*, 37–96.

37. W. E. B. Du Bois, *Souls of Black Folk*, 3–5, 11; W. E. B. Du Bois, *Oxford W. E. B. Du Bois Reader*, 497–509, 594–608.

38. Dawson, *Behind the Mule*, 10.

39. W. E. B. Du Bois, *Darkwater*, 1, 17, 35; W. E. B. Du Bois, *Souls of Black Folk*, 1.

40. W. E. B. Du Bois, *Souls of Black Folk*, 11.

41. W. E. B. Du Bois, *Darkwater*, 29.

42. Barker, Jones, and Tate, *African Americans and the American Political System*, 14.

43. King, *Why We Can't Wait*, 128–29; King, *Where Do We Go From Here?*, 161–66.

44. Full Employment and Balanced Growth Act, U.S.C. 3151 (1978).

45. Robert C. Smith, *We Have No Leaders*, 198, 205.

46. Wilson, *Truly Disadvantaged*, 155 (emphasis minimized); see also 129–32, 150–54.

47. Pitkin, *Concept of Representation*, 62, 107, 128, 122.

48. See Frymer, *Uneasy Alliances*, 178.

49. Perry and Parent, *Blacks and the American Political System*, 3–9, 11–34.

50. See *United States v. Carolene Products*. This case is notable for its n. 4, in which the Court acknowledged that "prejudice against discrete and insular minorities may be a special condition which tends seriously to curtail the operation of those political processes ordinarily relied upon to protect minorities." This statement, with its strongly implied immutability of race, led eventually to multiple levels of review in equal protection cases involving suspect classifications. See also *Regents of the University of California v. Bakke*, including concurrences and dissents, for a provocative discussion of the implications of n. 4 and as an example of the narrowing jurisprudential scope of those implications.

51. Canon, *Race, Representation, and Redistricting*, 3, 148.

52. Yamamoto, "Critical Race Praxis," 852.

53. Langston Hughes, "Let America Be America Again," in Hughes, *Collected Poems*, 189–91.

Bibliography

Note: A list of court decisions follows the bibliography.

Abrams, K. A. "Raising Politics Up: Minority Vote Dilution and Section 2 of the Voting Rights Act." *New York University Law Review* 63 (1988): 449–531.

"Administration Draws Fire from Civil Rights Groups on Voting Rights Position." *Congressional Quarterly Weekly Report,* January 30, 1982, 170–71.

Aleinikoff, Alexander, and Samuel Issacharoff. "Drawing Constitutional Lines after *Shaw v. Reno.*" *Michigan Law Review* 92 (1993): 588–651.

All About Redistricting. "Litigation in the 2010 Cycle." http://redistricting.lls.edu/cases.php#GA. Accessed December 15, 2011.

Allen, Robert. *Black Awakening in Capitalist America.* Garden City, N.Y.: Anchor, 1970.

Arizona Free Enterprise Club v. Bennett. Slip Opinion No. 10-238.

Awkward, Michael. *Negotiating Difference: Race, Gender, and the Politics of Positionality.* Chicago: University of Chicago Press, 1995.

Balkin, Jack, and Reva Siegel, eds. *The Constitution in 2020.* New York: Oxford University Press, 2009.

Ball, Howard, Dale Krane, and Thomas P. Lauth. *Compromised Compliance: Implementation of the 1965 Voting Rights Act.* Westport, Conn.: Greenwood, 1982.

Barker, Lucius, Mack Jones, and Katherine Tate. *African Americans and the Political System.* 4th ed. Upper Saddle River, N.J.: Prentice Hall, 1999.

Bell, Derrick. "*Brown v. Board of Education* and the Interest Convergence Dilemma." In *Critical Race Theory: The Key Writings,* edited by Kimberlé Crenshaw, Neil Gotenda, Gary Peller, and Kendall Thomas, 20–29. New York: New Press, 1995.

Berger, Raoul. *Government by Judiciary: The Transformation of the Fourteenth Amendment.* 2nd ed. Indianapolis: Liberty Fund, 1997.

Bonilla-Silva, Eduardo. *Racism without Racists: Color-Blind Racism and Racial Inequality in Contemporary America.* 3rd ed. New York: Rowman and Littlefield, 2010.

Bositis, David, ed. *Black Elected Officials: A Statistical Summary 2000.* Lanham, Md.: University Press of America, 2000.

Bositis, David. *The Congressional Black Caucus in the 103rd Congress.* Lanham, Md.: University Press of America, 1994.

Bositis, David, ed. *Redistricting and Minority Representation.* Lanham, Md.: University Press of America, 1998.

Bositis, David, ed. *Voting Rights and Minority Representation: Redistricting, 1992–2002.* Lanham, Md.: University Press of America, 2006.

Brandwein, Pamela. "A Judicial Abandonment of Blacks? Rethinking the 'State Action' Cases of the Waite Court." *Law and Society Review* 41 (2007): 343–86.

Brandwein, Pamela. *Reconstructing Reconstruction: The Supreme Court and the Production of Historical Truth.* Durham: Duke University Press, 1999.

Brown, Elsa Barkley. "To Catch the Vision of Freedom: Reconstructing Southern Black Women's Political History, 1865–1880." In *African American Women and the Vote, 1837–1965,* edited by Ann Gordon and Bettye Collier-Thomas, 66–99. Amherst: University of Massachusetts Press, 1997.

Brown, Michael, Martin Carnoy, Elliott Currie, Troy Duster, David B. Oppenheimer, Marjorie M. Schultz, and David Wellman, eds. *Whitewashing Race: The Myth of a Color-Blind Society.* Berkeley: University of California Press, 2003.

Burin, Eric. *Slavery and the Peculiar Solution: A History of the American Colonization Society.* Gainesville: University Press of Florida, 2005.

Burman, Steven. *The Black Progress Question: Explaining the African-American Predicament.* Thousand Oaks, Calif.: Sage, 1995.

Canellos, Peter. "Elena Kagan: Better for Liberals than They Believed." *Boston Globe,* September 9, 2011. http://www.boston.com/bostonglobe/editorial_opinion/blogs/the_angle/2011/08/elena_kagan_may.html. Accessed December 13, 2011.

Canon, David. *Race, Representation, and Redistricting.* Chicago: University of Chicago Press, 1999.

Canon, David. "Renewing the Voting Rights Act: Retrogression, Influence, and the *Georgia v. Ashcroft* Fix." *Election Law Journal* 7 (2008): 3–24.

"Capital Boxscore." *Congressional Quarterly Weekly Report,* September 5, 1981, 1726.

Civil Rights Act of 1964. 42 U.S.C. Chapter 21.

"Civil Rights Victory: Voting Rights Act Extension Cleared for President Reagan." *Congressional Quarterly Weekly Report,* June 26, 1982, 1503–4.

"Confirmation Hearing on the Nomination of John G. Roberts, Jr. To Be Chief Justice of the United States." Hearing before the Committee on the Judiciary, United States Senate, 109th Congress, September 12–15, 2005, 169–73. http://www.gpofdsys/pkg/GPO-CHRG-ROBERTS/Content_detail.gov/.html. Accessed April 4, 2012.

Clayton, Dewey. *African-Americans and the Politics of Congressional Redistricting.* New York: Garland, 2003.

Clayton, Dewey. *The Presidential Campaign of Barack Obama: A Critical Analysis of a Racially Transcendent Strategy.* New York: Routledge, 2010.

Coleman, Willi. "Architects of a Vision: Black Women and Their Quest for Political and Social Equality." In *African American Women and the Vote, 1837–1965,* edited by Ann Gordon and Bettye Collier-Thomas, 24–39. Amherst: University of Massachusetts Press, 1997.

Collins, Paul, Jr. *Friends of the Supreme Court: Interest Groups and Judicial Decision Making.* Oxford: Oxford University Press, 2008.

"Congress Clears Voting Rights Act Extension." *Congressional Quarterly Almanac* (1975), 521–33.

Crenshaw, Kimberlé. "Demarginalizing the Intersection of Race and Sex: A Black Feminist Critique of Antidiscrimination Doctrine, Feminist Theory, and Antiracist Politics." *University of Chicago Legal Forum* 1989 (1989): 139–67.

Crenshaw, Kimberlé, Neil Gotenda, Gary Peller, and Kendall Thomas, eds. *Critical Race Theory: The Key Writings.* New York: New Press, 1995.

Dahl, Robert. *Dilemmas of Pluralist Democracy: Autonomy vs. Control.* New Haven: Yale University Press, 1982.

Davidson, Chandler, and Bernard Grofman, eds. *Quiet Revolution in the South.* Princeton: Princeton University Press, 1994.

Davidson, R. H., and W. J. Oleszek. *Congress and Its Members.* 4th ed. Washington, D.C.: Congressional Quarterly, 1994.

Dawson, Michael. *Behind the Mule.* Princeton: Princeton University Press, 1994.

Delany, Martin. *The Condition, Elevation, Emigration, and Destiny of the Colored People of the United States Politically Considered.* 1852. http://infomotions.com/etexts/gutenberg/dirs/1/7/1/5/17154/17154.htm. Accessed February 18, 2011.

Delany, Martin. *The Origin of Races and Color.* 1879; Baltimore: Black Classic, 1991.

Delgado, Richard, ed. *Critical Race Theory: The Cutting Edge.* Philadelphia: Temple University Press, 1995.

Delgado, Richard, and Jean Stefancic. *Critical Race Theory: An Introduction.* New York: New York University Press, 2001.

DeNavas-Walt, Carmen, Bernadette D. Proctor, and Jessica C. Smith. *Income, Poverty and Health Insurance Coverage in the United States: 2009.* U.S. Census Bureau Current Population Reports, P60-238. Washington, D.C.: U.S. Government Printing Office, 2010.

Derfner, Jeremy. "The New Black Caucus." *American Prospect,* March 27–April 10, 2000, 16–19.

Dittmer, John. "The Education of Henry McNeal Turner." In *Black Leaders of the Nineteenth Century,* edited by Leon Litwack and August Meier, 253–74. Urbana: University of Illinois Press, 1988.

"Dole Seeking Compromise: Disputes, Maneuvers Delay Voting Rights Markup." *Congressional Quarterly Weekly Report,* May 1, 1982, 1017.

Douglass, Frederick. *My Bondage and My Freedom.* 1855; New York: Dover, 1969.

Douglass, Frederick. "What the Black Man Wants." In *Let Nobody Turn Us Around,* edited by Manning Marable and Leith Mullings. Lanham, Md.: Rowman and Littlefield, 2000.

Drange, Matt. "California Citizens Redistricting Commission Approves Final Draft Maps; Litigation Expected to Follow." *Times-Standard,* July 30, 2011. http://www.times-standard.com/localnews/ci_18584957.

Dray, Phillip. *Capitol Men.* Boston: Houghton Mifflin, 2008.

Du Bois, Ellen Carol. *Feminism and Suffrage.* Ithaca: Cornell University Press, 1978.

Du Bois, W. E. B. *Darkwater: Voices from within the Veil.* 1920; Mineola, N.Y.: Dover Thrift, 1999.

Du Bois, W. E. B. *Dusk of Dawn.* 1940; New Brunswick, N.J.: Transaction, 1984.

Du Bois, W. E. B. *The Oxford W. E. B. Du Bois Reader.* Edited by Eric Sundquist. New York: Oxford University Press, 1996.

Du Bois, W. E. B. *The Souls of Black Folk.* 1903; New York: Penguin, 1989.

Duverger, Maurice. *Political Parties: Their Organization and Activity in the Modern State.* Translated by Barbara North and Robert North. London: Wiley, 1954.

Dyson, Michael Eric. *I May Not Get There with You: The True Martin Luther King Jr.* New York: Free Press, 2000.

Edsall, Thomas B., and Mary D. Edsall. *Chain Reaction.* New York: Norton, 1992.

Eggen, Dan. "Gonzales Defends Approval of Texas Redistricting by Justice." *Washington Post,* December 3, 2005.

Eggen, Dan. "Justice Staff Saw Texas Redistricting as Illegal." *Washington Post,* December 2, 2005.

Engstrom, Richard L. "Influence Districts and the Courts: A Concept in Need of Clarity." Paper presented at the Roscoe C. Siciliano Forum on "The Future of the Voting Rights Act: Democracy in Danger?" University of Utah, October 12, 2006.

Epps, Garrett. *Democracy Reborn: The 14th Amendment and the Fight for Equal Rights in Post–Civil War America.* New York: Holt, 2006.

Epstein, David. *Dividing Lines: Racial Redistricting and Substantive Representation.* Forthcoming.

Epstein, David, Richard Pildes, Rodolfo de la Garza, and Sharyn O'Halloran, eds. *The Future of the Voting Rights Act.* New York: Sage, 2006.

"Expansion of Voting Rights Act Urged." *Congressional Quarterly Weekly Report,* April 12, 1975, 761–62.

Fannie Lou Hamer, Rosa Parks, and Coretta Scott King Voting Rights Act Reauthorization and Amendments Act of 2006.

"Fannie Lou Hamer, Rosa Parks and Coretta Scott King Voting Rights Act Reauthorization and Amendments Act of 2006 (Part I)." Congressional hearing, May 4, 2006.

Fenno, Richard F. *Congressmen in Committees.* Boston: Little, Brown, 1973.

Fenno, Richard F. *Going Home: Black Representatives and Their Constituents.* Chicago: University of Chicago Press, 2003.

Fields, Reginald. "State Sen. Nina Turner Says More than 14,000 Wrong-Precinct Ballots Were Disqualified in 2008: Politifact Ohio." *Plain Dealer,* July 5, 2011. http://www.cleveland.com/open/index.ssf/2011/07/state_sen_nina_turner_says_mor.html. Accessed December 13, 2011.

Flexner, Eleanor. *A Century of Struggle.* Cambridge: Belknap Press of Harvard University Press, 1996.

Foner, Eric, ed. *Freedom's Lawmakers: A Directory of Black Officeholders during Reconstruction.* Rev. ed. Baton Rouge: Louisiana State University Press, 1996.

Ford, Ellen. *Women and Politics: The Pursuit of Equality.* Boston: Houghton Mifflin, 2002.

Frymer, Paul. *Uneasy Alliances.* Princeton: Princeton University Press, 1999.

Galderisi, Peter, ed. *Redistricting in the New Millennium.* Lanham, Md.: Lexington, 2005.

Garnet, Henry Highland, ed. *Walker's Appeal in Four Articles; An Address to the Slaves of the United States of America.* Salem, Mass.: Ayer Company, 1984.

Gerstein, Josh. "Eric Holder: Voter ID Law Hurts Minorities." *Politico,* December 13, 2011. http://www.politico.com/news/stories/1211/70400.html. Accessed December 13, 2011.

Gillespie, Andra, ed. *Whose Black Politics? Cases in Post-Racial Black Leadership.* New York: Routledge, 2009.

Gillette, William. *The Right to Vote: Politics and Passage of the Fifteenth Amendment.* Baltimore: Johns Hopkins University Press, 1965.

Golub, Mark. "Plessy as 'Passing': Judicial Responses to Ambiguously Raced Bodies in *Plessy v. Ferguson.*" *Law and Society Review* 39 (2005): 563–600.

Gordon, Ann, and Bettye Collier-Thomas, eds. *African American Women and the Vote, 1837–1965.* Amherst: University of Massachusetts Press, 1997.

Gotanda, Neil. "A Critique of 'Our Constitution Is Color Blind.'" In *Critical Race Theory: The Key Writings,* edited by Kimberlé Crenshaw, Neil Gotenda, Gary Peller, and Kendall Thomas, 257–75. New York: New Press, 1995.

Graber, Mark. *Dred Scott and the Problem of Constitutional Evil.* New York: Cambridge University Press, 2008.

Greenhouse, Linda. "The Chief Justice on the Spot." *New York Times,* January 9, 2009.

Grofman, Bernard, ed. *Race and Redistricting in the 1990s.* New York: Agathon, 1998.

Grofman, Bernard. "Would Vince Lombardi Have Been Right If He Had Said: 'When It Comes to Redistricting, Race Isn't Everything, It's the Only Thing?'" *Cardozo Law Review* 14 (1997): 1237–76.

Grofman, Bernard, and Thomas Brunell. "The Art of the Dummymander: The Impact of Recent Redistrictings on the Partisan Makeup of Southern House Seats." In *Redistricting in the New Millennium,* edited by Peter Galderisi, 183–99. Lanham, Md: Lexington, 2005.

Grofman, Bernard, Lisa Handley, and Richard Niemi. *Minority Representation and the Quest for Voting Equality.* New York: Cambridge University Press, 1992.

Guinier, Lani. "Groups, Representation, and Race-Conscious Districting: A Case of the Emperor's Clothes." *Texas Law Review* 71 (1993): 1589–1642.

Guinier, Lani. "More Democracy." *University of Chicago Legal Forum* 1 (1995): 1–22.

Guinier, Lani. *The Tyranny of the Majority.* New York: Free Press, 1994.

Hallett, George, Jr. *Proportional Representation, the Key to Democracy.* New York: National Municipal League, 1940.

Hammond, Susan Webb. *Congressional Caucuses in National Policy-Making.* Baltimore: Johns Hopkins University Press, 2001.

Harmon-Jones, Eddie, and Judson Mills, eds. *Cognitive Dissonance: Progress on a Pivotal Theory in Social Psychology.* Washington, D.C.: American Psychological Association, 1999.

"Hatch vs. Civil Rights Groups: Amid Intense Lobbying, Senate Faces Decision on Voting Rights Act." *Congressional Quarterly Weekly Report,* March 6, 1982, 520–21.

Henderson, Lenneal, ed. *Black Political Life in the U.S.: A Fist as the Pendulum.* San Francisco: Chandler, 1972.

Higginbotham, A. Leon. *In the Matter of Color.* New York: Oxford University Press, 1978.

Higginbotham, A. Leon. *Shades of Freedom.* New York: Oxford University Press, 1996.

Higginbotham, A. Leon, Gregory Clarick, and Marcella David. "*Shaw v. Reno:* A Mirage of Good Intentions with Devastating Racial Consequences." *Fordham Law Review* 62 (1994): 1593–1659.

Holder, Eric. Remarks, Department of Justice African American History Month Program, February 18, 2009. http://www.justice.gov/ag/speeches/2009/ag-speech -090218.html. Accessed April 4, 2012.

"House Judiciary Committee Passes Compromise Version of Voting Rights Renewal." *Congressional Quarterly Weekly Report,* August 1, 1981, 1422.

"House Opens Hearings on Voting Rights Act." *Congressional Quarterly Weekly Report,* May 9, 1981, 819.

"House Passes Bill to Extend Voting Rights Act." *Congressional Quarterly Almanac* (1981), 415–18.

"House Passes Bill to Extend Voting Rights Act." *Congressional Quarterly Weekly Report,* October 10, 1981, 1965–66.

"House Passes Strong Voting Rights Extension." *Congressional Quarterly Weekly Report,* June 7, 1975, 1200–1203.

Hughes, Langston. *The Collected Poems of Langston Hughes.* Edited by Arnold Rampersad. New York: Knopf, 1994.

"'Intent' a Key Issue in Voting Rights Debate." *Congressional Quarterly Weekly Report,* January 9, 1982, 42.

Issacharoff, Samuel, Pamela Karlan, and Richard Pildes. *The Law of Democracy.* New York: Foundation, 2002.

Jefferson, Thomas. *Notes on the State of Virginia.* http://etext.lib.virginia.edu/toc/mod eng/public/JefVirg.html. Accessed February 18, 2011.

Joint Center Database, Number of Black Elected Officials in the United States, by State and Office. http://www.jointcenter.org/research/national-roster-of-black-elected-officials. Accessed April 4, 2012.

Joseph, Peniel. *Dark Days, Bright Nights: From Black Power to Barack Obama.* New York: Basic Civitas, 2010.

"Judiciary Panel Approves Voting Rights Bill." *Congressional Quarterly Weekly Report,* July 25, 1981, 1343.

"Justice Department Rejects N.C. Plan." *Congressional Quarterly Weekly Report,* December 12, 1981, 2448.

Karlan, Pamela. "*Georgia v. Ashcroft* and the Retrogression of Retrogression." *Election Law Journal* 3 (2004): 21–36.

Katznelson, Ira, and Helen V. Milner, eds. *Political Science: The State of the Discipline.* New York: Norton, 2002.

Kearney, Joseph D., and Thomas W. Merrill. "The Influence of *Amicus Curiae* Briefs on the Supreme Court." *University of Pennsylvania Law Review* 148 (2000): 743–854.

Key, V. O. *Politics, Parties, and Pressure Groups.* New York: Crowell, 1958.

Keyssar, Alexander. *The Right to Vote: The Contested History of Democracy in the United States.* New York: Basic Books, 2000.

King, Martin Luther, Jr. "I Have a Dream" [speech], August 23, 1963. http://www.ameri canrhetoric.com/speeches/mlkihaveadream.htm. Accessed February 18, 2011.

King, Martin Luther, Jr. *Stride toward Freedom: The Montgomery Story.* New York: Harper and Row, 1959.

King, Martin Luther, Jr. *Where Do We Go from Here: Chaos or Community?* New York: Harper and Row, 1967.

King, Martin Luther, Jr. *Why We Can't Wait.* 1963; New York: Signet Classic, 2000.

Klarman, Michael. *From Jim Crow to Civil Rights: The Supreme Court and the Struggle for Racial Equality.* New York: Oxford University Press, 2004.

Kousser, J. Morgan. *Colorblind Injustice: Minority Voting Rights and the Undoing of the Second Reconstruction.* Chapel Hill: University of North Carolina Press, 1999.

Kousser, J. Morgan. "The Strange, Ironic Career of Section 5 of the Voting Rights Act, 1965–2007." *Texas Law Review* 86 (2008): 667–775.

Lawson, Stephen F. *In the Pursuit of Power.* New York: Columbia University Press, 1985.

Layton, Azza. *International Politics and Civil Rights Policies in the United States, 1941–1960.* Cambridge: Cambridge University Press, 2000.

Lennertz, James. "In Dixieland We'll Take Our Stand . . . Judicial Review of Racial Gerrymandering, North and South." Paper presented at the annual meeting of the American Political Science Association, Atlanta, September 1999.

Litwack, Leon, and August Meier, eds. *Black Leaders of the Nineteenth Century.* Urbana: University of Illinois Press, 1988.

Lowndes, Joseph, Julie Novkov, and Dorian T. Warren, eds. *Race and American Political Development.* New York: Routledge, 2008.

Lublin, David I. *The Paradox of Representation: Racial Gerrymandering and Minority Interests in Congress.* Princeton: Princeton University Press, 1997.

Lustig, Jeffrey R. *Corporate Liberalism: The Origins of Modern American Political Theory, 1890–1920*. Berkeley: University of California Press, 1982.

Marable, Manning. *From the Grassroots*. Boston: South End, 1980.

Marable, Manning. *How Capitalism Underdeveloped Black America*. Boston: South End, 1983.

Marable, Manning. *Race, Reform, and Rebellion*. 2nd ed. Jackson: University Press of Mississippi, 1991.

Marable, Manning, and Leith Mullings, eds. *Let Nobody Turn Us Around*. Lanham, Md.: Rowman and Littlefield, 2000.

Marx, Karl. *Capital*. 1867. http://www.marxists.org/archive/marx/works/1867-c1/. Accessed February 18, 2011.

Mathews, John Mabry. *Legislative and Judicial History of the Fifteenth Amendment*. Baltimore: Johns Hopkins University Press, 1909.

McCloskey, Robert G. *The American Supreme Court*. 2nd ed. Chicago: University of Chicago Press, 1994.

McMurry, Linda. *To Keep the Waters Troubled: The Life of Ida B. Wells*. New York: Oxford University Press, 1998.

Meier, August, Elliott Rudwick, and Francis Broderick, eds. *Black Protest Thought in the Twentieth Century*. 2nd ed. New York: Macmillan, 1971.

Merriam, Charles, and Harold Gosnell. *The American Party System*. 4th ed. New York: Macmillan, 1949.

Middleton, Stephen, ed. *Black Congressmen during Reconstruction: A Documentary Sourcebook*. Westport, Conn.: Praeger, 2002.

Mill, John Stuart. *On Liberty*. Edited by Alburey Castell. 1859; Arlington Heights, Ill.: Harlan Davidson, 1947.

Moses, Wilson. *Alexander Crummell: A Study of Civilization and Discontent*. New York: Oxford University Press, 1989.

Moses, Wilson. *Creative Conflict in African-American Thought*. New York: Cambridge University Press, 2004.

Murray, Charles. *Losing Ground: American Social Policy, 1950–1980*. New York: Basic Books, 1994.

National Conference of State Legislatures. "Voter Identification Requirements." http://www.ncsl.org/default.aspx?tabid=16602. Accessed December 15, 2011.

North Carolina General Assembly. "1992 Congressional Base Plan #10." http://wsww.ncga.state.nc.us/representation/Content/Plans/PlanPage_DB_1991.asp?Plan=1992_Congressional_Base_Plan_10&Body=Congress. Accessed April 4, 2012.

"Opposition Fading to Voting Act Renewal." *Congressional Quarterly Weekly Report*, June 20, 1981, 1111.

Painter, Nell Irvin. "Martin Delany: Elitism and Black Nationalism." In *Black Leaders of the Nineteenth Century*, edited by Leon Litwack and August Meier, 149–72. Urbana: University of Illinois Press, 1988.

Painter, Nell Irvin. *Sojourner Truth: A Life, a Symbol*. New York: Norton, 1996.

Pallasch, Abdon. "GOP Chairman: African-Americans Not Given Good Reason to Vote for Party." *Chicago Sun-Times*, April 10, 2010.

Pearson, Rick. "African-American Groups Seek to Defend Democratic Map in Court." *Chicago Tribune*, September 12, 2011.

Peller, Gary. "Race Consciousness." *Duke Law Journal* 4 (1990): 758–847.

Pergram, Scott. "GOPers West and Scott Welcome in Congressional Black Caucus." No-

vember 9, 2010. http://politics.blogs.foxnews.com/2010/11/09/gopers-west-and
-scott-welcome-congressional-black-caucus. Accessed February 18, 2011.

Perry, Huey, and Wayne Parent. *Blacks and the American Political System.* Gainesville:
University Press of Florida, 1995.

Persily, Nathan. "The Promise and Pitfalls of the New Voting Rights Act." *Yale Law Journal* 117 (2007): 174–253.

Pildes, Richard A. "The Decline of Legally Mandated Minority Representation." *Ohio State Law Journal* 68 (2007): 1139–61.

Pitkin, Hannah F. *The Concept of Representation.* Berkeley: University of California Press, 1967.

Piven, Frances Fox, and Richard Cloward. *Why Americans Don't Vote.* New York: Pantheon, 1989.

Piven, Frances Fox, Lorraine C. Minnite, and Margaret Groarke. *Keeping Down the Black Vote: Race and the Demobilization of American Voters.* New York: New Press, 2009.

Reilly, Ryan J. "Kagan: SCOTUS Ruling against Arizona Public Financing Is 'Chutzpah.'" *TPM Muckraker,* June 27, 2011. http://tpmmuckraker.talkingpointsmemo.com/2011/06/kagan_supreme_court_ruling_against_arizona_public.php. Accessed December 13, 2011.

Rivers, Christina. "'Conquered Provinces'? The Voting Rights Act and State Power." *Publius: The Journal of Federalism* 36 (2006): 421–42.

Rollin, Frank [Frances Rollin Whipper]. *The Life and Public Services of Martin R. Delany.* Boston: Lee and Shepard, 1868.

Rosenbaum, David, and Eric Lichtblau. "New Twist in Texas Districting Dispute." *New York Times,* December 3, 2005.

"Rules Committee Action: Voting Rights Extension." *Congressional Quarterly Weekly Report,* May 17, 1975, 1042–44.

Sanders, Katie. "Voter Registration Groups Sue over New Florida Election Law." *Saint Petersburg Times,* December 15, 2011. http://www.tampabay.com/news/politics/legislature/voter-registration-groups-sue-over-new-florida-election-law/1206508. Accessed December 15, 2011.

"Section 5 Recommendation Memorandum: December 12, 2003." *Washington Post.* http://www.washingtonpost.com/wp-srv/nation/documents/texasDOJmemo.pdf. Accessed February 18, 2011.

"Senate Judiciary Approves Voting Rights Bill." *Congressional Quarterly Weekly Report,* May 8, 1982, 1041–43.

"Senate Panel Approves Voting Rights Bill." *Congressional Quarterly Weekly Report,* March 27, 1982, 680.

"Senate Passes Extension of Voting Rights Act." *Congressional Quarterly Weekly Report,* June 19, 1982, 1456.

"Senators Try to Protect Voting Rights Options." *Congressional Quarterly Weekly Report,* October 17, 1981, 2028.

Shadd, Adrienne. "Mary Ann Shadd Cary: Abolitionist." http://www.collectionscanada.gc.ca/northern-star/033005-2200-e.html. Accessed February 18, 2011.

Sheinin, Aaron Gould. "State Sues for Approval of New Legislative Maps." *Atlanta Journal-Constitution,* October 6, 2011. Accessed on-line, December 15, 2011.

Siegel, Stephen. "The Federal Government's Power to Enact Color-Conscious Laws: An Originalist Inquiry." *Northwestern University Law Review* 92 (1998): 477–589.

Singh, Robert. *The Congressional Black Caucus: Racial Politics in the U.S. Congress.* Thousand Oaks, Calif.: Sage, 1997.

Smith, John D. *Black Judas: William Hannibal Thomas and "The American Negro."* Athens: University of Georgia Press, 2000.

Smith, Robert C. *We Have No Leaders.* Albany: State University of New York Press, 1996.

Smith, Steven S., and C. J. Deering. *Committees in Congress.* Washington, D.C.: Congressional Quarterly Press, 1984.

Somashekhar, Sandhaya. "Louisiana Redistricting Case Seen as Crucial Test of Voting Rights Act." *Washington Post,* June 4, 2011. http://www.washingtonpost.com/politics/louisiana-redistricting-case-seen-as-crucial-test-of-voting-rights-act/2011/05/25/AGCKT1IH_story.html. Accessed December 15, 2011.

"Some Republicans Unhappy with Voting Rights Plan Adopted by Judiciary." *Congressional Quarterly Weekly Report,* August 8, 1981, 1446.

Sotomayor, Sonia. "A Latina Judge's Voice." 2001. Reprinted in *New York Times,* May 14, 2009.

Spann, Girardeau. *Race against the Court.* New York: New York University Press, 1993.

Stewart, Maria W. *Maria W. Stewart, America's First Black Woman Political Writer.* Edited and introduction by Marilyn Richardson. Bloomington: Indiana University Press, 1987.

Stuckey, Sterling. *Going through the Storm: The Influence of African American Art in History.* New York: Oxford University Press, 1994.

"Subcommittee Action: Voting Rights Act." *Congressional Quarterly Weekly Report,* April 26, 1975, 876.

Swain, Carol. *Black Faces, Black Interests.* Cambridge: Harvard University Press, 1995.

Swain, Carol. "Reauthorization of the VRA: How Politics and Symbolism Failed America." *Georgetown Journal of Law and Public Policy* 5 (2007): 29–39.

"Talks on Voting Rights Act Now in Progress." *Congressional Quarterly Weekly Report,* July 18, 1981, 1289.

Tate, Katherine. *Black Faces in the Mirror.* Princeton: Princeton University Press, 2003.

Thernstrom, Abigail. *Whose Votes Count?* Cambridge: Harvard University Press, 1987.

Thomas, Clarence. *My Grandfather's Son.* New York: HarperCollins. 2007.

Times-Picayune. "Legislative Black Caucus Will Not Challenge New Louisiana Congressional Map." *Times-Picayune,* August 6, 2011. http://www.nola.com/politics/index.ssf/2011/08/legislative_black_caucus_will.html. Accessed December 15, 2011.

"To Examine the Impact and Effectiveness of the Voting Rights Act." Congressional hearing, October 18, 2005.

Turner, Henry McNeal. *Respect Black: The Writings and Speeches of Henry McNeal Turner.* Compiled and edited by Edwin Redkey. New York: Arno, 1971.

U.S. Congress. House. Committee on Judiciary. *Hearings before the Subcommittee on Civil and Constitutional Rights on the Extension of the Voting Rights Act.* 94th Cong., 1st sess., February 25–26, March 3–6, 13–14, 17, 20–21, 24–25, 1975.

U.S. Congress. House. Committee on Judiciary. *Hearings before the Subcommittee on Civil and Constitutional Rights on the Extension of the Voting Rights Act.* 97th Cong., 1st sess. May 6–7, 13, 19–20, 27–28, June 3, 5, 10, 12, 16–18, 23–25, July 13, 1981.

U.S. Congress. House. Committee on Judiciary. *Hearings before the Subcommittee on the Constitution on the Extension of the Voting Rights Act.* 109th Cong., 1st sess., November 9, 2005.

U.S. Congress. Senate. Committee on the Judiciary. *Hearings on the Nomination of John Roberts as Chief Justice of the Supreme Court.* 109th Cong., 1st sess., September 12–15, 2005.

Valelly, Richard. *The Two Reconstructions: The Struggle for Black Enfranchisement.* Chicago: University of Chicago Press, 2004.

Valelly, Richard, ed. *The Voting Rights Act: Securing the Ballot.* Washington, D.C.: Congressional Quarterly Press, 2006.

Vose, Clement. *Caucasians Only: The Supreme Court, the NAACP, and the Restrictive Covenant Cases.* Berkeley: University of California Press, 1959.

Vose, Clement. "Litigation as a Form of Pressure Group Activity." *Annals of the American Academy of Political and Social Science,* July–November 1958, 20–31.

Vose, Clement. "NAACP Strategy in the Covenant Cases." *Western Reserve Law Review* 6 (1955): 101–16.

"Voting Rights Act: Debate on Extension Begins." *Congressional Quarterly Weekly Report,* March 8, 1975, 489–92.

"Voting Rights Act Extended, Strengthened." *Congressional Quarterly Almanac* (1982), 373–77.

"Voting Rights Act Extension Approved." *Congressional Quarterly Weekly Report,* May 3, 1975, 925–26.

Voting Rights Act of 1965. 42 U.S.C. 1973.

"Voting Rights Act Renewal to Spark Fight in Congress." *Congressional Quarterly Weekly Report,* April 11, 1981, 633–37.

"Voting Rights Act: Evidence of Continued Need." Congressional hearing, March 8, 2006.

"Voting Rights Act: An Examination of the Scope and Criteria for Coverage under the Special Provisions of the Act." Congressional hearing, October 25, 2005.

"Voting Rights Act: The Judicial Evolution of the Retrogression Standard." Congressional hearing, November 9, 2005.

"Voting Rights Act: Section 5—Preclearance Standards." Congressional hearing, November 1, 2005.

Walker, David. *David Walker's Appeal to the Coloured Citizens of the World.* Edited by Peter Hinks. University Park: Pennsylvania State University Press, 2000.

Walker, David. *David Walker's Appeal to the Coloured Citizens of the World.* Edited by James Turner. Baltimore: Black Classic, 1993.

Walker, David. *Walker's Appeal in Four Articles and an Address to the Slaves of the United States of America.* Edited by Henry Highland Garnet. 1848; Salem, MA: Ayer, 1984.

Walton, Hanes, Jr. *African American Power and Politics: The Political Context Variable.* New York: Columbia University Press, 1997.

Walton, Hanes, Jr. *Invisible Politics: Black Political Behavior.* Albany: State University of New York Press, 1985.

Walton, Hanes, Jr., and Robert C. Smith. *American Politics and the African American Quest for Universal Freedom.* 5th ed. New York: Longman–Prentice Hall, 2010.

Washington, Booker T. "The Atlanta Exposition Address." In *Let Nobody Turn Us Around,* edited by Manning Marable and Leith Mullings, 182–85. Lanham, Md.: Rowman and Littlefield, 2000.

Wells-Barnett, Ida B. *Crusade for Justice: The Autobiography of Ida B. Wells.* Edited by Alfreda M. Duster. Chicago: University of Chicago Press, 1970.

Wells-Barnett, Ida B. *The Red Record.* http://www.gutenberg.org/files/14977/14977-h/14977-h.htm. Accessed February 18, 2011.

Williams, Kim M. *Mark One or More: Civil Rights in Multiracial America.* Ann Arbor: University of Michigan Press, 2006.

Williams, Linda F. *The Constraint of Race: Legacies of White Skin Privilege in America.* University Park: Pennsylvania State University Press, 2003.

Wills, Garry. *The Negro President: Jefferson and the Slave Power.* Boston: Houghton Mifflin, 2003.

Wilson, William J. *The Truly Disadvantaged.* Chicago: University of Chicago Press, 1987.

X, Malcolm. *Malcolm X Speaks: Selected Speeches and Statements.* Edited by George Breitman. New York: Grove Weidenfield, 1990.

Yamamoto, Eric K. "Critical Race Praxis: Race Theory and Political Lawyering Practice in Post–Civil Rights America." *Michigan Law Review* 95 (1997): 821–900.

Yarema, Allan. *The American Colonization Society: An Avenue to Freedom?* Lanham, Md.: University Press of America, 2006.

COURT DECISIONS

Adarand Constructors, Inc. v. Peña, 515 U.S. 200 (1995)

Allen v. State Board of Elections, 393 U.S. 544 (1969)

Arizona Free Enterprise Club's Freedom Club PAC v. Bennett 100 U.S. 10-238 (2011) (Slip Opinion)

Arlington Heights v. Metropolitan Housing Dev. Corp., 429 U.S. 252 (1977)

Baker v. Carr, 369 U.S. 186 (1962)

Bartlett v. Strickland, 129 S. Ct. 1231 (2009)

Beer v. United States, 425 U.S. 130 (1976)

Boerne v. Flores, 521 U.S. (1997)

Bowers v. Hardwick, 478 U.S. 186 (1986)

Bradwell v. Illinois, 83 U.S. 130 (1872)

Branch v. Smith, 538 U.S. 254 (2003)

Bush v. Vera, 517 U.S. 952 (1995)

Brown v. Board of Education, 347 U.S. 483 (1954)

Brown v. Board of Education II, 349 U.S. 294 (1955)

City of Richmond v. U.S., 442 U.S. 387 (1975)

Civil Rights Cases, 109 U.S. 3 (1883)

Colegrove v. Green, 328 U.S. 549 (1946)

Davis v. Bandemer, 478 U.S. 109 (1986)

Dred Scott v. Sandford, 60 U.S. 393 (1857)

Fullilove v. Klutznick, 448 U.S. 448 (1980)

Gautreaux v. Chicago Housing Authority, 297 F. Supp. 907 (N.D. Ill. 1969)

Georgia v. Ashcroft, 539 U.S. 461 (2003)

Gomillion v. Lightfoot, 364 U.S. 339 (1960)

Gratz v. Bollinger, 539 U.S. 244 (2003)

Growe v. Emison, 507 U.S. 25 (1993)

Grutter v. Bollinger, 539 U.S. 306 (2003)

Guinn v. U.S., 238 U.S. 347 (1915)

Holder v. Hall, 512 U.S. 874 (1994)

Howell v. Netherland (1770, Virginal colonial case), http://oll.libertyfund.org/?option =com_staticxt&staticfile=show.php%3Ftitle=800&chapter=85803&layout =html&Itemid=27. Accessed February 18, 2011.

Karcher v. Daggett, 462 U.S. 725 (1983)

Kelo v. City of New London, 545 U.S. 469 (2005)

Lawrence v. Texas, 539 U.S. 558 (2003)

League of United Latin American Citizens et al., v. Perry, 548 U.S. 399 (2006)

Marbury v. Madison, 5 U.S. 137 (1803)

McLaughlin v. Florida, 347 U.S. 184 (1964)

McLaurin v. Oklahoma, 339 U.S. 637 (1950)

Miller v. Johnson, 515 U.S. 900 (1995)

Milliken v. Bradley, 418 U.S. 717 (1974)

Minor v. Happersett, 88 U.S. 162 (1874)

Missouri v. Jenkins, 491 U.S. 274, 276 (1989); 495 U.S. 33 (1990); 515 U.S. 70 (1995)

Mobile v. Bolden, 466 U.S. 55 (1980)

Nixon v. Herndon, 273 U.S. 536 (1927)

Northwest Austin Municipal Utility District Number 1 v. Holder, 129 S. Ct. 2504 (2009)

Parents Involved in Community Schools v. Seattle School District Number 1 et al., 551 U.S. 701 (2007)

Planned Parenthood of Southeastern Pennsylvania v. Casey, 505 U.S. 833 (1992)

Plessy v. Ferguson, 163 U.S. 537 (1896)

Regents of the University of California v. Bakke, 438 U.S. 265 (1978)

Reno v. Bossier Parish School Board I, 520 U.S. 471 (1997)

Reno v. Bossier Parish School Board II, 528 U.S. 320 (2000)

Reynolds v. Sims, 337 U.S. 533 (1964)

Richmond v. J. A. Croson Co., 488 U.S. 469 (1989)

Rodgers v. Lodge, 458 U.S. 613 (1982)

Roe v. Wade, 410 U.S. 113 (1973)

Sale (McNary)/I.N.S. v. Haitian Centers, 509 U.S. 155 (1993)

Shaw v. Hunt, 517 U.S. 899 (1996)

Shaw v. Reno, 509 U.S. 630 (1993)

Slaughter-House Cases, 83 U.S. 36 (1873)

Smith v. Allwright, 321 U.S. 649 (1944)

South Carolina v. Katzenbach, 383 U.S. 301 (1965)

Strauder v. West Virginia, 100 U.S. 303 (1879)

Sweatt v. Painter, 339 U.S. 629 (1950)

Terry v. Adams, 345 U.S. 461 (1953)

Thornburg v. Gingles, 438 U.S. 30 (1986)

United Jewish Organizations Inc. v. Carey, 430 U.S. 144 (1977)

U.S. v. Carolene Products, 304 U.S. 144 (1938)

U.S. v. Charlottesville Redev. and Housing Authority, 718 F. Supp. 461 (W.D. Va. 1989)

U.S. v. Cruikshank, 92 U.S. 542 (1876)

U.S. v. Hays, 515 U.S. 737 (1995)

U.S. v. Reese, 92 U.S. 214 (1876)

Wards Cove Packing Co. v. Atonio, 490 U.S. 642 (1989)

White v. Regester, 412 U.S. 755 (1973)

Wright v. Rockefeller, 376 U.S. 52 (1964)

Zimmer v. McKeithen, 485 F. 2nd 1297; 5th Cir. (1973)

Index

Note: Page numbers in italics refer to tables and figures.

Abernathy, Ralph, 78
abolition, 21, 37, 38, 39, 40, 42, 44, 47, 62, *107*
    black women, 36, 48–50, 57, 58
    pacifism, 37, 43
    white, 47
accommodationism, 30, 45, 46, 53, 60,
        61–62, 67, *107*
    and Bruce, Blanche K., 53
    Congressional Black Caucus (CBC), 67
    and integration, 60
    and Turner, Henry McNeal, 55–56, 60
    and Washington, Booker T., 46, 61–62
Adarand v. Peña, 105, 119, 184n24, 187n26
Adegbile, Debo, 185n43
affirmative action, 104, 111, 123, 161
    CBC, 9
    in higher education, 3, 142, 145, 185n42
    race-based districting, 30
    See also specific court cases, e.g., *Grutter
        v. Bollinger*
AFL-CIO, 78
African Civilization Society, 42, 45
African Methodist Episcopal Church, 38, 55
Alabama, 61, 124, 128, 169n7
    See also Mobile, AL; Tuskegee Institute
Alaska, 77, 169n7, 180n47
Alito, Samuel, 12, 186n2
Allen, Robert, 38, 44
Allen v. State Board of Education, 80, 81
American Anti-Slavery Society, 48
American Colonization Society, 39, 41, 42,
    45

American Woman Suffrage Association,
    58
amicus curiae briefs, 87, 125
    Congressional Black Caucus as, 6, 8, 14,
        15, 18, 63, 65, 124
    Adarand v. Peña, 105, 119, 184n24,
        187n26
    Astroline v. Shurberg, 105
    Ayers v. Mabus, 105
    Branch v. Smith, 105, 109, 184n1
    color blindness, 151
    Gratz v. Bollinger, 104, 105
    Grutter v. Bollinger, 3, 104, *105,* 123,
        145, 185n42, 187n26
    Jean v. Nelson, 105
    McNary v. Haitian Centers, 105
    Metro Broadcasting v. F.C.C., 105
    Miller v. Johnson, 111–17
    minority voting rights litigation, 4,
        102–9
    *Northwest Austin Municipal Utility
        District Number 1 v. Holder,* 5,
        12, 15, 102, *105,* 106, *109,* 120–23,
        126, 144, 173n4, 182n107, 185n51
    Supreme Court opinion, 143–46,
        148
    Rodgers v. Lodge, 109–11
    Shaw v. Hunt, 10, 15, 100, 102, *105,*
        106, 108, 117–20, 123, 124, 126,
        141–43, 145, 148, 151, 156, 158,
        185n43, 186n2, 187n31
    University of Michigan, 169n4

Printed and bound by CPI Group (UK) Ltd, Croydon, CR0 4YY

09/06/2025